UNCONTAINABLE ROMANTICISM

Uncontainable Romanticism

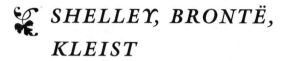 *SHELLEY, BRONTË, KLEIST*

Carol Jacobs

THE JOHNS HOPKINS UNIVERSITY PRESS
Baltimore and London

© 1989 The Johns Hopkins University Press
All rights reserved
Printed in the United States of America

The Johns Hopkins University Press
701 West 40th Street
Baltimore, Maryland 21211
The Johns Hopkins Press Ltd., London

The paper used in this publication meets the
minimum requirements of American National
Standard for Information Sciences—Permanence
of Paper for Printed Library Materials,
ANSI Z39.48-1984.

Library of Congress Cataloging in Publication Data

Jacobs, Carol.
    Uncontainable romanticism : Shelley, Brontë, Kleist /
Carol Jacobs.
        p. cm.
    Bibliography: p.
    Includes index.
    ISBN 0-8018-3786-3 (alk. paper)
    1. English literature—19th century—History and
criticism. 2. Romanticism—England. 3. Shelley,
Percy Bysshe, 1792–1822—Criticism and interpretation.
4. Brontë, Emily, 1818–1848—Criticism and
interpretation. 5. Kleist, Heinrich von, 1777–1811—
Criticism and interpretation. 6. Literature,
Comparative—English and German. 7. Literature,
Comparative—German and English. 8. Romanticism—
Germany. I. Title.
PR457.J25   1989
820'.9'145—dc19   88–7852
                                                        CIP

For that first teller of "law-stories,"
whose narrations prefigured so much
of what is here

Contents

Preface: The Dagger of Language

Ever since its inception (if such a concept makes sense) Romanticism has denied itself a historically limitable field. If I have called this volume *Uncontainable Romanticism*, then, it is not because Shelley, Brontë, and Kleist fall neatly into that historical abyss we tend to label Romantic. What Romanticism has come to mean in recent years, in any case, is a yielding of its own temporal limits to register critical claims of a much more overwhelming kind.[1] "Romanticism" as it appears here is uncontainable as well because what takes place in these pieces is an uncontrollable moving beyond all those parameters seemingly fixed within the texts, because of the insistence in each text that it stage its own critical performance. Repeatedly rehearsed are the forces of control—representation, authority (artistic, political, theological, legal), and criticism—unbound precisely in the moment, or rather process, of their triumph, an unbinding that perpetually undoes the various gestures of teleological closure. Thus this volume would seem to end by reading stories about the possibility of telling the truth, somewhere between history and fiction, with a narrator or interpreter who might seem to have the last laugh. What is put into movement here (if we might turn to two authorities on the question) is the relentless thrust towards a criticism (as Friedrich Schlegel would have it) that floats between that which is represented and that which represents, and since literature can only be reflected by literature, it is a criticism in which (as Walter Benjamin would have it) we the masters are not at home.

Each of the texts in the pages that follow gives a critical performance with similar stakes, playing out in more or less theatrical ways the possibility of its own linguistic status. The most deceptively straightforward meditation on authority and representation is Shelley's "On the Medusa of Leonardo da Vinci in the Florentine Gallery." Ostensibly an unproblematic, poetic description of a mimetic painterly enterprise, it directly confronts the issue of representation in the arts. It is a text, however, whose utter simplicity soon places the imaged Medusa, the painting, and the viewer in dangerous involutions, involutions that imply a similar inextricability of the poem along with its referent, as well as both the poet and the reader.

If the "Medusa" disintegrates conventional representation, and with it the perspectives of authority (painter, poet, reader), it is in the lyrical drama *Prometheus Unbound* that Shelley sets such questions on a political and theological stage. The hero, whose liberation promises the downfall of false gods and the coming to power of proper authority, cannot, from the beginning to the very end, corroborate the authority of his own voice. The *telos* of the transvaluation unbound in the text is less a political arena finally governed by a philosopher king than the site of a poetical enterprise of differential instability (act 3, scene 3) and an ever to be renewed repetition of revolution.

In *Wuthering Heights* one enters the fiction along with its would-be narrator and interpreter. The conjunction is not reassuring, for like Prometheus, Lockwood can never confirm the authority in either of his roles. Lockwood's attempts to understand this realm and control its narration are met by the violent assaults of Wuthering Heights's textual center. In a series of dreams Lockwood experiences a remarkable pre-figuration of the novel's critical concerns, and all this takes place as a dislocation of those same themes that might seem to promise stability of authority and meaning.

In Kleist's *Prince Friedrich von Homburg, Michael Kohlhaas,* and "The Duel" the question of authority is linked to the concepts of political and theological power and to a crisis of interpretation. Each of these works revolves around the figure of a legal text whose status resists definition. In each there is a force that counters that text's readability. In *Homburg* it is the recurrent play within the play, in *Michael Kohlhaas* the gypsy woman's text, and in "The Duel" the more illusive configuration of the holy trial of combat before God that makes it uncertain just what the law decides and when, or even if, it decides it.

These readings begin with the apparently simplistic problem of reproductive representation, and they close, or pretend to close, with the vertiginous tales of Kleist's narrator in "Improbable Veracities." The movement is not insignificant. Everything comes together in this text—authority, denomination, figuration, history, stories, and, more explicitly than in the earlier essays, the question of the stories we tend to call criticism, unleashed in forms that are, by definition, impossible to summarize. In very different ways, none of the writers that are read here can be contained by the question of a representation and authority situated in the realm of the other—the author, his or her language, and its referent. The ironic reverberations of each essay are such that a crisis of interpretation is bound to explode, an explosion thematically insisted on in many of the literary works but uncontainable within their confines. It is in chapter 8, "The Style of Kleist," that I attempt to work out, if not to master, some of the implications of the ironical critical stance within each text.

If I have failed to gloss, and in doing so gloss over (as prefaces are wont to do), the "central point" of one of the essays, this is perhaps as it should be. The omission of *Penthesilea* is, in a strange way, more rigorously emblematic of what is to come than anything I have written above. Nevertheless, I would like to reflect briefly on at least one passage from that text, Penthesilea's final monologue.

It is not that I want the figure of Penthesilea to speak for me: how could she, who was never quite able to speak for herself, much less to speak for another? This monologue is unheard of, properly unheard and incomprehensible in the moment of its utterance. Therefore, it is not that *Penthesilea* is exemplary, in that precisely the *same thing* could be seen to take place in the other literary texts read here. Doubtless, I could just as well have prefaced the pages to come by taking any of them as example, but not with the same economy. I confess, moreover, that I am drawn to dwell on this text here because on occasion it has been regarded as something of a scandal and especially because of the ironical discrepancy between what Goethe's sensibility no doubt found unacceptable and what remains far more unsettling, as well as far less obvious.

Almost at the close of Kleist's *Penthesilea* (for it is not the heroine who has the final word) the unthinkable takes place. Her passion for Achilles first betrayed the laws of the Amazon state and then destroyed her lover. And now, with an utterly mad lucidity, Penthesilea, in a manner of speaking, takes her own life.

For now I climb down into my breast,
Like a shaft, and dig forth for myself, cold
Like ore, an annihilating feeling.
This ore, I purify in the fires of woe
Hard, for myself, to steel; steep it then,
With the hot corroding venom of remorse, through and through;
Carry it then to hope's eternal anvil,
And whet and sharpen it for me to a dagger;
And to this dagger now I reach my breast:
Thus! Thus! Thus! Thus! And once more.—Now it is good.
    [*She falls and dies*]

Setting this passage as emblematic of the text to come, entitling this preface "The Dagger of Language," is a gesture of risk. Perhaps no other image could offer itself up so openly to a predictable misreading.

For most of Kleist's readers this gesture resolves the earlier error of madness in which Penthesilea slayed Achilles with rather appalling violence. Here, it would seem, she atones for her crime by taking her own life, a gesture that is often read either as a triumph of self-mastery or as a tragic suicide. *Penthesilea* may bear the label "tragedy," but it is far less Penthesilea's end than the absolutely conventional comments of her Amazon sisters that situate the text within the bounds of the tragic genre. In the play's last lines the High Priestess and Prothoe go on to bemoan Penthesilea's fragility; the Amazon queen, nevertheless, insistently celebrates her end as "good." Moreover, just before her final monologue, Penthesilea contemplates a death of a more traditional kind: taking her life with the very real dagger at her side or with the same arrow she used to fell her lover. But Kleist has her withdraw from this seduction, no doubt because it would have produced a more definitive tragic closure.

Penthesilea openly chooses to shift the ground of her fall to that of language. To regard this shift to language as a simple rejection of the real for its other would be to miss the point. The Amazon queen's monologue comes only after long meditations on her own misconceived uses of speech by which she explains her attack on Achilles, so that her final lines mark a comprehension of another order. Her rhetoric, moreover, lies beyond the desire to persuade and stands no longer as metaphor for something else that simply needs decoding—the two forms of language and understanding that war with one another for so many of the play's opening scenes. Nor is it a matter of either pure aestheticism or pure action. What all this may suggest in the context of the play is something to be worked out in chapter 4. What it does *not* signify is crucial for all the chapters to come.

Penthesilea's dagger startles the reader and is far more scandalous, if far less readable, than the scene of physical violence that preceded it. That dagger startles with a shock to the eyes, the ears, and the understanding from which one can recover only by repressing the way in which she speaks in favor of the apparent outcome and content of her speech. Its scandal, then, has something to do with the manner in which we forge on through it in an effort not to see and not to hear what actually takes place. This is because we can neither relegate it to a nonthreatening realm of *mere* language, mere imagination, nor regard it as language's nihilistic threat to a realm of substance otherwise left whole. Penthesilea forges her weapon from rhetorical figures mined in the depths of her own breast and takes her life, such as it is, by bringing dagger and breast once more together. The relation of the breast, as conventional locus of life, feeling, and self, to language and the relation within language between the literal and figural are anything but simple. In a passage where action and its linguistic description cannot be extricated from one another language does not send a dagger to attack a life, self, authority, and reason outside itself. Each is constituted by and ungrounded in the other. The dagger arises from a movement through language that claims the dagger to be forged from those same life forces it may then seem to menace. The breast becomes its simile (the shaft), in which a "feeling" is dug forth; the feeling in turn becomes *its* simile (the ore), and this simile then produces an object real enough to take Penthesilea's life. Such is the conjuring trick that creates substance from a slip of the tongue, a slip between apparently simple denomination and rhetorical figure, and this is said to destroy substance in turn. It is a forgery in which the difference between what she says and what she does can no longer be located.

One might call this turn of events either self-mastery or tragic suicide—the taking of a life, the loss of the self—but nothing is happening to the concepts of life and self that did not arise out of them to begin with. All this takes place, moreover, in a manner that is at once dead serious and a pure flight of the imagination. The concept of life in contradistinction to mere image is utterly undone. It is undone in the name of a self that no longer desires an effect on the world outside, that apparently gains perfect mastery through an act of inconceivable will. But it does so only with the gesture of self-destruction, in a linguistic performance that leaves self, substance, and that which critically undercuts them indistinguishable.

Acknowledgments

I would like to thank both the American Council of Learned Societies and the Camargo Foundation for their generous support. I am enormously grateful to Linda Bogdan for her patient and precise work in the technical preparation of the manuscript, to Joanne Allen for her careful editing, and to Johann Pillai for his fine proofreading and the preparation of the index.

Chapter 1 first appeared in *Yale French Studies* 69 (1985): 163–79; chapter 3 in *Boundary II*, Spring 1979, 49–71; chapter 8 in *Diacritics*, December 1979, 47–61.

I

❧ *PERCY BYSSHE SHELLEY*

Head of Medusa, Uffizi Gallery, Florence

1

On Looking at Shelley's Medusa

On the Medusa of Leonardo da Vinci in the Florentine Gallery

I

It lieth, gazing on the midnight sky,
    Upon the cloudy mountain-peak supine;
Below, far lands are seen tremblingly;
    Its horror and its beauty are divine.
5 Upon its lips and eyelids seems to lie
    Loveliness like a shadow, from which shine,
Fiery and lurid, struggling underneath,
The agonies of anguish and of death.

II

Yet it is less the horror than the grace
10   Which turns the gazer's spirit into stone,
Whereon the lineaments of that dead face
    Are graven, till the characters be grown
Into itself, and thought no more can trace;
    'Tis the melodious hue of beauty thrown
Athwart the darkness and the glare of pain,
16 Which humanize and harmonize the strain.

III

And from its head as from one body grow,
    As   grass out of a watery rock,
Hairs which are vipers, and they curl and flow
20   And their long tangles in each other lock,
And with unending involutions show
    Their mailèd radiance, as it were to mock
The torture and the death within, and saw
The solid air with many a raggèd jaw.

IV

25   And, from a stone beside, a poisonous eft
    Peeps idly into those Gorgonian eyes;
Whilst in the air a ghastly bat, bereft
    Of sense, has flitted with a mad surprise
Out of the cave this hideous light had cleft,
30   And he comes hastening like a moth that hies
After a taper; and the midnight sky
Flares, a light more dread than obscurity.

V

'Tis the tempestuous loveliness of terror;
    For from the serpents gleams a brazen glare
35   Kindled by that inextricable error,
    Which makes a thrilling vapour of the air
Become a   and ever-shifting mirror
    Of all the beauty and the terror there—
A woman's countenance, with serpent-locks,
40   Gazing in death on Heaven from those wet rocks.

Additional Stanza

It is a woman's countenance divine
    With everlasting beauty breathing there
Which from a stormy mountain's peak, supine
    Gazes into the   night's trembling air.
45   It is a trunkless head, and on its feature
    Death has met life, but there is life in death,
The blood is frozen—but unconquered Nature
    Seems struggling to the last—without a breath
The fragment of an uncreated creature.[1]

   "On the Medusa of Leonardo da Vinci in the Florentine Gallery"[2] has been disregarded by Shelley's most prominent readers. Thus such canonical critical works as Wasserman's *Shelley: A Critical Reading*, Bloom's *Shelley's Mythmaking*, or Baker's *Shelley's Major Poetry*, to list only a few, do not discuss the poem. One volume, Kroese's *The Beauty and the Terror*,[3] borrows its title from the text in question but never analyzes the poem. In *The Romantic Agony* Mario Praz entitles his first chapter "The Beauty of the Medusa"; it opens dramatically with a full citation of Shelley's poem, for, we are told, "it amounts almost to a manifesto of the conception of Beauty peculiar to the Romantics."[4] Yet despite the privileged place given to the piece, Praz seems all too eager to leave it behind rather than contemplate its intricacies in detail. To what can we attribute this critical oversight?[5] Such reticence makes good sense from several points of view. Significant problems abound with respect to establishing the correct text. There is the unresolved question of the final stanza, whether or not Shelley intended it to be attached to the main body of the poem,[6] as well as the lacunae Shelley left in several lines that necessarily challenge the comprehension of his reader. Moreover, despite its unusual literary grace, what kind of light can one hope to shed on a poem that seems simply to reproduce the lineaments of the well-known painting it describes?

In the case of Shelley, of course, we are confronted, not with a painting, but rather with a text that cites a painting as its subject matter. At least the title of the poem, "On the Medusa of Leonardo da Vinci in the Florentine Gallery," does this with the insistent and unpoetic precision of a catalog entry. The title functions, then, as a double frame, placing the reader at several levels of remove from the object of artistic representation, the dangerous head of the Medusa. Yet nowhere in the forty-nine lines that follow are we reminded that the poet describes a painting rather than the real thing. This poses unending problems in situating ourselves, in fixing the object of our scrutiny as text, painting, or Medusa to the exclusion of the other two. It raises a tangle of questions that are as predictable as they are maddening. Does Shelley gaze directly at the Gorgon, as suggested by the poem, or at the painting attributed to Leonardo, as suggested by the title? What does it mean to look at the Medusa? What does it mean to look at a work of art, to look at a painting, or, for that matter, to read a poem? Does the text expose *us* directly to the gaze of the Medusa, or does it function like the shield of Perseus, mirroring the Gorgon's head and protecting us from its effects?[7] How does a literary text operate whose fundamental gesture is to describe the objective world? another work of art? and what would it mean to describe? Who is the gazer—Perseus, his predecessors, the painter, the poet, the reader?

There are no clear-cut answers to the questions, although all six stanzas are bent on nothing if not on describing the scene at hand and situating the observer with respect to it. The poem immediately dispels any simple concept of mimetic description that the title might seem to have proposed, for neither the scene nor the perspective of the gazer is identical to that of the painting.[8]

> It lieth, gazing on the midnight sky,
>   Upon the cloudy mountain-peak supine;
> Below, far lands are seen tremblingly;

The Medusa gazes on the midnight sky, yet there is another line of vision, that of the viewer: "Below, far lands are seen tremblingly." This line of vision shifts the head to a level much lower with respect to the observer than that suggested by the canvas: he stands above the slain Gorgon as he views the lands beyond, tremblingly. This is not to say that either the gazer or the scene itself trembles; rather, despite his shift to the position once occupied by the triumphant Perseus, there is something precarious in his manner of seeing.

This is intensified, if not explained, by a sense of struggle in the contradictory attributes of his object of contemplation, both here and in the other stanzas that concentrate on the face of the Medusa, where its horror and its beauty, its loveliness and its agonies, are uttered in the same poetic breath.[9]

> Its horror and its beauty are divine.
> Upon its lips and eyelids seems to lie
>   Loveliness like a shadow, from which shine,
> Fiery and lurid, struggling underneath,
> The agonies of anguish and of death.

If we are to believe these lines (in a stanza perhaps all too suggestive of a pun on lies), loveliness veils "the agonies of anguish and of death." In a text that openly announces a work of art as its subject matter it would seem legitimate to read this as a nonironical version of Baudelaire's statement: "The intoxication of art is more apt than any other to veil the terrors of the eternal abyss."[10] Shelley himself was soon to write (although the passage is somewhat out of context):

> Poetry turns all things to loveliness; it exalts the beauty of that which is most beautiful, and it adds beauty to that which is most deformed: it marries exultation and horror, grief and pleasure, eternity and change; it subdues to union under its light yoke all irreconcilable things.[11]

Is it, then, the loveliness of art, of Leonardo's painting and of Shelley's poetry, that masks the horror of its object and protects the onlooker and reader? Is the representation of art such that it distances us from the effects of the Medusa?

At the end of the second stanza it is once again a question of the relationship between the beauty and the agony. The beauty at issue is now unmistakably that of the work of art, for the elements of painting and song (hue and melody) enter explicitly into play.

> 'Tis the melodious hue of beauty thrown
> Athwart the darkness and the glare of pain,
> Which humanize and harmonize the strain.

If art is here, as before, that which is cast athwart the pain, it is hardly that which conceals the terrors of death. For according to the unexpected plural forms of the verbs in line 16, it is not "the melodious hue of beauty" that mitigates the strain but rather, with an unexpected shift, "the darkness and the glare of pain." The loveliness of art, then, does not lessen the strain of the Medusa's agony: rather, the darkness and glare of pain humanize art and harmonize a strain that here, as elsewhere in Shelley, suggests the strain of poetry.[12]

The "melodious hue of beauty" is not like the mirror held by Perseus, which reflects its monstrous object while shielding him from its powers. For if the first stanza offers a conventional description of its supposed, external object, if it also takes pains to separate the Medusa's gaze from that of the observer, if at the same time (for these are necessarily bound to a unified concept of representation) it speaks of art as mask and balm, in the second stanza it is precisely this loveliness of art, its "grace," that menaces the gazer.

> Yet it is less the horror than the grace
>   Which turns the gazer's spirit into stone,

What kind of art is this that is more threatening to the gazer than the horror of looking directly at the Medusa? How does the mirror of art function? What is its mode of reflection? Suddenly, it is no longer the Medusa who is to be portrayed but the spectator, for the Medusa was, of course, something of an artist in stone. Yet whereas the myth would seem to speak of a reification of the physical attributes of the observer, what concerns Shelley is no longer physical reality, neither that of the poem's object, the painting of the Medusa, nor that of its onlooker: it is the gazer's *spirit* that is transformed into stone.[13]

Yet it is less the horror than the grace
  Which turns the gazer's spirit into stone,
Whereon the lineaments of that dead face
  Are graven, till the characters be grown
Into itself, and thought no more can trace;

To trace what transpires here is indeed impossible. Despite his positioning with respect to the Medusa in the first stanza, the fate of the gazer is more akin to that of Perseus's predecessors than to that of the hero. And if his spirit is turned to stone, this takes place not as a reifying process that preserves form but as a radical transformation. It is neither the features of the onlooker nor his spirit but rather the lineaments of the dead Gorgon's face that are graven at the point of articulation between the Medusa and the would-be Perseus. The gazer loses his identity, but this is not to say that the Medusa retains hers, for in Shelley's text it is no longer a question of who dominates whom. The contours of the Medusa's face are graven, but the monster as the single, fixed locus of petrifying powers is dead.

Nor are the "characters" in this performance of artistic production simply the features, the cast of countenance, delineated in stone. They include all those creatures we have seen the poem to conceive—the Medusa as object imitated, the gazer as poet, artist, reader, or beholder, and the graven work of art, poem or painting. What takes place is an inexorable process, to the point that each of these progressively and irreversibly grows into a single, if unfixable, "itself," an "itself" that might plausibly be designated as any and none of these.

Were it possible to extricate our gaze from this scene, we might be able to contemplate its critical implications. For Shelley's poem is about nothing if not about our own interpretative predicament as readers. The "characters" of line 12 are drawn into a process of unending involution in a notion of art that can no longer be regarded as preserving what happens to serve as the cornerstone of so much of our contemporary critical endeavor. In this scene of unthinkable creation each of these characters is dislocated as a possible point of valorization. Yet it is such valorization of the artist that determines much psychoanalytic and all biographical interpretation, such valorization of the object imitated that underlies, for example, historical criticism, and such privileging of the spectator on which the various forms of reader response commentary are based.[14] Nor are we witness to a pseudo-Mallarméan sacrifice of the object, artist, and beholder in favor of a work of art that can then be contemplated in isolation, aesthetically or semiotically, with no such points of reference. One begins to understand the reluctance of Shelley's interpreters with regard to this text.

The process of involution is such that "thought no more can trace." Can no longer trace what? one is tempted to ask, for Shelley breaks off his thought by leaving the usually transitive verb *trace* without an object. Thought is no longer the trace of something else, which is certainly not to say that the bizarre mirroring that takes place in this text would be one of simple and triumphant self-reflection. Perhaps we might make sense of the phrase by reading *thought* as the object of *trace*. But what is it, then, that can no longer trace thought? Either the thinking subject or the object of thought remains absent. What the text insists on is a lack in thought, and this lack is coincident with a grammatical failure, with the inability of language to complete its meaning.

If the relationship between thinking subject and object, between gazer and Medusa, is seen to tremble, if "thought no more can trace" takes place in the name of the grace of art rather than the horror of art's monstrous object, if the "darkness and the glare of pain" promises, as we have seen, to humanize and harmonize the strain of poetry (lines 14–16), one might nevertheless regard the second stanza as a moment of error and aberration in a poetry that now seems to return to a more harmonized and humanized concept of itself. Beginning with stanza 3, the text seems intent upon describing the painting attributed to Leonardo in a manner that no longer menaces or even problematizes the human beholder. Nowhere else in the poem does its voice seem more matter-of-fact, more true to the simple task of description posed by the title of the text. Or could it be that the beholder has already grown into "itself"? For if it is true that it no longer figures as the subject matter of the poem's statement, the gazer is implicitly involved, here as elsewhere, as the narrative voice. And the entire point of the narration in stanza 3 is that one cannot make heads or tails of it.

> And from its head as from one body grow,
>   As   grass out of a watery rock,
> Hairs which are vipers, and they curl and flow
>   And their long tangles in each other lock,
> And with unending involutions . . .

The unending involutions, the inextricable tangles that would make the matching of head and body impossible, are in no way problematic for the narrative voice. For while it insists on their inextricability, an inextricability that it will later even speak of as "error," the intent of this voice does not lie in rectifying the error. Contrary to appearance, though, this is not to say that the text simply reproduces their tortuous visual form in words. It is quite the other way around. At the same time that the stanza speaks of involutions with evident detachment, it performs far more radical gestures through the intricacies of its figural language. The hairs of the Medusa grow "from its head as from one body." What has happened to our head? What the last stanza of the poem will call a "trunkless head" here becomes a headless trunk, a body without a head of its own. It becomes the very inverse of what it was before the thrust of simile transformed it. Simile, here as elsewhere in Shelley, is certainly no sign of similarity,[15] nor is it, however, a limited operation of inversion or negation. One is not witness to a Persean decapitation, for figural language is no hero, severing the head of the monster and mastering her powers. The simile maintains the trunkless head in proximity to the headless trunk: each both completes the meaning of the other and makes it unreadable, for the two merge into that which thought no more can trace.

One is especially hard put as to the nature of such figures when Shelley compounds his first adverbial simile with a second.

> And from its head as from one body grow,
> As   grass out of a watery rock,

The Medusa head, first transformed into a headless trunk, now seems smitten by its own mythical force—turned to stone with a turn of phrase that compares it to a rock. At the very moment that the text apparently carries out the task of description, just when poetry would seem to devote itself to the most straightforward concept of representational art, a mimetic recreation of the canvas attributed to Leonardo, something utterly unspeakable takes place as well. The simile of line 17 divests the object of its identity, and that of line 18 leaves it as unlike itself as possible, for it becomes totally other, victim to its own power to transform into stone, a self-reflection gone awry. The force of the Medusa is allied with poetic figuration, and as we saw in stanza 2, this is hardly a force of mimetic reification. The Medusa is described as object, it is depicted as in the painting, but in the same breath the force of its figuration is such as to (in the language of the closing stanza) uncreate the same creature.[16] The Medusa, then, is both the object of these lines and the poetic strain that mocks and undoes the concept of object.[17] It is these two modes that are endlessly entangled in one another throughout the text.[18]

There are at least two ways, then, of looking at the Medusa. The one allows the spectator to regard it from a safe distance, as object; the other draws the beholder into a conception of the Medusa as the performance of a radical figural transformation—of itself, of the beholder, of the language that attempts to represent it. In stanza 4 these two roles are played by an eft that looks with neither interest nor sense of danger into the Gorgon's eyes and a "ghastly bat" that is driven mad by what it perceives.

> And, from a stone beside, a poisonous eft
>   Peeps idly into those Gorgonian eyes;
> Whilst in the air a ghastly bat, bereft
>   Of sense, has flitted with a mad surprise
> Out of the cave this hideous light had cleft,
>   And he comes hastening like a moth that hies
> After a taper; and the midnight sky
> Flares, a light more dread than obscurity.

The passage reads like a parody of Plato's "Allegory of the Cave,"[19] for the bat is drawn into the light of midnight rather than dragged into the light of the sun. The journey upwards also dazzles Plato's cave dweller, but there he who was previously doomed to seeing mere shadows of images seems promised, once outside the cave, a progression in enlightenment that will allow him to pass from shadows to reflections, to real objects, and finally to the contemplation of "the immediate source of reason and truth."[20] Plato's philosopher learns, then, to disentangle image from reality in the light of the intellectual world. But the bat in Shelley's text encounters a light that is "more dread than obscurity," for it reveals a situation in which one is "bereft / Of sense" and "thought no more can trace."

The Medusa herself is yet another version of those creatures in the cave, restrained from turning their heads, a fire lit above and behind them, for above and behind the Medusa, as the fifth stanza shows, is a light of dubious nature. "This hideous light" is not a heavenly body as in Plato but rather the "mailed radiance" of the serpentine involutions, the source of illumination for a remarkable scene played out before gazing eyes. The bat, then, leaves the cave of shadows, not for the sun of dazzling enlightenment, but only to confront the illusion of false figuration repeated in another form.[21] Indeed, this creature, suspended in that strangely "solid air," has every reason to be driven mad, witness as it is to the "tempestuous loveliness of terror" described in the lines that follow and, once again, in the final passage. As in stanza 2, where the grace of art rather than the horror of its subject matter turned the gazer's spirit into stone, so here the loveliness of terror involves a spectacular if bizarre mirroring.

> 'Tis the tempestuous loveliness of terror;
>   For from the serpents gleams a brazen glare
> Kindled by that inextricable error,
>   Which makes a thrilling vapour of the air
> Become a   and ever-shifting mirror
>   Of all the beauty and the terror there—
> A woman's countenance, with serpent-locks,
> Gazing in death on Heaven from those wet rocks.

Stanza 5 is where, as the saying goes, everything comes together, or fails to. A glare kindled by the "mailed radiance" of "long tangles" makes the air into a mirror of sorts that sets up a disconcerting model of reflective activity. If it makes good sense along with Neville Rogers to read "error" as the physical windings of the serpents,[22] one cannot entirely repress the more literal insistence on an "inextricable error," a mistake from which there is no recourse. It is this ineluctable error in both senses of the word that brings about the production of a mirror from the trembling vapors of the air, a looking glass that finds no fixed position but rather shifts its locus perpetually. What it reflects is "all the beauty and the terror there." Like a limited view of the painting or poetic text, it might seem to portray the Medusa, caught in a temporality that line 42 calls "everlasting," as a fixed object of description: "A woman's countenance, with serpent-locks." Strange that such a questionable reflecting device should, for the first time in the text, give us a clear and decisive breakdown of the elements of beauty and terror, the loveliness of the countenance on the one hand, the horror of the serpent-locks on the other. Strange also that it is only at this point in the poem that we are reassured of the human quality of the Gorgon, for until now she has always been referred to as "it." Striking that the endless involutions of serpents and "watery rock" that in stanza 3 marked the threat of figurative language as displacement, radical self-reflection, and transfor-mation should here be present as the most matter-of-fact objects, "serpent-locks" and "wet rocks." Of course, this all takes place just when the basis of such mirroring is clearly announced as error, its instrument as ever-shifting, its reflections, therefore, inevitably an illusion, the illusion, among others, of set distinctions between beauty and terror, the human and the monstrous, the literal and the figurative.

And yet, we have not even begun—and how could we begin among these unending involutions?—to trace the intricacies of speculation implicit at the close of the text. The mirror, we have seen, resembles both the painting and the poem that take the head of the Medusa as their model; but that reflection is also the image of a work of art produced from within the work of art. It becomes easier to visualize this passage if one looks to the painting, where there is indeed a very distinct vapor. It arises from the slightly parted lips of the Medusa. The "thrilling vapour of the air" that forms the psyche comes from the mouth of Medusa, not only as her breath but also, since the mirror appears as an image of poetry, as the spoken word. The last lines of the poem speak somewhat indirectly of this.

> It is a trunkless head, and on its feature
>   Death has met life, but there is life in death,
> The blood is frozen—but unconquered Nature
>   Seems struggling to the last—without a breath
> The fragment of an uncreated creature.

The Medusa's death is a birth of sorts out of which a certain creature arises. According to myth, Pegasus sprang from the blood of the Gorgon at the moment she was slain. In Shelley's text the figure for poetic inspiration results from a struggle between life and death, breath and its loss. It appears as a questionable source of poetry, a vaporous mirror that both reflects and withdraws the locus of reflection. This is why, in the closing verse of that "additional stanza," which has one line too many perhaps (and not only because it has nine lines instead of eight), the result of poetic reproduction is called "the fragment of an uncreated creature." For nothing in Shelley's work of art bears witness to completeness, and we have seen the manner in which the concept of creation is uncreated time and again.

We might think of the close of the text as itself uncreating what came before, rewriting the earlier lines as it draws them into itself in a final gesture of involution. If the opening verses focus descriptively upon the lips and eyelids of the Medusa's countenance, these features become the crucial points of a bizarre self-reflection in stanza 5. But it is not only a question here of uncreating the simplistic mimetic thrust that seems intermittently to govern the poem.[23]

The position of the spectator, and therefore the reader, is even more radically at stake than one could have realized. For the gazer's "spirit," transformed into an engraving in which death meets life (stanza 2), is mirrored later in the "thrilling vapour" (line 36) exhaled by the Gorgon. Spirit in both its etymological and conventional significance is breath, "the breath of life" as well as "the soul of a person passing out of the body in the moment of death,"[24] that struggle, of which we have read, between breath and its surrender. The figure of the external beholder is taken into the countenance of the Medusa in stanza 5, where she is once again seen "gazing."

She gazes "in death on Heaven" (line 40), or as the opening words of the poem would have it, "It lieth, gazing on the midnight sky." But what does it see? That "Heaven" or "midnight sky" is the same sky that earlier flared with "a light more dread than obscurity," a light that threatens thought and sight far more than the darkness of obscurity. This is no blank stare into the heavens above, for the last stanza has the Medusa gazing "into the   night's trembling air."

> It is a woman's countenance divine
>   With everlasting beauty breathing there
> Which from a stormy mountain's peak, supine
>   Gazes into the   night's trembling air.

The "trembling air" is that same "thrilling vapour of the air" that becomes an "ever-shifting mirror." What the Medusa contemplates, then, and it is indeed enough to rob one of one's senses, is the ever-shifting image of herself gazing into a mirror formed of a vapor that arises from her own mouth. The Medusa becomes, then, in a sense, if one can follow the windings of the points of articulation in this scene, the artist-poet from whose mouth the reflective work of art arises, the object depicted by that work of art, and the beholder of the work of art. All at once, one is tempted to say, and yet they cannot logically be conceived simultaneously.

The "characters" have "grown / Into itself," but this does not mean that we are witness to a perfect union. Quite the contrary. If our reading of the phrase "thought no more can trace" showed language necessarily lacking either object or subject, this is the object lesson taught, if never quite comprehended, in those closing lines. The Medusa views herself in a mirror that trembles between the "everlasting" and the "ever-shifting." Everlasting since what she sees might be represented as fixed in the manner of the painting at the Uffizi. But what she gazes on is an image of herself as the beholder of herself as the origin of an image that reflects herself as the beholder. . . . It is impossible for thought to hold the reflecting subject, the producing subject, and the object produced (which in turn reflects) all in the same time frame.[25] The refusal of closure, then, offers to view the production of the perpetually frag-mented "uncreated creature." In ways that would be too vertiginous to outline, one can imagine the endless involutions added to this by remembering those other beholders, painter and poet, spectator and reader, who may be envisioned not only within but also without the text.

All this is kindled by the light of the unending tangles we saw in stanza 3.[26] For from the moment that the subject or object in question is thought, that is to say, language,[27] the lack of which we have spoken is bound to take place. This becomes clear if we reflect once again on the turns of phrase in Shelley's similes, since the simile is to some extent emblematic of what happens in all figural language.

> And from its head as from one body grow,
>   As   grass out of a watery rock,

If these lines are the phrase "from its head . . . grow" in search of an analogon, what is their thrust, and that of all similes, if not the attempt of language to name itself—language in search of its own image. Such a moment not only mocks the pretention to denominate an objective realm located elsewhere but, as we have seen, more crucially mocks the concept of a subject identical to itself. In verses that are framed as a narrative subject naming the other (Medusa), verses that nevertheless show a linguistic subject naming itself, the force of the simile transforms the other into a self, and that self into yet another, everlastingly, ever-shiftingly. Figurative language, which for Shelley is the same as literary language, mocks itself, like the Medusa gazing on her trembling vapor of the air—such is the inextricable error of the text.

Errors of this sort cannot be confined to the particularities of the poem at hand, to the Medusa and the particular kind of art she inspires, as though we might mark the limits of the monstrousness and protect ourselves from its theoretical implications. Such a gesture would deny the inextricability of beauty and horror on which Shelley insists; it would repeat the historical repression of the final stanza, where the text openly gives life to an "uncreated creature" that, metaphorically, can be none other than poetic inspiration in general. In Shelley's most definitive statement on the nature of the literary text, written less than two years after the poem, we encounter precisely the same complex of elements, except, tellingly, that man rather than the Medusa is the locus of reflection.

"Poetry," Shelley writes in "A Defence of Poetry," "in a general sense, may be defined to be 'the expression of the Imagination': and poetry is connate with the origin of man."[28] This is no banal historical assertion of poetry's role in the youth of the world. Poetry is connate with the origin of man because man is, only insofar as there is poetry. Of poets Shelley will go on to say: "Their language is vitally metaphorical; that is, it marks the before unapprehended relations of things" (482). What can it mean that the language of poets is vitally figural?[29] On the one hand poetry "strips the veil of familiarity from the world, and lays bare the naked and sleeping beauty which is the spirit of its forms" (505). Yet this stripping of the veil hardly gives us a privileged proximity to that which lies beneath. "Poetry lifts the veil from the hidden beauty of the world, and makes familiar objects be as if they were not familiar" (487). This is because although poetry may lay bare the "naked . . . beauty which is the spirit of [the world's] forms," that beauty is never present to us as meaning. "Veil after veil may be undrawn, and the inmost naked beauty *of the meaning* never exposed" (500, emphasis mine). This strange lifting of a veil that refuses meaning and renders the once familiar a chaos is equivalent to spreading the curtain of figural language, that is to say, of poetry. "And whether it spreads its own figured curtain or withdraws life's dark veil from before the scene of things, it equally creates for us a being within our being. It makes us the inhabitants of a world to which the familiar world is a chaos" (505).

Poetry, then, which renders the familiar unfamiliar and denies us access to any core of meaning, poetry as the expression of the imagination in figural language, is connate with man. Shelley goes on now to speak of man in this context through a series of metaphors and similes.

> Poetry, in a general sense, may be defined to be "the expression of the Imagination": and poetry is connate with the origin of man. Man is an instrument over which a series of external and internal impressions are driven, like the alternations of an ever-changing wind over an Aeolian lyre, which move it by their motion to ever-changing melody. But there is a

principle within the human being, and perhaps within all sentient beings, which acts otherwise than in the lyre, and produces not melody, alone, but harmony, by an internal adjustment of the sounds or motions thus excited to the impressions which excite them. (480)

Were man merely an instrument, he would simply produce "reflected image[s]" (480) of the impressions driven over him. But there is a principle within him that makes him other than the lyre to which he is first compared, that alters these reflections, "the sounds or motions thus excited," so that they respond to the impressions that excited them to begin with. What is at stake here in the contrast between the passive and the active lyre is the relationship between Reason and Imagination, for just before man is called an instrument, we read, "Reason is to Imagination as the instrument to the agent" (480).

> [Reason] may be considered as mind contemplating the relations borne by one thought to another, however produced; and [Imagination], as mind acting upon those thoughts so as to colour them with its own light, and composing from them, as from elements, other thoughts, each containing within itself the principle of its own integrity. (480)

Imagination is that which acts so as to alter; it acts upon thoughts to produce other thoughts, and each of these contains "the principle of its own integrity."

What is the principle of the integrity of the thoughts produced by Imagination, poetry, figural language? Shelley does not tell us, but he performs it. For to clarify his distinction between man as an Aeolian lyre and man who acts other than the lyre, he goes on to write:

> It is as if the lyre could accommodate its chords to the motions of that which strikes them. . . ; even as the musician can accommodate his voice to the sound of the lyre. (480)

The first part of the sentence is clear enough, for it simply reiterates the gesture that came before, a call for "the internal adjustment of the sounds . . . to the impressions which excite them" (480). But Shelley then offers us a simile. The lyre that does more than be passively driven, that *adjusts* its chords to the ever-changing wind, is like a musician who accommodates his voice to the lyre. The second "lyre," it would seem, can no longer be understood as part of the extended metaphor. If we are to make common sense of what we read, the term should be read literally, the metaphorical frame forgotten. The reader, nevertheless, cannot help but hear the vibrations from the recent metaphorical use of *lyre* at the beginning of the sentence, and this, of course, is the point.

What the musician does in adapting his voice is to respond to and comment on the lyre, a lyre that can also be read metaphorically, as the figure of Reason. This means, first of all, that Reason and Imagination are not to be imagined as two separate faculties, for Imagination contains Reason within it as a moment of its fictional history. But in a harmony whose reverberations get quite out of hand, the lyre in question could just as well be that in the first clause of the sentence—no passive lyre of Reason, but one that, in turn, has already "accommodate[d] its chords to the motions of that which strikes them." The precise phrasing of the second clause would speak for this, for it is not simply a singer who accommodates his voice but a musician, he who plays the lyre of Imagination to begin with. The "principle of its own integrity" (480) that each thought contains within itself is one that ruptures all attempts to circumscribe its limits, for there is no way to fix the frame of its figurality.

> Poetry enlarges the circumference of the imagination by replenishing it with thoughts of ever new delight, which have the power of attracting and assimilating to their own nature all other thoughts, and which form new intervals and interstices whose void for ever craves fresh food. (488)

> [Poetry] is a strain which distends, and then bursts the circumference of the hearer's mind. . . . (485)[30]

As in the "Medusa," where the beholding subject, the producing subject, and the object produced can never coincide, where all takes place under the aegis of an endless mirroring in which thought no more can trace, poetry or Imagination can never close definitively on that to which it makes its internal adjustment. "Lift[ing] the veil from the hidden beauty of the world" as it spreads the curtain of figural language, it must always refuse to expose meaning, creating, rather, intervals of noncoincidence with that upon which it reflects. It is in this sense that criticism, too, another attempt to behold, might well be regarded as an act of the Imagination.

2

Unbinding Words

How does one begin to read the text entitled *Prometheus Unbound?*
How does one read the monologue that breaks the silence of the
night in which the first scene is set, a scene that explicitly promises the
dawning of a new day? For this monologue is spoken by the figure who
"gave man speech," a speech that then "created thought" (2.4.72).[1]

> He gave man speech, and speech created thought,
> Which is the measure of the Universe;
> And Science struck the thrones of Earth and Heaven
> Which shook but fell not; and the harmonious mind
> Poured itself forth in all-prophetic song.
>
> (2.4.72–76)

How to think this speech, how to measure it, caught as one is in
the all too familiar double bind of thinking that which makes thought
possible and speaking the possibility of speech. The distress of this
reader-baffling situation is assuaged, if not fully alleviated, by the thrust
of Prometheus's words. For it seems to go without saying that Shelley's
text is about the release of the Titan—a restoration to his proper place
and proper authority, then, of the origin of speech and thought—and
about the downfall of all that menaces him.

In the opening lines, Prometheus himself speaks of nothing if not
this. For alongside his insistence on a temporality beyond measure in
which each endlessly divided moment seems the forever of long years
(1.12–15), alongside the stasis that promises "No change, no pause, no
hope!" (1.24), he is yet certain of the advent of the revolutionary hour to
come.

And yet to me welcome is Day and Night,
Whether one breaks the hoar frost of the morn,
Or starry, dim, and slow, the other climbs
The leaden-coloured East; for then they lead
Their wingless, crawling Hours, one among whom
—As some dark Priest hales the reluctant victim—
Shall drag thee, cruel King, to kiss the blood
From these pale feet . . .

$$(1.44-51)^2$$

If the sway of teleology is to overcome an aimless passage of time,[3] the authority in whose name this revolution is to take place is nevertheless somewhat difficult to situate. The originary, compelling moment of this sequence of events took place thousands of years before the opening scene the reader is called to witness. And although we may encounter it belatedly, only through hearsay and a strange ritual of repetition, it would seem to attest to the fact that Prometheus's strength, then as now, lay in his voice. For in contradistinction to Aeschylus's Prometheus, this hero has not acted his defiance but rather spoken it. Shelley, who attempted, as we know, to translate *Faust*,[4] inverts the radical mistranslation that Faust performs in Goethe's play. There too, after all, it is a question of words that make their appearance at the originary moment. In one of the opening scenes Faust announces: "I feel an urge to open up the fundamental text . . . the sacred original" (1.1220–22). And here he begins to translate "In the beginning was the Word"—a "Word" that first becomes "sense," then "force," and ultimately "deed."[5] If Faust turns originary word to deed, Shelley, conversely, transforms the mythological Promethean deed into an originary act of words, the annunciation of the curse.

At that critical juncture, then, Prometheus uttered his devastating curse and set the stage for all to come, for with these words, as Prometheus relates it, he placed his "all-enduring will" against "the fierce omnipotence of Jove," making "his agony / The barrier" to the "else all-conquering foe" (1.114–19) of Earth and her sons.

THE EARTH
And at thy voice [my] pining sons uplifted
Their prostrate brows from the polluting dust
And our almighty Tyrant with fierce dread
Grew pale. . . .

$$(1.159-62)$$

Prometheus's voice has ever since been treasured as a repository of power and value. Earth and her sons "Preserve [that curse], a treasured spell" and "meditate / In secret joy and hope those dreadful words" (1.184–85). The Titan's words, then, shield and preserve and can be preserved in turn as a resource of power.

Yet as the elements of nature recount the effect of Prometheus's voice, they are entirely counter to any promise of deliverance from former sufferings.

> By such dread words from Earth to Heaven
> My still realm was never riven:
>
> (1.99–100)

> Nor any power above or under
> Ever made us mute with wonder!
>
> (1.89–90)

> And we shrank back—for dreams of ruin
> To frozen caves our flight pursuing
> Made us keep silence—thus—and thus—
> Though silence is as hell to us.
>
> (1.103–6)

> Never such a sound before
> To the Indian waves we bore.—
> A pilot asleep on the howling sea
> Leaped up from the deck in agony
> And heard, and cried, "Ah, woe is me!"
> And died as mad as the wild waves be.
>
> (1.93–98)

How are we to understand this double language, which betrays others and itself, which brings with it the violence of madness and rending, which imposes a tyrannical voicelessness on those who would speak? Can such utterance be reconciled with the benevolent figure Asia later describes—he who gave man speech, thought, and Science, a power, as she tells it, able to strike "the thrones of Earth and Heaven" (2.4.74)?

But as no reader of *Prometheus Unbound* can fail to note, the same figure that once defied the omnipotence of Jupiter had also empowered him (1.381–82; 2.4.43–45);[6] the same utterance that shielded those of the earth had also called for their suffering.

Aye, do thy worst. Thou art Omnipotent.
  O'er all things but thyself I gave thee power,
And my own will. Be thy swift mischiefs sent
  To blast mankind, from yon etherial tower.
  Let thy malignant spirit move
  Its darkness over those I love:
  On me and mine I imprecate
  The utmost torture of thy hate

(1.272–79)

What kind of voice is this that claims to be a barrier to the agony of others and also the source of the power to inflict it? And what is the only realm that Prometheus preserves here from the violence of Jove if not that of his own will (1.274), the authority of his own words?

The economy of renunciation is such, however—is this not what we are to understand, and what so many of Shelley's readers have understood before us?—that the hatred and violence of the curse (an invocation that has brought suffering to Earth and Prometheus alike) have been, rather, Prometheus's greatest error. Its reiteration is therefore the path to conscious self-understanding and the means to undo the evil of that speech.[7]

PROMETHEUS
  It doth repent me: words are quick and vain;
  Grief for awhile is blind, and so was mine.
  I wish no living thing to suffer pain.

(1.303–5)

But if such a countercurrent is easy to understand, there are others that make it quite difficult to define the almost unfathomable situation at the opening of the text. Prometheus, hero of the drama, knows that the curse was uttered but cannot recall its content. This lapse marks the loss of something beyond a particular moment of speech, for if he fails to induce the Mountains, Springs, Air, and Whirlwinds to repeat his curse of long ago, what is at stake is nothing less than the present power of his word.

              If then my words had power
  —Though I am changed so that aught evil wish
  Is dead within, although no memory be
  Of what is hate—let them not lose it now!
  What was that curse? for ye all heard me speak.

(1.69–73)

Prometheus desperately seeks the repetition of those words as an affirmation of the power of his voice, and it also would seem to signify the affirmation of his identity.

> I hear a sound of voices—not the voice
> Which I gave forth . . .
> . . . .
> . . . Know ye not me,
> The Titan? . . .
>
> (1.112—18)

What does it mean to have a figure who represents the origin of the spoken word and thought yet forgets his own most critical declamation—whose strange amnesia extends, moreover, to a loss of sense of self and of his own authority? What does it mean that not only is Prometheus bound to a ravine of icy rocks, as the stage directions would have it, but *Prometheus Unbound* opens in the abyss between an obliterated originary moment that it takes three hundred lines to recall and a revolution deferred for yet two acts?

Let us begin with the deferral. It is in fact where the text begins. If Prometheus's penitence is indeed the critical gesture of the drama, the inner revolution required to bring about a transformation of the outer realm, if the moment of recall seems pivotal in that it should summon the past, empty it of its morally negative content, and precipitate us into a new era, how are we to explain the events that follow?[8] For no sooner does he bring about a repetition of the originary linguistic act, no sooner is the gap in memory accounted for, than Prometheus admits its failure to provide the sense of recognition he sought in hearing the voice that he gave forth: "Were these my words, O Parent?" (1.302).

Not only does the repetition of the curse fail to solve the crisis of self-identity and authority, the revolution itself is not measurably closer at hand. Mercury, messenger of Jupiter, immediately appears on the scene, and his errand is revealing.

> Even now thy Torturer arms
> With the strange might of unimagined pains
> The powers who scheme slow agonies in Hell,
> And my commission is, to lead them here,
> Or what more subtle, foul or savage fiends
> People the abyss, and leave them to their task.
> Be it not so! . . . There is a secret known

> To thee and to none else of living things
> Which may transfer the sceptre of wide Heaven,
> The fear of which perplexes the Supreme . . .
> Clothe it in words and bid it clasp his throne
>
> (1.365–75)

For Jupiter, it seems, as for Prometheus and Earth, language, knowledge, and power are inextricably linked. But there, too, Prometheus must confess his impotence: were he willing, he would have neither knowledge nor language to express what Jupiter desires.

> MERCURY
> Thou knowest not the period of Jove's power?
> PROMETHEUS
> I know but this, that it must come.
>
> (1.412–13)

What does it mean to have a figure who promises the coming of the millennium, whose very name, in fact, marks him as a fore-thinker (Prometheus), but who cannot name the hour of his enemy's fall?

The punishment for this refusal has a strange if perhaps predictable relationship to that which came before. Mercury has been accompanied by the Furies, who joyously assault their victim as "ministers of pain and fear" (1.452). Prometheus's words, it seems—willy-nilly—do indeed retain their power, for in the curse, as spoken by the Phantasm of Jupiter, we read:

> Rain then thy plagues upon me here,
> Ghastly disease and frenzying fear;
> And let alternate Frost and fire
> Eat into me and be thine ire
> Lightning and cutting hail and legioned forms
> Of furies, driving by upon the wounding storms.
>
> (1.266–71)

If his tormentors appear as something of the perfectly literal fulfillment of Prometheus's original curse,[9] what has happened to his will to recall that moment of blind fury? "The Curse / Once breathed on thee I would recall" (1.58–59), Prometheus announced in his opening monologue. He wishes, of course, not only to remember his words but also to revoke them. Yet their recitation not only prompts no genuine recall in the sense of recollection; it fails to bring about the desired nullification. Prometheus, it seems, is as little able to empty his words of their power as he is to guarantee their fullness.

And how could it be otherwise when the crucial term in question is *recall?* It is this word that has set the critics by the ears, creating a turmoil with regard to fixing the Titan's exact intent.[10] For *recall,* here as often in Shelley, performs with all the complexity—and none of the ordered control—of the Hegelian term *Aufhebung.* It suggests a calling back to memory and even a more general summoning back, a restoration, a making present once again. How to reconcile this with its sense as revoking or annulling the purport of a text—and this again with its sense as "re-call," to call again, a second time?[11] None of these meanings is able to hold its own in the strategy of Shelley's first act. The curse is summoned back, in a manner of speaking, but is never made present enough to mind to become remembrance. It is called again, but hardly just as it was uttered three thousand years earlier. And the will to revoke, it seems, at least for now, is as doomed as the desire to re-call it precisely.

Prometheus, then, cannot effect his revolution with the gesture of *recall,* and perhaps this explains the manner in which the Furies choose to cause him anguish. As Prometheus's curse undergoes its literal fulfillment, the Furies enter the scene by staging the disasters of past revolutions, the two attempts at moral transvaluation that most resemble that of the Titan. Just as Prometheus's impotence to control the intention of his own language is taking place, at the same moment when his will to revoke a past performative utterance results rather in its perfect success, we read the echo of similar disparities between the effect of language and authorial intent.[12]

Christ, it seems, brought ruin to the world through words that outlived him, words that lived on without him, despite his will to revoke, turning on the truth and peace they were meant to bring about.

> One came forth, of gentle worth,
> Smiling on the sanguine earth;
> His words outlived him, like swift poison
>   Withering up truth, peace and pity.
> . . . .
> Hark that outcry of despair!
> 'Tis his mild and gentle ghost
>   Wailing for the faith he kindled.
>
> (1.546–55)

The promise of the French Revolution was a univocity of sacred names. But this gave way to a confusion and strife reminiscent of what followed the building of Babel.[13]

> Names are there, Nature's sacred watchwords—they
> Were borne aloft in bright emblazonry.
> The nations thronged around, and cried aloud
> As with one voice, "Truth, liberty and love!"
> Suddenly fierce confusion fell from Heaven
> Among them—there was strife, deceit and fear;
> Tyrants rushed in, and did divide the spoil.
> This was the shadow of the truth I saw.
>
> (1.648—55)

If the error of Christ and that of the French Revolution is a naive belief in the power of the word, Prometheus, too, as the Furies would have it, is bound to, and in a sense by, a mistaken concept of language—that concept of a language giving rise to thought and science. The Titan thought to have communicated to mankind the possibility of "clear knowledge," but such delusions of circumscription gave way to structures of open-endedness—hope, love, doubt, desire.

> Dost thou boast the clear knowledge thou waken'dst for man?
> Then was kindled within him a thirst which outran
> Those perishing waters; a thirst of fierce fever,
> Hope, love, doubt, desire—which consume him forever.
>
> (1.542—45)

Prometheus's repentance cannot, for now, close what his gifts have opened. What takes place, however, when Prometheus finally comes into his own? Does this mean that he will come to know his own voice, his self, his past, his future? When all we know of him is liberated, he is indeed unbound, but how are we to understand such unbinding? In this text so concerned with tyrants and slaves, the Titan has met, if not his master, at least his match, one who is neither Jupiter nor his representatives but rather an adversary that even in its name is the counterforce to Prometheus. For it is on the figure of *recall* in all its implications that this crucial scene hangs. It is this that unbinds Prometheus, makes his relationship to words no longer necessarily binding—and not only those of the curse. This is not to say that the intentional link between authority, knowledge, and language is definitively severed. On the contrary. Far more unsettling is that Prometheus may never know whether he is in a

position to recall either as confirmation—to remember, restore, re-call—
or as annulation—to revoke or, for that matter, to find a language that
might fulfill the promise of his own name by naming that which is to
come.

The immediate revolution that Prometheus's readers might like to
foresee, then, does not take place, not least of all because the conventional temporality of revolution is unhinged. For if the difference
between annulling the past and restoring it cannot be designated, how is
one to know whether one is coming or going? There is, however, no
question that a revolution of sorts is what *Prometheus Unbound* is about,
and this is, at least in part, the temporal and linguistic apocalypse that
recall exemplifies. In a sense, then, the moment of recall is indeed the
critical force of revolution, but it fulfills neither the desires of Prometheus nor those of his readers. Prometheus wishes to repent and
thereby to prove the power of his words, to reaffirm his own identity or
even to become conscious of his past errors in order to transcend them.
And if he cannot authentically renounce his will to power, this might be
because the very desire for repentance reasserts that will: "The Curse /
Once breathed on thee I *would* recall" (1.58–59, emphasis mine). Prometheus cannot give up his power, but his words can and do unsay their
speaker.[14] If the moment of recall operates as the vortex of a revolution,
it is because another notion of language is at play in which the authority
of the speaker's will is thoroughly disordered. Recalling cannot at this
moment continue to serve as the remembrance of a particular consciousness, the repetition of a particular voice, or a revocation brought about
by the will of a particular subject. The radical re-nunciation that first
begins to take place here will later reverberate in Prometheus's proleptic
description of the cave (3.3), in the "harmonies divine," the "difference
sweet," and the "echoes of the human world" (3.3.38, 39, 44). It is not
that one will there transcend the contra-diction—such double-talk as
that we saw in Prometheus's original curse, both barrier to and cause of
the same effect. It is just that such "difference" will no longer bear the
onus of moral inconsistency.

Not only is *recall* a word that performs the dissemination of its
varied meanings, these meanings oddly recapitulate some of our most
treasured (if mutually exclusive) theories about how language functions—as a making present in full restoration of that which it names, or
as a bringing to mind of that which is nevertheless recognized as past, or
as that which annuls that of which it speaks. Much of act 1 becomes an

echo chamber for these questions—for the questions of relationship between a subject and its language, between its language and the thing it names—and also for the question of dialogue.[15] The complex problematic of the recall, a language that may well revoke itself in the moment of its affirmation, takes over the entire scene. Earth's ultimate response to Prometheus's desire to take possession of his own words says more than she can know, for she speaks with an irony that can hardly be intentional.

PROMETHEUS
But mine own words, I pray, deny me not.
THE EARTH
They shall be told.—Ere Babylon was dust,
The Magus Zoroaster, my dead child,
Met his own image walking in the garden.
That apparition, sole of men, he saw.
For know, there are two worlds of life and death:
One that which thou beholdest, but the other
Is underneath the grave, where do inhabit
The shadows of all forms that think and live
Till death unite them, and they part no more;
Dreams and the light imaginings of men
And all that faith creates, or love desires,
Terrible, strange, sublime and beauteous shapes,
There thou art, and dost hang, a writhing shade
'Mid whirlwind-peopled mountains; all the Gods
Are there, and all the Powers of nameless worlds,
Vast, sceptred phantoms; heroes, men, and beasts;
And Demogorgon, a tremendous Gloom;

(1.190–207)

This other world is fundamentally one of language, inhabited as it is by images, the images of "all forms that think and live." Prometheus's desire to maintain the power of his voice in having his past words made present to him ("If then my words had power . . . let them not lose it now!"), his desire to confirm his self-identity, is answered by the necessary confrontation with a denial of such possibilities. A form can meet its image, a subject its dreams and imaginings, only by way of death. As always in Shelley's texts, this is no literal death, but a death within life. The passage demands maintaining the disjunction between the image and what it shadows forth. At the very moment of their union the world of shades is a realm of no will to power: here reside names without power and powers without names ("all the Powers of nameless worlds" are there). Thus the attempt to unite power and name, to give speech to a shape, or authority to an image, is a violent and unsuccessful ventriloquism. The figure who speaks the curse will experience that voice as total alterity, as the invasion of an other that rends him from within.

> PHANTASM OF JUPITER
>   What unaccustomed sounds
> Are hovering on my lips, unlike the voice
> With which our pallid race hold ghastly talk
> In darkness? . . .
> . . . .
> A spirit seizes me, and speaks within:
> It tears me as fire tears a thunder-cloud!
>
> (1.242–45, 254–55)

Like Prometheus, the Phantasm hears unaccustomed sounds unlike the voice that might assure him of his own identity. His words belie any possible coincidence between thought and speech—a disjunction that should give us pause, since Prometheus was said to have given speech which then created thought (2.4.72).[16]

> PROMETHEUS
>   Speak the words which I would hear,
> Although no thought inform thine empty voice.
>
> (1.248–49)

Such is the voice that has no thought to "in-form" it, to give shape to the shape. For if the world of this phantasm can be said to consist of anything, it is empty shapes and shades, shadows and images, the violent questionability of representation performed by the figure of the recall.

The first act requires a confrontation with the realm of the dead and all that realm implies; it remains caught in the involutions of recalling the past. However, the second act moves forward, it would seem, with a sense of momentum to the point of transformation and actual revolution. Asia is joined by Panthea, and together they follow the call of Echoes to Demogorgon's abode. There they are carried away by the Car of the Hour in the apocalyptic passage that concludes with Asia's monologue: "My soul is an enchanted Boat."

For all this, the opening lines of the second act seem an uncanny repetition of the crises of act 1. The setting of the earlier scene pledged the dawning of a new day ("Morning slowly breaks" [act 1, scene description]) only to be followed by a peculiarly inexorable temporal dilemma. In the second act Asia, too, announces what seems to be the coming of a new era. This spring, however, is a season more immediately bound to memory than to regeneration. The entire act moves between an imperfect recuperation of past dreams and the dream of a future that is not quite realized.

> Yes, like a spirit, like a thought which makes
> Unwonted tears throng to the horny eyes
> And beatings haunt the desolated heart
> Which should have learnt repose,—thou hast descended
> Cradled in tempests; thou dost wake, O Spring!
> O child of many winds! As suddenly
> Thou comest as the memory of a dream
> Which now is sad because it hath been sweet;
>
> (2.1.2–9)

These are no "soft winds," no "mild winds," from which the "snow-storms flee," as the chorus of spirits prophesies at the close of act 1 (lines 791–98). Spring comes "suddenly," cradled in the tempests and blasts of Heaven—an awakening that ruptures repose rather than guaranteeing new fullness. Spring's abruptness is "like a thought" (2.1.2), like a movement "of the human mind" (preface, p. 133), that undoes the valence of its object, a reflection on past operations of the mind, a memory that inverts the value of what it reflects, turning sweetness to sadness. If, as Asia goes on to proclaim, "This is the season, this the day, the hour" (2.1.13), it is the season of poorly camouflaged violence as it swiftly descends, less, it would seem, as the spirit of new beginnings than as a disfigurement of the past—of past dreams and of reality.

> Like genius, or like joy which riseth up
> As from the earth, clothing with golden clouds
> The desart of our life. . . .
> This is the season, this the day, the hour;
>
> (2.1.10–13)

But is this the season, the day, the hour? When spring appears as a memory that fails to recapture the dream of the past, the advent of the long-awaited moment seems nevertheless to be at hand. Such immediacy, however, quickly gives way to a temporality of delay.

> This is the season, this the day, the hour;
> At sunrise thou shouldst come, sweet sister mine,
> Too long desired, too long delaying, come!
> How like death-worms the wingless moments crawl!
> The point of one white star is quivering still
> Deep in the orange light of widening morn
> Beyond the purple mountains; through a chasm
> Of wind-divided mist the darker lake
> Reflects it—now it wanes—it gleams again
> As the waves fade, and as the burning threads
> Of woven cloud unravel in pale air. . . .
> 'Tis lost! . . .
>
> (2.1.13–24)

As in act 1, the present moment is caught between the loss of the past and a deferral of the future, as though it had no other definition of its own. For even before Panthea enters, the present moment of "this . . . the season, this the day, the hour" has been lost—the golden clouds to which the springtime had just been compared (2.1.11) have come unraveled: "the burning threads / Of woven cloud unravel in pale air. . . ." (2.1.22–23). And on her arrival, Panthea's eyes, "Like stars half quenched in mists of silver dew" (2.1.29), appear there only to reiterate another emblem of belatedness of which Asia had just spoken, the waning of the morning star in the waves of the lake (2.1.17–22).

>   —hear I not
> The Æolian music of her sea-green plumes
> Winnowing the crimson dawn?
>   [Panthea *enters*]
>   I feel, I see
> Those eyes which burn through smiles that fade in tears
> Like stars half quenched in mists of silver dew.
> Beloved and most beautiful, who wearest
> The shadow of that soul by which I live,
> How late thou art! the sphered sun had climbed
> The sea, my heart was sick with hope, before
> The printless air felt thy belated plumes.
>
> (2.1.25–34)

Panthea's arrival marks the coming of an "Æolian music." Yet strangely enough, this music, created as Panthea's plumes "winnow . . . the crimson dawn," appears also as a writing. It is this displacement that

takes shape over and over throughout the scene. The slide is between
plume and plume, from nature to text and from the promise of immediate perception ("I feel, I see") to a more questionable print produced in
the temporality of delay ("The printless air felt thy belated plumes"),
marked upon the otherwise blank page of the printless air.

If this music is not offered to view, there is another kind of text that
Asia wishes to read, a text that she is sure Panthea carries with her. For if
spring implied a transvaluation of past dreams, most of the scene now
turns on the narration of half-remembered dreams.

> PANTHEA
> Pardon, great Sister! but my wings were faint
> With the delight of a remembered dream
> As are the noontide plumes of summer winds
> Satiate with sweet flowers. . . .
> . . . .
> ASIA
>   Lift up thine eyes
> And let me read thy dream.—
>
> (2.1.35–38, 55–56)

How does one read in the eyes of another? What kind of reading is
this, and what can one hope to find there? It is as though Asia expects to
take in that dream as something one can really sense, as one takes in, say,
the perfume of sweet flowers carried on summer winds. She forgets,
perhaps, to listen to Panthea's words to her: "I am made the wind /
Which fails beneath the music that I bear / Of thy most wordless
converse" (2.1.50–51). When Panthea insists on the spoken word, upon
telling the story of her dream ("As I have said" [2.1.56], she continues),
such mediating converse is lost upon Asia. Asia declares words the
empty equivalent of air.

> ASIA
>   Thou speakest, but thy words
> Are as the air. I feel them not. . . . oh, lift
> Thine eyes that I may read his written soul!
> PANTHEA
> I lift them, though they droop beneath the load
> Of that they would express—what canst thou see
> But thine own fairest shadow imaged there?
>
> (2.1.108–13)

The written soul, the text that Asia searches for in place of the disconcerting narration, is nevertheless an ambiguous creature of shadow or
shade. Perhaps "thine own fairest shadow," as Panthea calls it, an image
of Asia herself, or of Panthea, whom Prometheus had called the shadow
of Asia (2.1.70), or of Prometheus, as Asia would have it, for these three
are image and shadow of one another.

> There is a change: beyond their inmost depth
> I see a shade—a shape—'tis He, arrayed
> In the soft light of his own smiles which spread
> Like radiance from the cloud-surrounded moon.
> Prometheus, it is thou—depart not yet!
>
> (2.1.119–23)

If it is indeed Prometheus who appears, if Asia's desire for the immediate
"[reading of] his written soul" (2.1.110) would seem fulfilled, this figure is
nevertheless just as immediately driven out by another, another shape,
another dream, whose content is the purest message of necessary deferral
and transience.[17]

> DREAM
>   Follow, follow!
> PANTHEA
> It is mine other dream.—
> ASIA
>   It disappears.
>
> (2.1.131–32)

Just prior to this, Panthea had spoken of the dream Asia wishes to
grasp within her sister's eyes. That discourse, had Asia been able to
follow it, spoke of the necessary ambiguity of the direct presence that
Asia seeks. As in act 1, no simple plenitude of recall is possible without
the reverberations of loss: "Then two dreams came. One I remember
not" (2.1.61). Yet it is not only the distance of its retelling that brings a
forgetfulness and consciousness of obliteration. Panthea's dreamed experience of presence bespeaks loss of yet another kind.

> Then two dreams came. One I remember not.
> But in the other, his pale, wound-worn limbs
> Fell from Prometheus, and the azure night
> Grew radiant with the glory of that form
> Which lives unchanged within, and his voice fell
> Like music which makes giddy the dim brain

Faint with intoxication of keen joy:
"Sister of her whose footsteps pave the world
With loveliness—more fair than aught but her
Whose shadow thou art—lift thine eyes on me!"
I lifted them— . . .

(2.1.61–71)

Prometheus's call to Panthea to lift her eyes on him echoes Asia's insistent requests: "Lift up thine eyes / And let me read thy dream.—" (2.1.55–56; see also lines 109–10). Panthea's initial refusal, her determination to narrate her tale rather than allow it to be read directly, may reflect her understanding (for this is what the dream is about) that there is no light in this drama without shadow, no direct presence without the necessity of veiling and the risk of dissolution.

I lifted them—the overpowering light
Of that immortal shape was shadowed o'er
By love; which, from his soft and flowing limbs
And passion-parted lips, and keen faint eyes
Steam'd forth like vaporous fire; an atmosphere
Which wrapt me in its all-dissolving power
As the warm ether of the morning sun
Wraps ere it drinks some cloud of wandering dew.
I saw not—heard not—moved not—only felt
His presence flow and mingle through my blood
Till it became his life and his grew mine
And I was thus absorbed— . . .

(2.1.71–82)

Prometheus's power dissolves whatever it encounters, and this absorption is not altogether one of ecstatic union: for his voice "fell / Like music which makes giddy the dim brain" (2.1.65–66), so that Panthea neither saw, nor heard, nor moved. And when Panthea's being is once again condensed, she finds her thoughts unable to articulate what she has heard.

My being was condensed, and as the rays
Of thought were slowly gathered, I could hear
His voice, whose accents lingered ere they died
Like footsteps of far melody. Thy name,
Among the many sounds alone I heard
Of what might be articulate . . .

(2.1.86–91)

In a sense, is this not as it should be—a testimony to the overwhelming glorification of Prometheus to come, the overpowering light
of the new godhead? It is a glory of which Asia, too, would seem to
partake, if we are to believe the song that precedes her self-proclaimed
enchantment at the close of the act. For there a voice bids Asia to screen
her smiles:

> then screen them
> In those looks where whoso gazes
> Faints, entangled in their mazes.
>
> (2.5.51–53)

> And all feel, yet see thee never
> As I feel now, lost forever!
>
> Lamp of Earth! where'er thou movest
>   Its dim shapes are clad with brightness
> And the souls of whom thou lovest
>   Walk upon the winds with lightness
> Till they fail, as I am failing,
> Dizzy, lost . . . yet unbewailing!
>
> (2.5.64–71)

Like Prometheus, Asia cannot be directly gazed upon, and just as his
transfiguration brought intoxication that baffled thought, her glory, too,
leaves the gazer dizzy and lost forever.

If this particular voice is unbewailing in the face of such menacing
splendor, Ione seems to look upon the matter somewhat differently. In
the wake of Panthea's dream:

> Ione wakened then, and said to me:
> "Canst thou divine what troubles me tonight?
> I always knew what I desired before
> Nor ever found delight to wish in vain.
> But now I cannot tell thee what I seek;
> I know not—something sweet since it is sweet
> Even to desire—. . . .
>
> (2.1.93–99)

As Ione lies asleep, Panthea locked within her arms (2.1.46), in immediate proximity to the figure who dreams of immediate proximity, something unheard of takes place. Something is displaced. Embittering the
sweetness of desire is a troubling blank in the possibilities of thought. If
Ione always knew before what it was she desired, the object of her

longing can no longer be told or known. Her encounter with the
dreaming Panthea seems to instill an open-ended thirst of love and
desire,[18] a desire that precludes her knowing or naming its object,
precludes, then, any possibility of teleological fulfillment.

Thus, if, according to the "voice" at the close of act 2, Asia's "lips
enkindle / With their love the breath between them" (2.5.48–49), Ione
offers an accusatory explanation for the source of such warmth.

> "—it is thy sport, false sister!
> Thou hast discovered some inchantment old
> Whose spells have stolen my spirit as I slept
> And mingled it with thine;—for when just now
> We kissed, I felt within thy parted lips
> The sweet air that sustained me; and the warmth
> Of the life-blood for loss of which I faint
> Quivered between our intertwining arms."
>
> (2.1.99–106)

While Panthea lay "pressed within / The folded depth of [Ione's] life-
breathing bosom" (2.1.48–49), at least as Ione would have it, Panthea's
spells stole her sister's spirit and absorbed it into hers. Thus Ione feels
that the "sweet air that [once] sustained" her is now elsewhere—within
the parted lips of Panthea—and in her arms she finds the warmth of her
own lifeblood. The dreaming of Panthea, a seeming response to the
desire for completion and fulfillment, brings about a theft and emptying,
and perhaps a warning against misreading the significance of the revolution to come.

The opening scene of *Prometheus Unbound* enacts the crisis of
knowing one's own voice, of coming to terms with one's self, and places
this dilemma in the broader matrix of a rupture in our conventional
temporal and linguistic structures. Act 2 repeats these crises, this time in
the context of a mystified sense of oneness with the other.[19] For the
relationship between Asia and Panthea, who, despite appearances, do
not quite see eye to eye, is negatively echoed by that of Panthea to the
dreamed shape of Prometheus, by that of the transfigured Asia to those
around her, as well as by that of Ione to Panthea. These intersubjective
unions, which fall dangerously short of simple ecstasy, now give way to
narrations that insistently juxtapose a temporality of incipience over
against deferral, a promise of presence over against a writing that
dislocates.

Once Asia has witnessed in Panthea's eyes the displacement of Prometheus by another shade, Panthea goes on to speak of this, her second dream. Like that which Asia will soon relate, Panthea's dream concerns the meaning of their present encounter:

DREAM
> Follow, follow!

PANTHEA
It is mine other dream.—

ASIA
> It disappears.

PANTHEA
It passes now into my mind. Methought
As we sate here the flower-infolding buds
Burst on yon lightning-blasted almond tree,
When swift from the white Scythian wilderness
A wind swept forth wrinkling the Earth with frost . . .
I looked, and all the blossoms were blown down.

(2.1.131–38)

Like that springtime that left the opening of act 2 more a rupture than a period of generation, a springtime that descended upon us "From all the blasts of Heaven," "Cradled in tempests" and "child of many winds" (2.1.1–7), the springtime of Panthea's dream is a bursting grafted onto that which is already blasted ("the flower-infolding buds / Burst on yon lightning-blasted almond tree"), a blossoming coincident, as well, with a violent wind. And not just any wind, nor just a wind that tears the flowers from the trees in the season of their unfolding, blowing them down in the very moment of their blowing.

> But on each leaf was stamped—as the blue bells
> Of Hyacinth tell Apollo's written grief—
> *O follow, follow!*

(2.1.139–41)

The inscription on each leaf is, perhaps, the counterpromise of this brutal spring, but a counterpromise not to be misinterpreted as the seemingly banal optimism of that other misread wind—"O Wind, / If Winter comes, can Spring be far behind?" ("Ode to the West Wind," 69–70)—an optimism that Shelley's most famous line, in any case, belies with the rhetorical question. In act 2 of *Prometheus Unbound* there is no springtime that is separate from the blast of the wind, a wind that is neither the destroyer of a fullness that established itself before nor the harbinger of another era yet to come.

How are we then to understand the message on each leaf, the doubly inscribed leaf that forces us from the botanical realm of organic continuity to that of the written text: how are we to read this volume of scattered pages? The mode of their stamping, we are told, is like the grief of Apollo inscribed on the blue bells of Hyacinth. Whatever the echoed call to follow may indicate, in recalling the plight of Apollo it cannot offer the promise of fulfillment. For that myth reiterates the inevitably failed attempt to eradicate the difference between self and other, and reiterates it with a vengeance. This is a vengeance, tellingly enough, both by and on him who would presume to take language as his medium— and to take it in a particular sense. Apollo, as the first god to desire one of his own sex,[20] fell in love with the lad Hyacinthus. Yet Apollo is strangely doubled by a human rival who, like his divine counterpart, bears the title of poet. Thamyris so blindly exulted in that title that he boasted of talents superior to those of the Muses (*Iliad* 695–700). Apollo had only to report this insolent pride for the Muses to deprive the human poet of sight, voice, and memory (to leave him, then, much as Panthea was left on her encounter with Prometheus).

Having destroyed his rival in love by denying him his power of lyrical poetry, as though the one were somehow the enabling metaphor for the other, as though what was being undone were a language whose utterance fulfills desire, Apollo presumes himself now the possessor of Hyacinthus. But the divine poet fares no better than Thamyris before him: he, too, learns the rude lesson that forces him out of his usual mode of composition. Apollo in turn incurs the jealousy of the West Wind, and like the wind of Panthea's dream, which tears each blossom from the branch and stamps it with words of dislocation, the West Wind of the myth is the force of a brutally significant and complex transformation. For as Apollo instructs Hyacinthus in the throw of the discus, the Wind changes that object hurled away from the youth into something of a boomerang which strikes him dead with his own missile.[21]

Hyacinthus's blood is changed into the flower that bears the same name. Indeed it bears several senses of the same name. Just as the discus is made to retrace its path and recoil on its author, Apollo must learn to write in a mode of language that simultaneously affirms and denies the object of his desire. On its petals Apollo, who is now metamorphosed into a poet of another order, inscribes the letters that at once name his lover and tell his written grief. For alpha iota are the initial letters of Hyacinthus's name, a seeming call to presence, at the very least an insistence on memory, and also the cry of woe that acknowledges the irrevocability of his loss.

Panthea's dream leaves the reader in a rather baffling situation. For if it is presented in the unmistakable guise of the prophetic dream, as a scenario whose interpretation is bound to clarify the future, everything in its structure and content belies that possibility. It is, after all, almost more immediately forgotten than remembered: "Then two dreams came. One I remember not" (2.1.61). Whereas the traditional prophetic dream presupposes a correlation between dream text and event, a memory before the event, so to speak, this particular prophetic moment nearly defies that link. Not only does the dream first figure as a blank in consciousness, not only does its appearance finally take shape as the displacement of Prometheus's presence to Asia,[22] as a disjunction rather than a prophecy of their future union; the very content of that dream warns of misreading fulfillment where there is none, of misreading apparent signs of generation as the harbingers of a plenitude to come. Panthea's dream tells of undercutting the continuity on which the structure of organic growth, as well as the structure of prophecy, is based. The bursting of buds upon the almond trees does not unfold the first flowers of spring but takes place, rather, with a double rupture in our expectations. Those blossoms are blown down by the natural, if seemingly perverse, force of the wind from the Scythian wilderness. But perhaps more significant is the at first imperceptible displacement from leaf to leaf, from vernal growth to the printed page. And yet it is not the stamped message alone that makes the printed leaf a disruption of its natural counterpart, nor is it a simple crossing out of the kind of teleology associated both with organic nature and with successful prophecy. What is printed on the leaf, as the text goes on to say, is a mocking of their voices rather than their realization (2.1.162–63), one that is emphatically and appropriately made to rhyme with "hollow" (2.1.175). "*O follow, follow!*" (2.1.141) is at once the structure of prophecy and its denial, a pointing towards or a call to move in the direction of— but without an endpoint. The leaves of Panthea's dream are like "the blue bells / Of Hyacinth [that] tell Apollo's written grief" (2.1.139–40), because each tells the tale of the impossibility of its telling. The substitution of the flower for the boy takes place with an inscription whose double register denies the voice of lyrical affirmation that might recuperate the past, and with it the gesture of the metaphor. Thus the substitution of the prophetic text for imminent reality comes about in a narration that insists on the dislocation of such continuities. What becomes predictable, then—if predictability were to remain a viable concept—is nothing more, and nothing less, than the production of the peculiar kind of writing encountered in these metaphors for the impossibility of metaphor.

But it seems to go without saying that despite all, Panthea's dream is about that which is to follow. Such writing appears at the critical moment of the revolution, or—at least at the moment of revolution in Shelley's text—at what seems to be the beginning of a new era, which could well be read as the substitution of a new authority in the place of a morally degenerate one. At the juncture of Jupiter's downfall reverberates a certain cry, a cry whose syllables are printed nowhere else in all of Shelley's poetry but one which nevertheless echoes significantly. For what Jupiter calls is that same *"ai"* that the god of wisdom and poetry must learn to write, the "Ai!" of Apollo's written grief."

> Let Hell unlock
> Its mounded Oceans of tempestuous fires,
> And whelm on them into the bottomless void
> The desolated world and thee and me,
> The conqueror and the conquered, and the wreck
> Of that for which they combated.
>   Ai! Ai!
> The elements obey me not . . . I sink . . .
> Dizzily down—ever, forever, down—
> And, like a cloud, mine enemy above
> Darkens my fall with victory!—Ai! Ai!

$$(3.1.74-83)$$

If Panthea's dream is prophetic of the revolution to come—and such a coincidence in Jupiter's spoken grief would seem to leave room for no other interpretation—it is a revolution that teaches us to rethink the nature of revolution. For the revolutionary wail and the revolutionary script tell us the no longer now of "Ai!" or the not here, not yet, of "follow"; they mark a questioning of the concept of revolution as teleology and of language as metaphor.

This is a language, then, that speaks of its own rupture, and it is perhaps because of this that it is the pauses in Panthea's narration which speak most meaningfully to Asia.

As you speak, your words
Fill, pause by pause my own forgotten sleep
With shapes. . . .

(2.1.141–43)

What the gaps in Panthea's narration lead Asia to partially remember is her own dream, a dream that both alters and echoes that of her sister. Asia, too, speaks of moments of incipience that give way to a written call to deferral.

And the white dew on the new-bladed grass,
Just piercing the dark earth, hung silently—
And there was more which I remember not;
But, on the shadows of the morning clouds
Athwart the purple mountain slope was written
Follow, O follow! as they vanished by,
And on each herb from which Heaven's dew had fallen
The like was stamped as with a withering fire;
A wind arose among the pines—it shook
The clinging music from their boughs, and then
Low, sweet, faint sounds, like the farewell of ghosts,
Were heard—*O follow, follow, follow me!*
And then I said: "Panthea, look on me."
But in the depth of those beloved eyes
Still I saw, *follow, follow!*

(2.1.148–62)

The *"follow, follow"* of Asia's dream comes once again as the answer to the desire to find immediate presence in her sister's eyes. Once again Asia has asked Panthea to "lift / Thine eyes," presumably so "that I may read [Prometheus's] written soul!" (2.1.109–10), but her dream insists on the "withering fire" of another inscription. This refusal of "a [reassuring] shade—a shape" (2.1.120), this other kind of inscription, is undoubtedly a call to read differently. In a manner of speaking, Asia follows its call, although what she follows are "Echoes," voices whose origins are not their own, voices dislocated from the source of authority. But whether Asia has learned to read is yet to be answered.

ECHOES
In the world unknown
    Sleeps a voice unspoken;
By thy step alone

Can its rest be broken,
Child of Ocean!

(2.1.190—94)

Asia, it seems, is called to break the rest of a "voice unspoken." Will
she then come to know the realm of Demogorgon, formerly "the world
unknown"? will she bring the "voice unspoken" to full speech, or will
she merely break the rest of a voice that must forever remain, in some
sense, unspoken, awakening its refusal of open voice?[23] It depends, of
course, on how one reads what Shelley has to say.

> PANTHEA
> Hither the sound has borne us—to the realm
> Of Demogorgon, and the mighty portal,
> Like a volcano's meteor-breathing chasm,
> Whence the oracular vapour is hurled up
> Which lonely men drink wandering in their youth
> And call truth, virtue, love, genius or joy—
> That maddening wine of life, whose dregs they drain
> To deep intoxication, and uplift
> Like Mænads who cry loud, Evoe! Evoe!
> The voice which is contagion to the world.
>
> (2.3.1—10)

The entrance to Demogorgon's abode, at any rate, is inauspicious
enough, for it hurls an oracular vapor that intoxicates to a misapprehension of truth, that causes those who drink of it to cry in the mænadic
voice that accompanied the dismemberment of the prototypical lyric
poet. To be sure, all this seems put to rights once Jupiter is deposed
(3.3.124—47), and Asia herself is not one to question, much less rend, the
integrity of the lyrical utterance.

On the contrary. Her entire dialogue with Demogorgon is a
celebration of the power of the word, albeit an ironized celebration. For
if earlier Asia's concept of reading was the direct perception of Prometheus's "written soul" (2.1.110), "a shape . . . arrayed / In the soft light
of his own smiles which spread / Like radiance from the cloud-sur-
rounded moon" (2.1.120—22), her confrontation with Demogorgon
systematically inverts each value of that image.

> PANTHEA
> I see a mighty Darkness
> Filling the seat of power; and rays of gloom

Dart round, as light from the meridian Sun,
Ungazed upon and shapeless—neither limb
Nor form—nor outline . . .

(2.4.2–6)

From the question of negative perception the text immediately shifts to that of knowledge, or perhaps quite literally to that of knowledge as question.

DEMOGORGON
> Ask what thou wouldst know.

ASIA
What canst thou tell?

DEMOGORGON
> > All things thou dar'st demand.

(2.4.7–8)

What Asia is slow to grasp is that Demogorgon may bid her ask but promises only to "tell" rather than answer. And what he will tell is no more and no less than what she will ask.[24] It seems fitting, then, that the guides to Demogorgon's realm are echoes. For Demogorgon's particular form of oracular pronouncement is ultimately not unlike the echo, however misunderstood that form of expression must necessarily be.

Thus at the close of their dialogue Asia admits that Demogorgon can only echo what her own soul would answer.

ASIA
So much I asked before, and my heart gave
The response thou hast given; and of such truths
Each to itself must be the oracle.—
One more demand . . . and do thou answer me
As my own soul would answer, did it know
That which I ask. . . .

(2.4.121–26)

To the end, however, Asia remains blinded by a desire for a certain kind of knowledge.[25] Thus she asks exactly the same question that Jupiter earlier posed through Mercury. For from the very beginning of their encounter, Asia has sought a means to name power.

ASIA
Who made the living world?

DEMOGORGON
> > God.

ASIA
                              Who made all
That it contains—thought, passion, reason, will,
Imagination?
DEMOGORGON
                 God, Almighty God.

                                              (2.4.9–11)

Apparently satisfied with the self-evident significance of Demogorgon's response, Asia goes on to seek a name for the authority behind the forces of evil. But here Demogorgon offers no name but rather a force as action.

ASIA
And who made terror, madness, crime, remorse?

. . . .

DEMOGORGON
                                              He reigns.
ASIA
Utter his name—a world pining in pain
Asks but his name; curses shall drag him down.
DEMOGORGON
He reigns.
ASIA
              I feel, I know it—who?
DEMOGORGON
                                   He reigns.

                                              (2.4.19, 28–31)

More precisely, it is not the name per se that Asia desires, for the long speech that follows proves that she, too, could pronounce it if she wished. What Asia seeks is the control that accompanies naming, domination through the curse, language as authority: she thus reiterates the various calls to and recalls of power of Prometheus and Earth in act 1.

If Demogorgon refuses to answer, if he insists on performing the unspokenness of his own voice, Asia fills in that void abysm of the refusal of a language of power with her own narration. Her long speech (2.4.32–109) recounts the historical tale of the beginning of the world, its rule by Saturn, and, through Prometheus's gift of wisdom, its fall to Jupiter, during whose reign Prometheus has done all possible to give men dominion over the world around them, to grant "The birthright of their being, knowledge, power" (2.4.39). The Titan may stand at the origin of speech, which creates thought, prophetic song, and music, he may stand at the origin of Science, which challenges "the thrones of Earth and Heaven" (2.4.74), but Asia's description is peculiarly punctuated by a replication of those same structures of false power.

> And he tamed fire, which like some beast of prey
> Most terrible, but lovely, played beneath
> The frown of man, and tortured to his will
> Iron and gold, the slaves and signs of power,
> And gems and poisons, and all subtlest forms
> Hidden beneath the mountains and the waves.
>
> (2.4.66–71)

Prometheus, as she would have it, has instituted new relations of power and slavery in place of old ones. Asia, too, is less interested in abolishing thrones altogether than in establishing a new hierarchical order.

> ASIA
> While yet [Jupiter's] frown shook Heaven, aye when
> His adversary from adamantine chains
> Cursed him, he trembled like a slave. Declare
> Who is his master? Is he too a slave?
> DEMOGORGON
> All spirits are enslaved who serve things evil:
> Thou knowest if Jupiter be such or no.
> ASIA
> Whom calledst thou God?
> DEMOGORGON
> I spoke but as ye speak—
> For Jove is the supreme of living things.
> ASIA
> Who is the master of the slave?
>
> (2.4.106–14)

Just what is at stake in Demogorgon's continued refusal to answer? To be sure, the imperative that drives him here has nothing to do with an unwillingness to upset the mastery of Jupiter. This, after all, is the crucial event that takes place only one scene later. Demogorgon's reticence arises, rather, from Asia's fundamental misapprehension of the nature of truth and language.

DEMOGORGON
                              —If the Abysm
Could vomit forth its secrets:—but a voice
Is wanting, the deep truth is imageless;
For what would it avail to bid thee gaze
On the revolving world? what to bid speak
Fate, Time, Occasion, Chance and Change? To these
All things are subject but eternal Love.

                                             (2.4.114–20)

Demogorgon's "deep truth" is that of the abysm. It has no ground, no voice, no possibility of being represented. One can gaze on the revolving world ruled by "Fate, Time, Occasion, Chance and Change." Indeed poetry's "figured curtain," as we have seen Shelley call it elsewhere,[26] a realm of images, is just this world—and the only realm, in one form or another, to which we may have access. But nowhere, and certainly not by way of Demogorgon, can "the deep truth" be voiced as Asia wishes, as a presence, as the present, as a here and now that endures.[27]

Thus, in answer to Asia's final question, "When shall the destined hour arrive?" (2.4.128), she beholds cars that seem to be borne between the fear of that behind them and a desire that is repeatedly deferred:

DEMOGORGON
                              Behold!
ASIA
The rocks are cloven, and through the purple night
I see Cars drawn by rainbow-winged steeds
Which trample the dim winds—in each there stands
A wild-eyed charioteer, urging their flight.
Some look behind, as fiends pursued them there
And yet I see no shapes but the keen stars:
Others with burning eyes lean forth, and drink
With eager lips the wind of their own speed
As if the thing they loved fled on before,
And now—even now they clasped it; their bright locks
Stream like a comet's flashing hair: they all
Sweep onward.—

                                             (2.4.129–40)

But surely there is a "far goal of Time" (3.3.174), a resting place, promised by the Spirit of the hour (2.4.173), announced by Asia at the end of act 2 and by Earth in act 3 and implicit, most certainly, in the overall trajectory of the drama. Asia and Panthea arrive at the Caucasus, borne by the car and accompanied by the spirit who was Demogorgon's answer to Asia's "when." Prometheus is unbound by Hercules, and in the moment of his unbinding he performs the fore-thought promised by his name. For here Prometheus tells of an era, now only ever so slightly deferred, when he and Asia, Panthea, and Ione will pass their time out of time in a place that escapes the conventional parameters of locality.

Still it is not that Prometheus envisions space and time as finally becoming the stable here and now after which Asia so longed, for while he may claim to speak of a state of permanence, the passage describes a perpetual interchange between the cave and two realms that define it through their otherness—the abode of nature and the realm of man.

> And there is heard the ever-moving air
> Whispering without from tree to tree, and birds,
> And bees; and all around are mossy seats
> And the rough walls are clothed with long soft grass;
> A simple dwelling, which shall be our own,
> Where we will sit and talk of time and change
> As the world ebbs and flows, ourselves unchanged—
>
> (3.3.18–24)

The difference between the cave and its exterior is easy to define but difficult to maintain. The world ebbs and flows, the air is ever-moving, as are the bees and birds; and yet those within remain "unchanged." This same natural world, nevertheless, is at once outside the cave and inside the cave (3.3.20–21), at once both of these and the border that separates the two.

> There is a Cave
> All overgrown with trailing odorous plants
> Which curtain out the day with leaves and flowers
>
> (3.3.10–12)

This curtain, like so many veils in Shelley,[28] rises less to reveal than to insist on a blindness. It curtains out the day but curtains it in as well—"the . . . walls are clothed with long soft grass"—and curtains in not only the verdant growth of that realm without but also, apparently, its perpetual change.

> A simple dwelling, which shall be our own,
> Where we will sit and talk of time and change
> As the world ebbs and flows, ourselves unchanged—

What can hide man from Mutability?—
And if ye sigh, then I will smile, and thou
Ione, shall chant fragments of sea-music,
Until I weep, when ye shall smile away
The tears she brought, which yet were sweet to shed;
We will entangle buds and flowers, and beams
Which twinkle on the fountain's brim, and make
Strange combinations out of common things
Like human babes in their brief innocence;
And we will search, with looks and words of love
For hidden thoughts, each lovelier than the last,
Our unexhausted spirits, and like lutes
Touched by the skill of the enamoured wind,
Weave harmonies divine, yet ever new,
From difference sweet where discord cannot be.

(3.3.22–39)

If the natural world ebbs and flows, if man cannot escape Mutability, what Prometheus envisages for himself, nevertheless, is also mutability, a permanent if entirely "sweet" mutability. When Asia sighs, he will smile. When Prometheus weeps, Asia will smile, a differentiation to be brought about by Ione's chanting of sea-music. For the entire experience takes place under the aegis of music and poetry: the group will "talk of time and change," making "Strange combinations out of common things," "search[ing] with looks and words of love / For hidden thoughts," "Weav[ing] harmonies divine." It marks a break from what preceded it, for Prometheus has moved from the theater of political struggle, in which "discord" displays a decisive will to authority, to that of an apparently will-less interior scene of poetic creation.

Nevertheless, the fixed closure implied by the metaphor of withdrawal is belied not only by the unremitting interchange with the world outside but also by the "difference sweet" of the perpetual activity within. The flowers and birds of the natural realm enter into strange combination with the beams of the fountain in a creation that takes place as ever new juxtapositions and harmonies. Here, however, a flower is never treated as a flower, for nothing can remain itself or maintain its self-identity: every element enters into play only in relation to its other. Like that other flower that could not be itself, the syllable *ai* written by the god of poetry that named the flower and much else as well, the poetry of the cave brings about endless self-differentiation, but without the pathos of desire and grief.[29] Nothing is uttered here without the difference implicit in a recall that is at once repetition and renunciation, restoration and revocation.

The natural object enters the cave to lose all semblance of organic unity—a nonviolent version of the rupture-into-text of the leaves in Asia's and Panthea's dreams. For the cave, on the other hand, the unremitting interchange with the natural world signifies a surrender of any illusory claim to a necessity of the poetic enterprise within that might escape substance. Nor therefore can a claim to natural essence be recuperated in the name of a poetry that, precisely through such substantiality, might escape the dislocations of representation. The passage is constructed with a startling symmetry that sets everything off balance.

For no sooner are we assured of the "difference sweet" and harmonies divine that arise from within than Prometheus turns to the other sounds that come to the cave from without: "the echoes of the human world" (3.3.44).[30] For unlike the natural sounds, all that enters from the human world comes by way of "mediators" (3.3.58). All sounds and shapes come forth as "echoes," murmurs, "apparitions," "phantoms," "shadows" (3.3.44–57). A new version, then, of "Mont Blanc"'s "cave of the witch Poesy," where the "ceaseless motion" and "unremitting interchange" lead to a meditation on the phantasy of the human mind.[31] As in that earlier text, a "legion of wild thoughts," "swift shapes and sounds" (3.3.60) seem murmured in a voice too low and too "unresting"[32] to be grasped.

The apparitions that visit Prometheus are bound to disquiet any seduction into a poetics of immediacy or duration. The imagery that earlier denoted the world outside the cave—winds, bees, flowers—here returns as the apparently incidental matter of description and simile. But what could be more unsettling to the natural earthly realm to which such imagery refers than a mythological allusion to Enna, the meadow whose ground collapsed at the moment Hades carried off Persephone. For, as the myth tells us, when the god of the underworld abducted Demeter's daughter, the goddess of fruit and harvest went into mourning, so that Hades carried off the earth's natural plenitude as well.[33]

> And hither come, sped on the charmed winds
> Which meet from all the points of Heaven, as bees
> From every flower aerial Enna feeds
> At their known island-homes in Himera,

> The echoes of the human world, which tell
> Of the low voice of love . . .
>
> (3.3.40—45)

It is not a question here of simply counterbalancing two realms of absolutes outside the cave, the one the here and now of natural substance, the other the space of pure representation. It is not that Prometheus's naming of the human implies the displacement of reality by image and art. The human world performs, in the structure of an echo, as menace to the natural realm. Thus Prometheus re-calls the elements of nature in a gesture that simultaneously causes the bees and flowers of "aerial Enna" to stand in the service of a myth that underscores their potential disappearance.

This echo chamber of representation[34] is, for Prometheus, now no cause for grief, no sign of loss like the earlier attempt at recall nor a sign of empty deferral like the "follow" of prophecy in act 2. It is rather

> The wandering voices and the shadows these
> Of all that man becomes, the mediators
> Of that best worship, love, by him and us
> Given and returned, swift shapes and sounds which grow
> More fair and soft as man grows wise and kind,
> And veil by veil evil and error fall . . .
>
> (3.3.57—62)

Evil and error may fall here veil by veil, but as in "A Defence of Poetry," no inner core of essential truth results. What remains is, forever, "swift shapes and sounds" that simply grow more fair as shapes and sounds.

All this takes place in the name of (the mediators of) love and leads us back to the admonishment of Demogorgon.

> —If the Abysm
> Could vomit forth its secrets:—but a voice
> Is wanting, the deep truth is imageless;
> For what would it avail to bid thee gaze
> On the revolving world? what to bid speak
> Fate, Time, Occasion, Chance and Change? To these
> All things are subject but eternal Love.
>
> (2.4.114—20)

If eternal Love is not subject to "Fate, Time, Occasion, Chance and Change," this is because Love is not a thing but precisely the force that drives eternal change as endless mediation.[35]

As in "On the Medusa of Leonardo da Vinci in the Florentine Gallery," we have reached a moment of uncontainable self-reflection—in the case of *Prometheus Unbound*, what might rather be called a landscape of limitless recall. For as Prometheus describes "the cave and place around" (3.3.63), he both reiterates and transforms several of the most critical moments of the text that precedes it. The abyss of Demogorgon, the "revolving world" of shapelessness as perpetual transformation, Demogorgon's refusal to be reified, his refusal to speak a language that delimits its referent, now appears as the very possibility of art.

> And lovely apparitions dim at first
> Then radiant . . .
>
> . . . .
> Shall visit us, the progeny immortal
> Of Painting, Sculpture and rapt Poesy
> And arts, though unimagined, yet to be.
>
> (3.3.49–50, 54–56)

As in the opening scene of recall, which violates the structure of origin and repetition, here, too, the production of these apparitions is such that phantoms of forms take temporal precedence over reality.

> And lovely apparitions dim at first
> Then radiant—as the mind, arising bright
> From the embrace of beauty (whence the forms
> Of which these are the phantoms) casts on them
> The gathered rays which are reality—
>
> (3.3.49–53)

But whereas the earlier disruption was one of crisis, a crisis of authority, of the power of words, and a crisis in the concept of linear temporality, the dissolution at the cave is matter for rapture in which no will to self-identity takes place. Thus the human realm of echoes outside the cave doubles and transforms the realm of the dead as Earth described it earlier: there, too, it was a question of "beauteous shapes" and the power of man's imagination.

> For know, there are two worlds of life and death:
> One that which thou beholdest, but the other
> Is underneath the grave, where do inhabit
> The shadows of all forms that think and live
> Till death unite them, and they part no more;
> Dreams and the light imaginings of men

And all that faith creates, or love desires,
Terrible, strange, sublime and beauteous shapes.

(1.195–202)

If representation casts the spell of death on reality in this earlier moment of the drama, it is now indistinguishable from reality's point of origin (3.3.51–53). Nevertheless, art at this juncture is not an absolute, neither the absolute emptiness of empty shade nor the fullness of that error Shelley calls life (3.4.190). The "echoes of the human world," the scene of production of art as love, is one of a series of gestures that unbalance the weight of the absolute. If the earlier pages of *Prometheus Unbound* were fraught with the dangers of falling from power, of being bound to the earth, this moment in the pseudo-teleological structure is menaced with the threat of falling up. Thus act 3 closes—and this was Shelley's initial point of completion—with the threat, apparently circumvented, of being "Pinnacled dim in the intense inane" (3.4.204). For as *Prometheus Unbound* was meant to close, man is

Nor yet exempt, though ruling them like slaves,
From chance and death and mutability,
The clogs of that which else might oversoar
The loftiest star of unascended Heaven
Pinnacled dim in the intense inane.

(3.4.200–204)

Only man's mortality (all that is suggested by Earth's description of the "two worlds of life and death" and by Demogorgon's "revolving world") prevents him from a fate far worse than death, an oversoaring that would rob him of his reason and his definition. For if his death unsettles him in another sense, it does not allow him to fall up into delusions of the absolute.

Chance, death, and mutability, as we saw, are the ruling forces in the scene of the cave, not only because mutability by that other name of difference might seem far sweeter but because the entire performance of that scene is structured on a system of perpetual unbalance. Just as man's mutability prevents him from soaring to the intense inane of a seemingly heavenly absolute, so each of the three realms that Prometheus specifies—nature, the cave of harmonies, man's realm of poetic image—is that which trips the balance of the others.

But the cave, after all, does not mark the endpoint of the text. Act 3 goes on to celebrate the coming of the revolution to man, a revolution that liberates from the structure of hierarchy so completely that even the revolution's own claim to have created heaven on earth (3.4.160) is counterweighted, as we have seen. Act 4 is its heavenly counterpart: it takes place, if not, strictly speaking, in heaven, nevertheless with all the aura of a cosmic perspective. It is a perspective, however, that sings and dances of the impossibility of its own totalizing gesture. For this celebration repeats with more grandiose stakes the disbalance that preceded it.

And yet this act, like the first, begins with the promise of an era come to an end, this time a promise already fulfilled.

> Here, oh here!
> We bear the bier
> Of the Father of many a cancelled year!
> Spectres we
> Of the dead Hours be,
> We bear Time to his tomb in eternity.
>
> (4.9–14)

Time is borne "to his tomb in eternity," and this signals (as *Prometheus Unbound* has suggested from the beginning) the end of traditional temporal concepts; but what replaces those concepts is an "eternity" that only the closing lines of the text can account for. In the meantime, let us say simply that it is a matter less of the closure of time than of a continual movement of closing and rupturing. Thus the choruses of these pages call alternately:

> But now—oh weave the mystic measure
> Of music and dance and shapes of light
>
> (4.77–78)

and

> Break the dance, and scatter the song;
> Let some depart and some remain.
>
> (4.159–60)

Act 4 begins with a dirge and continues with a wedding song, but what it buries is not quite what one thinks, and the marriage it celebrates will never achieve duration. What starts as "dear disunion," in Panthea's words (4.200), and moves to a celebration of oneness will be effaced by "a mighty Power" (4.510) to which all resolution in *Prometheus Unbound* must give way. But even before this climactic dissolution, what takes place in the seeming harmony of the spheres is once again a movement of "difference sweet." The Moon and Earth confront each other as opposites abstractly emblematic of the forces at play throughout the text. The Moon appears as a figure of stillness within definitive linear movement, and Earth as the very force of "self-destroying" (4.249), self-contradictory whirling.

> A sphere, which is as many thousand spheres,
> Solid as chrystal, yet through all its mass
> Flow, as through empty space, music and light:
> Ten thousand orbs involving and involved,
> Purple and azure, white and green and golden,
> Sphere within sphere, and every space between
> Peopled with unimaginable shapes
> Such as ghosts dream dwell in the lampless deep
> Yet each intertranspicuous . . .
>
> (4.238–46)

If Earth and Moon do indeed unite, their coming together is predicated on a ritual of delight in Jupiter's fall (4.350–55) and the celebration of man's new powers.

> All things confess his strength.— . . .
> . . . .
> Language is a perpetual Orphic song,
> Which rules with Dædal harmony a throng
> Of thoughts and forms, which else senseless and shapeless were.
>
> (4.412–17)

But Jupiter's relegation to the deep and man's shape-giving rule of thoughts and forms through language are quite explicitly eclipsed by a power far mightier than the momentary harmony of Earth and Moon.[36]

> Peace! peace! a mighty Power, which is as Darkness,
> Is rising out o' Earth, and from the sky
> Is showered like Night, and from within the air
> Bursts, like eclipse which had been gathered up
> Into the pores of sunlight— . . .
>
> (4.510–14)

Demogorgon, figure of shapelessness ("neither limb / Nor form—nor outline" [2.4.5–6]) replaces the "stream of sound" of Moon and Earth (4.506) with "a sense of words" (4.517). This is a language that is anything but the "perpetual Orphic song" and "Dædal harmony" attributed to man, which guaranteed the sense and shape of thought.[37]

Here the dance is broken, and the song scattered, as indeed they must be. For even the liberation from hierarchy on earth, the differential harmony in heaven, and the virtue of perpetual displacement in Prometheus's cave run the danger of reification, of becoming that other virtue of the morally fixable—of becoming place as a ground to stand on. This is why the text insists not only on the cosmic eclipse of the marriage of Earth and Moon but also on the terrible and strange proximity, the coincidence rather, that no good reader has missed of the locus of the cave and the entrance to Demogorgon's abode. At this point there is the possibility once again of an oracular vapor hurled up to intoxicate to naive belief in "truth, virtue, love, genius or joy" (2.3.4–10). "Such virtue has the cave and place around" (3.3.63). For despite Earth's insistence on the transformation of that "destined Cave" (3.3.124–75), a new intoxication threatens to let one read "this far goal of Time" (3.3.174) as telos, to let Prometheus and all he might come to symbolize assume a form of mastery no less misplaced than that of Jupiter.

For where is Demogorgon in all of this—the anti-figure who refuses form and outline (2.4.5–6), demystifier of the power of conventional rhetoric—if not displaced just beneath that virtuous cave, with Jupiter as his prisoner.

> This is the Day which down the void Abysm
> At the Earth-born's spell yawns for Heaven's Despotism,
>   And Conquest is dragged Captive through the Deep;
> Love from its awful throne of patient power
> In the wise heart, from the last giddy hour
>   Of dread endurance, from the slippery, steep,
> And narrow verge of crag-like Agony, springs
> And folds over the world its healing wings.
> Gentleness, Virtue, Wisdom and Endurance,—
> These are the seals of that most firm assurance
>   Which bars the pit over Destruction's strength;
>
>   (4.554–64)

At the very juncture of conquering Jupiter, at the very moment when, in Asia's words, the master seems to have become a slave (2.4.109), what is dragged "Captive through the Deep" is less he who can be named "Jupiter" (as Asia might have preferred) than "Conquest" itself. Love may have sprung forth, but the abysm beneath remains slippery and steep. The danger, however, is once again not so much a fall below as a fall upwards. It is over and against this that Demogorgon serves as

> The clogs of that which else might oversoar
> The loftiest star of unascended Heaven
> Pinnacled dim in the intense inane.

> (3.4.202–4)

Thus the seals of assurance against the strength of Destruction are less that which maintains the status quo (of Prometheus's or man's or Earth and Heaven's conquest) than that which brings about a new revolution:

> And if, with infirm hand, Eternity,
> Mother of many acts and hours, should free
>   The serpent that would clasp her with his length—
> These are the spells by which to reassume
> An empire o'er the disentangled Doom.

> (4.564–69)

Demogorgon seems to close *Prometheus Unbound* with the spells of the final stanza (4.570–78), to offer the power-filled words to put the serpent, Jupiter, back in his place should he escape. The text that began with the crisis of the curse would close then with a new "spell," one whose potency is presumably far better assured than the involutions of Prometheus's original words and all their forms of "recall." But the spatial and temporal disruptions of *Prometheus Unbound* require that from the beginning, even before the conquest of Jupiter, the Doom that threatens to disentangle itself in Demogorgon's last monologue is already there. For the spirits that guide Asia and Panthea to Demogorgon sing of it as "underneath his throne."

> SONG OF SPIRITS
>   Resist not the weakness—
>   Such strength is in meekness—
>   That the Eternal, the Immortal,
>   Must unloose through life's portal

> The snake-like Doom coiled underneath his throne
> By that alone!
>
> (2.3.93—98)

The necessity of Demogorgon is such that he "Must unloose . . . / The snake-like Doom." For who figures forth "Eternity" if not Demogorgon—not only in the "Song of Spirits" but also in his own words. At the moment when Jupiter is thrust from power Demogorgon has this to say:

> JUPITER
> [*The Car of the* Hour *arrives.* Demogorgon *descends and moves towards the Throne of* Jupiter]
> Awful Shape, what art thou? Speak!
> DEMOGORGON
> Eternity—demand no direr name.
> Descend, and follow me down the abyss;
>
> (3.1.51—53)

Eternity is the name assumed by Demogorgon, he who refuses to be named. He is there as the potential power of otherness, the liberator of the serpent (4.565—67), whose liberation at the apparent "close" of the text might just as well reinstate Jupiter, or at least all the powers he embodies.

"Eternity" here implies anything but a state of permanence,[38] for it operates rather as the perpetual disruption of temporal and spatial stasis, a disruption already at play, in a sense, in Prometheus's first monologue. As in "The Necessity of Atheism,"[39] eternity (or necessity) is the questioning of the concept of origin; it is the pronounced incomprehensibility of first cause and, it goes without saying, then, of telos. This is why *Prometheus Unbound* is not "about" a restoration to his proper place and proper authority of Prometheus as the origin of speech and thought, a movement towards apocalypse or utopia, a millennium or redemption,[40] but rather the performance of perpetual if unpredictable revolution.

II

EMILY BRONTË

3

At the Threshold of Interpretation

"Curiouser and curiouser!" cried Alice (she was so much surprised, that
for the moment she quite forgot how to speak good English).
—Carroll, *Alice's Adventures in Wonderland*

Is it Carroll who will articulate for us the dilemma of finding one's
way into a literary text? And if Carroll's articulation becomes
"curiouser and curiouser" and threatens the possibility of "good English," of the good text, could we not, nevertheless, regard it as a most
appropriate entrance into the realm of *Wuthering Heights*? The breakdown in linguistic control announced in the epigraph takes place in the
midst of a series of events that are key to the understanding of *Alice's
Adventures in Wonderland*. Alice, you will remember, has just fallen
down the interminably long rabbit hole only to discover a lengthy hall of
locked doors. A tiny gold key fits none of the normal-sized portals but
does allow her to open a very small door leading to a wondrous, if
dangerous, garden. Alice may enter this land only at the price of a radical
change in her own size, a change proving to be disastrous to the integrity
of her self. For at this point follows a shrinking, which "'might end, you
know,' said Alice to herself, 'in my going out altogether, like a candle.'"
The shrinking is followed by an equally problematic growing, which
first imposes a bizarre self-estrangement and finally leads Alice to completely doubt the identity of her own voice.

Like the entrance to Wonderland, the entrance to *Wuthering
Heights* is marked by the metaphor of the doorway. Passage through that
threshold will generate a crisis both in the voice of the self and in the
logic of the good text. As in Carroll's text, where the adventures in
Wonderland ultimately fall under the aegis of the dream, so in *Wuthering
Heights* one dreams of finding its center only to find that the center is a
dream.

We enter *Wuthering Heights* through the voice of Lockwood, who devotes the first three chapters of his narrative to what he twice calls the "repetition of my intrusion."[1] These intrusions are, to be sure, the literal incursions he makes into the house of Wuthering Heights, but they function no less as attempts to penetrate *Wuthering Heights-as-text*. The outsider, conventional in language as well as understanding, makes repeated efforts to force his way to the penetralium. Yet one knocks vainly for admittance at these locked doors, and on his second visit, the intruder enters only by means of a violence that almost matches that of Wuthering Heights itself. He penetrates to the innermost chamber of the structure and to the enclosed oaken bed within, and here he experiences the very center of Wuthering Heights as a dream, or, more accurately, as a series of nightmares. This dream-troubled night rapidly results in Lockwood's excommunication from Wuthering Heights, for the illness brought on by these events confines him to Thrushcross Grange. At the same juncture Nelly Dean replaces Lockwood in his role as narrator, for Lockwood becomes the mere recorder of Nelly's story.

How are we to interpret this curious point of articulation between the first three chapters of the novel and the narrative that follows? Certainly not by taking Lockwood at his word. He organizes his explanation by suppressing all further mention of the dreams and by linking the subsequent events into a simplistic causal chain. A sleepless night and a difficult journey through the snow bring on a bad cold. The illness, in turn, incapacitates him, and so he calls in the housekeeper to entertain him with her tales. A fiction surely, for if we return to chapter 3, we find that the texts of the dreams dislocate the possibility of such explanation. The exclusion of Lockwood from the Heights and the displacement of Lockwood as direct narrator of the novel, his excommunication from Wuthering Heights both as a banishment from its community and as a relegation to a position outside of communication, are already the common, if oblique, themes of the dreams themselves. They mark the disjunction not only between Lockwood and Wuthering Heights but also between Lockwood and *Wuthering Heights-as-text*. For these passages offer a commentary on the nature of the fictional space marked off as Nelly's narrative, a commentary made possible by setting off Lockwood as that which lies outside the fictional realm. The exact locus of this commentary will remain equivocal, for it lies somewhere between Lockwood's puzzlement and Nelly's explanation and yet again at the heart of *Wuthering Heights*.

Finally closeted within the paneled bed, Lockwood imagines that he has delineated a protective boundary between himself and the threat-ening realm without: "I slid back the panelled sides, got in with my light, pulled them together again, and felt secure against the vigilance of Heathcliff, and every one else" (*WH* 25). The diary records but two descriptive details of this apparently secure inner space: "a few mildewed books" lie piled in the corner of the window ledge, and the ledge itself is "covered with writing scratched on the paint" (*WH* 25). Having reached the very center of Wuthering Heights, Lockwood finds it inhabited by texts. And not just any texts. For the scratchings of Catherine and the books of her library, whose margins also contain her diary, figure most significantly in Lockwood's dreams. Each dream incorporates one of these three texts. In the first appear the specter-like letters etched on the sill. The second concerns the pious discourse of Jabes Branderham, which Lockwood had just begun reading. The third personifies the child Cathy, who speaks from the pages of her diary.

Lockwood's narrative elaborates a system of "careful causality" to establish the relationship between text and dream.[2] He describes himself reading Catherine's name and then dreaming of it. He wakes to find his candle burning one of the good books and so peruses them. He dreams once again of the text he has just been reading and is awakened by "a shower of loud taps on the boards of the pulpit, which responded so smartly that, at last, to my unspeakable relief, they woke me" (*WH* 29). He locates the dream source in the title of Jabes's sermon, and its noisy conclusion is easily explained away by assigning it to a referent in the "real world," the branch of the fir tree: "And what was it that had suggested the tremendous tumult, what had played Jabes's part in the row? Merely the branch of a fir tree that touched my lattice, as the blast wailed by, and rattled its dry cones against the panes!" (*WH* 29). Lockwood attributes his last dream to the reading of Cathy's diary: " 'The truth is, sir, I passed the first part of the night in—' here, I stopped afresh—I was about to say 'perusing those old volumes;' then it would have revealed my knowledge of their written, as well as their printed contents" (*WH* 32).

Lockwood interprets his dreams by rooting them firmly in his waking world. In this manner he attempts to establish the ascendancy of reality over dream and to dispense with a merely fictional terror by rational explication. Yet the terror of fiction is otherwise. After all, the "reality" by means of which Lockwood claims deliverance is, rather, a series of texts. And looking to the dreams themselves, we find they give those texts quite another interpretation. In each of the dreams the dreamer is engaged in a violent struggle, and it is precisely those apparently innocuous texts that function as his vicious adversaries.

The waking Lockwood imagines himself victorious in these conflicts, but the dreams themselves tell the story of a different mastery. First the glaring letters of Catherine's name swarm at Lockwood; then it is quite literally the text of Jabes Branderham's sermon that assaults him; and finally he struggles unsuccessfully with a figure arisen from Cathy's diary, or "an impression which personified itself" (*WH* 32) out of the name Catherine Linton.

In his second dream Lockwood is condemned to endure the endless sermon of Jabes Branderham. With each division of the sermon Lockwood rises to go, but he is forced each time to resume his seat:

> Oh, how weary I grew. How I writhed, and yawned, and nodded, and revived! How I pinched and pricked myself, and rubbed my eyes, and stood up, and sat down again, and nudged Joseph to inform me if he would *ever* have done!
>
> I was condemned to hear all out. (*WH* 29)

The forgiveness demanded of Lockwood strangely figures as forgiveness of the discourse itself rather than of the sins the text names. The length of the text and especially the repetitive nature of its structure make its textuality more prevalent than its content:

> "Sir," I exclaimed, "sitting here, within these four walls, at one stretch, I have endured and forgiven the four hundred and ninety heads of your discourse. Seventy times seven times have I plucked up my hat and been about to depart—Seventy times seven times have you preposterously forced me to resume my seat. The four hundred and ninety-first is too much." (*WH* 29)

The four hundred and ninety-first attempt to deny the text, this time by destroying Jabes Branderham, the refusal to forgive the four hundred and ninety-first head of the discourse, is the sin for which Lockwood cannot be forgiven. As anticipated, the sentence of excommunication is handed down:

> "*Thou art the Man!*" cried Jabes, after a solemn pause, leaning over his cushion. "Seventy times seven times didst thou gapingly contort thy visage—seventy times seven did I take counsel with my soul—Lo, this is human weakness; this also may be absolved! The First of the Seventy-First

is come. Brethren, execute upon him the judgment written! such honour
have all His saints!"

With that concluding word, the whole assembly, exalting their pilgrim's
staves, rushed round me in a body. (*WH* 29)

Although its violence is initially masked, it is ultimately the endless text
that wields the power to destroy Lockwood.

Lockwood's last dream displays a similar pattern. Here, too, he
must struggle with a textual emanation, a figure from the diary passage
just read. The child-specter clasps his hand, and Lockwood attempts to
disengage himself by pulling the child's wrist along the broken window
pane. Finally he beguiles her into letting go, and yet, as in his other
dreams, his struggle is never definitively won. Neither the piling of the
books before him as a barrier nor the stopping of his ears can rid him of
the terrifying child's voice.

The waking, rational Lockwood thinks to master this violence by
reestablishing the reality of certain texts, but his nightmares mock him.
They mimic the structure of his relationship to those same texts and
reverse the apparent order of ascendancy.

Lockwood dreams of the texts that lie at the center of Wuthering
Heights and in this manner confronts the text of *Wuthering Heights*,[3] the
actual narrative begun in chapter 4. Or is it quite the reverse? Perhaps,
after all, it is *Wuthering Heights* that dreams here, dreaming of a violent
struggle with its other, Lockwood, in order to define a space for its own
fiction. Whatever the pattern of confrontation, chapter 3 (its dreams, its
texts, its description of Lockwood's coming and going) anticipates all
that takes place in the pages that follow. And yet it does not merely
anticipate what takes place there *as event*.[4] If chapter 3 is a prefiguration
of the narrative to come, it operates as that which literally comes before
the figure. It is the image of the figure: *avant la lettre,* it transforms what
might otherwise seem to be simple narrative content into the fiction's
continual commentary on its own figuration. If the fundamental questions of chapter 3—of naming, usurpation, homelessness, and passion—
prove to also hold sway in Nelly's tale of *Wuthering Heights,* they do so
as questions previously inscribed as the text's mode of elaborating on its
own textuality.

No one has written more suggestively on this relationship between
dream and narrative than Frank Kermode. In his provocative essay "A
Modern Way with the Classic" Kermode uses the multiple inscriptions

of Catherine's names to elegantly account for the movement of events in the novel.[5]

> When you have processed all the information you have been waiting for, you see the point of the order of the scribbled names, as Lockwood gives them: *Catherine Earnshaw, Catherine Heathcliff, Catherine Linton.* Read from left to right they recapitulate Catherine Earnshaw's story; read from right to left, the story of her daughter, Catherine Linton. The names *Catherine* and *Earnshaw* begin and end the narrative. . . . this is an account of the movement of the book: away from Earnshaw and back, like the movement of the house itself. (*MW* 419–20)

To be sure, it is the permutation of names in *Wuthering Heights* that generates the movement of the text. But is that generation really quite as ordered as Kermode would have us believe? He openly ascribes the linear ordering of the names to Lockwood: "you see the point of the order of the scribbled names, as *Lockwood gives them*" (emphasis mine) from Catherine Earnshaw, to Heathcliff, to Linton. And yet those same names, as they appear first on the window ledge and then in the dream, elude the reification that Lockwood imposes. On the window ledge they are simply varied here and there from one name to the next: "This writing, however, was nothing but a name repeated in all kinds of characters, large and small—*Catherine Earnshaw,* here and there varied to *Catherine Heathcliff,* and then again to *Catherine Linton*" (*WH* 25). In the nightmare as well the names swarm at Lockwood in no apparent order.

Kermode's interpretation, as radical as it often seems, operates in strange complicity with Lockwood's. We have already seen the fundamental disparity between the texts and dreams at the center of Wuthering Heights, on the one hand, and Lockwood's account of them, on the other. Kermode here chooses Lockwood's version—and he has his own good reason: such a version allows him to assume the stance of a linear reading not only of the novel's plot "from left to right" (*MW* 419), from beginning to end (*MW* 419–20), but also of the interpretative experience from the "'hermeneutic' promise" of an early inscription to the fulfillment of that promise (*MW* 418). His reading functions as a processing of information (*MW* 419) from an indeterminacy of meaning to "the repair of indeterminancy" and "to the generation of meaning" (*MW* 426).

The linear reading of events gives the sense of a closed, happy ending,[6] for Kermode speaks of the "restoration" of true names (*MW* 419) and of "inheritance restored" (*MW* 418) that bring about the emergence of "a more rational culture" (*MW* 421). This restoration operates, of course, as a metaphor for Kermode's own hermeneutic enterprise, for the solution of the dream rebus given above appears precisely in terms of restoring names rationally to their proper place. But Kermode's gesture is double: if with one hand he seems to close the text of *Wuthering Heights,* with the other he opens it up to "the coexistence . . . of a plurality of significances" (*MW* 428). With the largesse of liberalism, he claims "to be reading a text that might well signify differently to different generations and different persons within those generations" (*MW* 429).

And yet *Wuthering Heights* tolerates neither the one gesture nor the other. If we look to the actual functioning of names and the pattern of inheritance within the text, they promise neither a restored rationality nor the comfortable coexistence of equally valid forces. Instead of "signifying differently to different generations," they generate differences.

The uncanny dearth of names may permit linear trajectories for each of the Catherines, but it also fabricates interrelationships between other characters that are hardly reducible to linearity. Others, too, change and gain their identities through the combinatory dance of names in which all major characters take part.[7] The assumption of another's name functions less to advance the plot line than to elaborate complex patterns of differentiation that govern the entire text. Thus the second Catherine Linton can take her mother's name only at the price of distinction:

> It was named Catherine, but he [Edgar] never called it the name in full, as he had never called the first Catherine short, probably because Heathcliff had a habit of doing so. The little one was always Cathy; it formed to him a distinction from the mother, and yet, a connection with her. (*WH* 152)

> She was the most winning thing that ever brought sunshine into a desolate house—a real beauty in face, with the Earnshaws' handsome dark eyes, but the Lintons' fair skin, and small features, and yellow curling hair. Her spirit was high, though not rough, and qualified by a heart sensitive and lively to excess in its affections. That capacity for intense attachments reminded me of her mother; still she did not resemble her. (*WH* 155)

If the text plays upon the imperfect repetition of names, it plays no less on the imperfect repetition of personality and feature,[8] for just as Cathy fails to resemble her mother, so Linton Heathcliff only partially resembles his uncle. Nelly describes him as a "pale, delicate, effeminate boy, who might have been taken for my master's younger brother, so strong was the resemblance; but there was a sickly peevishness in his aspect that Edgar Linton never had" (*WH* 163–64).

The paradox in this realm of dislocated identities is that characters nevertheless relate to one another as images of those they only half resemble. Edgar Linton's attachment to his daughter "sprang from its relation to" her mother (*WH* 152). Isabella and Linton are metaphors in Heathcliff's eye for Edgar Linton, and Hareton for his own youth: "Five minutes ago, Hareton seemed a personification of my youth, not a human being. I felt to him in such a variety of ways, that it would have been impossible to have accosted him rationally" (*WH* 255). Everything in Heathcliff's final world swarms as endless signs for Cathy:

> For what is not connected with her to me? and what does not recall her? I cannot look down to this floor, but her features are shaped on the flags! In every cloud, in every tree—filling the air at night, and caught by glimpses in every object by day, I am surrounded with her image! The most ordinary faces of men and women—my own features—mock me with a resemblance. The entire world is a dreadful collection of memoranda that she did exist, and that I have lost her! (*WH* 255)

In a realm in which all has become pure image, here, then, is the function of names. Throughout *Wuthering Heights* they resemble that to which they refer only to mark its absence. Surely this betokens something close to insanity rather than Kermode's promise of a rationality restored. But what of Kermode's other alternative, that of a multitude of equally valid significances? This also is ruled out, for the name as we have seen it to function despotically eliminates its referent, leaving room for neither plurality nor significance.

It is this same function of names that the pattern of inheritance repeatedly traces. For inheritance in *Wuthering Heights* takes place as a series of usurpations. The family name, once inextricably bound to its property (that of Earnshaw to Wuthering Heights and Linton to Thrushcross Grange), can no longer guarantee possession. On the contrary, the earliest episode of Nelly's tale, the arrival of the parentless, originless child, threatens disjunction between name and property.

Heathcliff, never granted the family name, named rather for that which does not exist, a dead child, enters speaking an incomprehensible "gibberish" (*WH* 39) to dislocate name from referent. This agency of usurpation governs the text, then, from the very beginning.

On what is this relentless will to usurpation based? It figures less as desire for possession[9] than as a bizarre desire for imitation. The object of imitation would seem to be the previous master in the chain of usurpations. Heathcliff, for example, assumes Hindley's place by misusing Hareton almost precisely as Hindley had misused Heathcliff:

> I can sympathise with all his feelings, having felt them myself. I know what he suffers now, for instance, exactly—it is merely a beginning of what he shall suffer, though. And he'll never be able to emerge from his bathos of coarseness and ignorance. I've got him faster than his scoundrel of a father secured me. (*WH* 178)

And yet because it is the unwillingness to forgive past infractions that motivates these usurpations, they operate less as imitations of a person than as imitations of the gesture of violation, less as the attempt to replace a fixed identity than as the repetition of displacement. As Isabella finally flees Wuthering Heights, she articulates this in terms of demanding an eye for an eye and a tooth for a tooth:

> But what misery laid on Heathcliff could content me, unless I have a hand in it? I'd rather he suffered *less*, if I might cause his sufferings and he might *know* that I was the cause. Oh, I owe him so much. On only one condition can I hope to forgive him. It is, if I may take an eye for an eye, a tooth for a tooth; for every wrench of agony, return a wrench, reduce him to my level. (*WH* 149)

Hardly a major character eludes the violence of this displacement. First, Hindley is forced from home. After old Earnshaw's death, Heathcliff in turn is driven away, returning some years later to repeat the dispossession of Hindley. On his death, Heathcliff is replaced by Hareton, who had been left virtually homeless on Heathcliff's return. Isabella's marriage wrenches her from home and leaves her bemoaning the impossibility of return. Even after her escape from Heathcliff, she is forced to live out her life away from Thrushcross Grange. Her son Linton Heathcliff is uprooted first to his uncle's home and then to his father's. The second Catherine is taken from Thrushcross Grange as Heathcliff's temporary prisoner and soon becomes his permanent one.

The ultimate figure of homelessness, of course, is the first Cathy, for it is she who creates her exile as a conscious act of the imagination:

> If I were in heaven, Nelly, I should be extremely miserable . . . I dreamt, once, that I was there. . . . Heaven did not seem to be my home; and I broke my heart with weeping to come back to earth; and the angels were so angry that they flung me out, into the middle of the heath on the top of Wuthering Heights; where I woke sobbing for joy. That will do to explain my secret, as well as the other. I've no more business to marry Edgar Linton than I have to be in heaven. (*WH* 72)

The marriage to Edgar fulfills this prophecy of homelessness from which only death promises a respite. Yet Cathy's death in turn is yet another self-imposed exile. Lockwood encounters her as the ghostly child-waif who has been wandering for twenty years:

> "Let me in—let me in!"
> "Who are you?" I asked, struggling, meanwhile, to disengage myself.
> "Catherine Linton," it replied, shiveringly (why did I think of *Linton*? I had read *Earnshaw* twenty times for Linton). "I'm come home, I'd lost my way on the moor!" . . .
> "It's twenty years," mourned the voice, "twenty years, I've been a waif for twenty years!" (*WH* 30)

The text casts us back here to Lockwood's dreams, where it is no coincidence that the ultimate figure of homelessness should first have appeared. The entire episode of Lockwood's visit is an allegory of homelessness and excommunication, an allegory that reads and is read by the narrative that follows. As soon as he enters Wuthering Heights, Lockwood senses his exile. The return home is impossible without a guide, and Wuthering Heights, of course, can offer him none.

> "I wonder you should select the thick of a snow-storm to ramble about in. Do you know that you run a risk of being lost in the marshes? People familiar with these moors often miss their road on such evenings. . . ."
> "Perhaps I can get a guide among your lads, and he might stay at the Grange till morning—could you spare me one?"
> "No, I could not." (*WH* 20)

Because no guide is willingly offered, the intruder desperately rushes for the nearest gate, snatching a lantern to light the dark path back from Wuthering Heights. But this attempt also fails, for Lockwood is attacked by "monsters," who extinguish this last hope for rational illumination:

"On opening the little door, two hairy monsters flew at my throat, bearing me down and extinguishing the light" (*WH* 24).

Lockwood is then forced even deeper into darkness as he enters the inner chamber of the house. He imagines he has located a haven in what proves to be the very center of dislocation. Lockwood dreams of, and on waking experiences, excommunication. This, at least, is the tale of the second nightmare. Lockwood dreams that in Joseph he has found a guide who will finally lead him from Wuthering Heights, but soon he discovers that the path they are taking will not bring him home:

> I thought it was morning, and I had set out on my way home, with Joseph for a guide. The snow lay yards deep in our road; and, as we floundered on, my companion wearied me with constant reproaches that I had not brought a pilgrim's staff, telling me I could never get into the house without one. . . .
> For a moment I considered it absurd that I should need such a weapon to gain admittance into my own residence. Then, a new idea flashed across me. I was not going there. (*WH* 28)

(Lockwood and Joseph journey instead to hear a text, the sermon of the famous Jabes Branderham. The text, whose interpretation we must temporarily defer, will offer the novel's most elaborate commentary on the nature of Lockwood's excommunication.)

What they head for is hardly a home: it is a chapel.

> We came to the chapel. I have passed it really in my walks, twice or thrice. . . . The roof has been kept whole hitherto, but, as the clergyman's stipend is only twenty pounds per annum, and a house with two rooms, threatening speedily to determine into one, no clergyman will undertake the duties of pastor. (*WH* 28)

It is a crumbling structure in which the crumbling of structure takes place, in which the integrity of the sanctuary is violently destroyed—an appropriate space for the scenario of Lockwood's excommunication.

The dream gives at least one reason for Lockwood's exclusion: "My companion wearied me with constant reproaches that I had not brought a pilgrim's staff, telling me that I could never get into the house without one, and boastfully flourishing a heavy-headed cudgel, which I understood to be so denominated" (*WH* 28). Lockwood comes without pilgrim staff and cudgel, emblems of wandering on the one hand and estrangement and hostility on the other. It is precisely these roles of wanderer and stranger that Lockwood cannot accept. This is why, although Wuthering Heights continually denies refuge to the wanderer, although its gates offer him "no sympathizing movement" (*WH* 13), the persistent intruder will nevertheless force his entry repeatedly: " 'At least, I would not keep my doors barred in the daytime. I don't care—I will get in!' So resolved, I grasped the latch and shook it vehemently" (*WH* 17–18).

If Lockwood is excommunicated from the Heights, it is also because he refuses to risk relationships that imply fundamental separation; these are, however, the only kind of relationships that Nelly's narrative describes. The novel opens with Lockwood's attempt to construe desolation as a basis for human sympathy. He pretends to have sought out "a situation . . . completely removed from the stir of society," yet on finding Heathcliff a "solitary" man, Lockwood attempts to reconcile the solitary man with the neighbor. "I have just returned from a visit to my landlord—the solitary neighbour that I shall be troubled with. This is certainly a beautiful country! In all England, I do not believe that I could have fixed on a situation so completely removed from the stir of society" (*WH* 13). The narrator names his new home a "misanthropist's Heaven," and yet misanthropy for Lockwood becomes the ground for communal sharing. "A perfect misanthropist's Heaven— and Mr. Heathcliff and I are such a suitable pair to divide the desolation between us. A capital fellow! He little imagined how my heart warmed towards him when I beheld his black eyes withdraw so suspiciously under their brows" (*WH* 13). Lockwood repeats with the young Cathy the same mistake he makes with respect to Heathcliff. Here Lockwood elicits no sign of sympathy but nevertheless fantasizes the possibility of marriage.

What is the nature of this fundamental estrangement that *Wuthering Heights* imposes on narrator and characters alike? Surely Lockwood's banal love fantasies (where desire dreams in vain of coincidence with its object) are but images of something else. The path that finally returns Lockwood to his residence, the space that marks the untraversable distance between Wuthering Heights and home,[10] tells the tale:

> The whole hill-back was one billowy, white ocean, the swells and falls not indicating corresponding rises and depressions in the ground: many pits, at least, were filled to a level; and entire ranges of mounds, the refuse of the quarries, blotted from the chart which my yesterday's walk left pictured in my mind. (*WH* 35)

The nature of this fundamental estrangement is that between signs and meaning, an impasse of interpretation. For in this remarkable snowscape there is no correspondence between surface and ground. The risk here is a potential loss of life; but more significantly, it is also the loss that has of necessity already taken place, a loss of reason, of the potential to re-mark, what the above passage calls a blotting of the chart of the mind. Lockwood continues:

> I had remarked on one side of the road, at intervals of six or seven yards, a line of upright stones, continued through the whole length of the barren: these were erected, and daubed with lime, on purpose to serve as guides in the dark, and also, when a fall, like the present, confounded the deep swamps on either hand with the firmer path: but, excepting a dirty dot pointing up here and there, all traces of their existence had vanished. (*WH* 35)

The homelessness imposed by *Wuthering Heights* is that of the trace. The trace of existence, and the trace *as existence,* has vanished, for it no longer functions as a substantial sign *of* something, no longer serves as guide, but as a random "dirty dot pointing up here and there" and leading nowhere.

Where, then, are we in *Wuthering Heights?* The theater of naming that governs the text stages a series of tyrannical displacements of the namesake. The pattern of inheritance displays a disjunction of name and property, for property is handed on through usurpation, a gesture that is less one of appropriation than an almost-repetition of the dislocating gesture that preceded it. Little wonder, then, that the problematics of naming and inheritance are paralleled by that of perpetual exile, and that this homelessness figures also as the homelessness of the trace, which has lost its powers to identify its referent.

Perhaps this enables us to reread in *Wuthering Heights* that one last refuge of identity, the passion between Catherine and Heathcliff, for this relationship defines itself in terms of those themes of disjunction that it would seem to transcend. Passion, as Cathy describes it, is a self-imposed usurpation, willed dispossession of self-unity.[11] Heathcliff is the way in which she names herself: "I *am* Heathcliff" (*WH* 74). He is an existence of Cathy beyond herself (*WH* 73–74), in her mind as her own being (*WH* 74), and is more Cathy's self than she is (*WH* 72). He provides a path of mediation to Cathy's self that at the same time marks the impossibility of coincidence with that self. Passion becomes a mode of self-naming, a self-reflection that is necessarily self-sundering. This is why when Cathy finally states her love for Heathcliff she must in the same breath declare her decision not to marry him. Her declaration of love signals their disunion: "It would degrade me to marry Heathcliff now; so he shall never know how I love him" (*WH* 72).[12]

From the very first mention of this passion (in chapter 3), it appears as separation as well as union, since the passage from Catherine's diary marks the first but definitive break between Heathcliff and herself. The text introduces obliquely or directly all the modes of disjunction already discussed—naming, inheritance, the refusal to forgive, usurpation, wandering, and passion. The passage is written as two separate entries. The first describes a rainy Sunday afternoon at the Heights shortly after the death of Earnshaw—a long sermon by Joseph, the beginning of Cathy and Heathcliff's rebellion by the destruction of good books, the writing of Cathy's diary in the back kitchen, and a proposed scamper on the moors. Here there is a break in the text, and when Cathy writes again the crucial first separation between her and Heathcliff has already taken place. The separation she writes of is that imposed by Hindley:

> My head aches, till I cannot keep it on the pillow; and still I can't give over. Poor Heathcliff! Hindley calls him a vagabond, and won't let him sit with us, nor eat with us any more; and, he says, he and I must not play together, and threatens to turn him out of the house if we break his orders. (*WH* 27–28)

The passage is not situated until later in the novel, when it becomes clear that Cathy had written on the first night she and Heathcliff were forced to sleep separately (*WH* 107, quoted below).

The first actual break between the child-lovers occurs at the gap in the diary text, a gap that marks their scamper to Thrushcross Grange, Cathy's first wandering away from Wuthering Heights, her initial encounter with Edgar Linton, and thus the beginning of the split in Cathy herself. That the proposed scamper on the moors takes them to Thrushcross Grange is not stated explicitly in the diary, but a number of details link the rainy Sunday's adventure under the dairy woman's cloak mentioned by Cathy with that described later in chapter 6. Nelly says that their run on the moors, like that of the diary, takes place on a rainy Sunday following a banishment from the sitting room:

> One Sunday evening, it chanced that they were banished from the
> sitting room, for making a noise, or a light offence of the kind, and when I
> went to call them to supper, I could discover them nowhere. . . . The
> household went to bed; and I, too anxious to lie down, opened my lattice
> and put my head out to hearken, though it rained. (*WH* 46)

And Heathcliff, on returning from Thrushcross Grange, speaks of the
same cloak already mentioned in the diary: "Mrs. Linton took off the
grey cloak of the dairy maid which we had borrowed for our excursion"
(*WH* 49–50).

   If the text that Lockwood discovers introduces Cathy's passion, it
does so only in terms of separation, and it also specifically prefigures the
other two gestures of self-exile, death and marriage. The diary entry
prefigures her death, because at the height of her fatal illness Cathy longs
to return to the bed in which Lockwood had read her text, and she recalls
the moment described in the second passage of her diary (*WH* 27–28,
quoted above). At the same time, she likens this moment to when she
was wrenched from Wuthering Heights on marrying Edgar:

> I thought as I lay there . . . that I was enclosed in the oak-panelled bed at
> home; and my heart ached with some great grief which, just waking, I
> could not recollect. . . . I was a child; my father was just buried, and my
> misery arose from the separation that Hindley had ordered between me
> and Heathcliff. I was laid alone, for the first time, and rousing . . . I lifted
> my hand to push the panels aside. . . . and then memory burst in. . . . I
> cannot say why I felt so wildly wretched . . . for there is scarcely cause.
> But, supposing at twelve years old, I had been wrenched from the
> Heights, and every early association, and my all in all, as Heathcliff was at
> that time, and been converted at a stroke into Mrs. Linton. . . . (*WH* 107)

   Cathy's diary first introduces the tale of *Wuthering Heights* that
Nelly will go on to narrate. The tale, then, does not begin at the
beginning but opens by marking the initial break in the only relationship
that approaches perfect identity. At the same time, it sets up the central
pattern of violent severance that organizes the novel. Strange that this
diary which stresses disjunction and rebellion should be found within
the covers of "good books." Cathy's diary has been penned as an
interpretation of the religious books of her library, an interpretation that
contributes to their dilapidation:

Catherine's library was select, and its state of dilapidation proved it to have
been well used, though not altogether for a legitimate purpose; scarcely
one chapter had escaped a pen and ink commentary—at least, the appearance of one—covering every morsel of blank that the printer had left.
(*WH* 26)

Perhaps not so coincidentally, this diary which devours the textual
margin also relates the initial step of Cathy's rebellion as the destruction
of the good books that Joseph forces her and Heathcliff to read.

Saying this, he compelled us so to square our positions that we might
receive . . . a dull ray to show us the text. . . .
I could not bear the employment. I took my dingy volume by the
scroop, and hurled it into the dog-kennel, vowing I hated a good book.
(*WH* 27)

On being banished to the back kitchen, Cathy continues her rebellion by
writing her diary alongside Jabes Branderham's pious discourse and thus
destroying the "good book."

Cathy wishes to destroy Jabes's pious writing, yet the text that
Cathy comments on, or at least the only version we have of it (that given
in Lockwood's dream), rather than being destroyed by the interpretation seems strangely to enter into the spirit of Cathy's world of non-
forgiveness and revenge. The text one expects to preach the turning of
the other cheek ultimately demands an eye for an eye and a tooth for a
tooth. When Lockwood finally fails to forgive the text by refusing to
listen further, when he accuses the text and demands the annihilation of
its source, Branderham accuses Lockwood in return and demands the
narrator's annihilation.

Jabes Branderham's sermon, like Cathy's diary, is itself a commentary on a "good book." The discourse, entitled "Seventy Times Seven,
and the First of the Seventy-First," interprets a passage from the New
Testament. Although Branderham's comments seem at first to violate
the text they interpret (for surely, here in the holiest of texts, one expects
to find a call to forgiveness),[13] in fact Matt. 18.21–35 already contains its
own dislocations. In the earlier verses, Jesus apparently preaches unending forgiveness:

[21]Then came Peter to him, and said, Lord, how oft shall my brother sin
against me, and I forgive him? till seven times?

²²Jesus saith unto him, I say not unto thee, Until seven times: but, Until seventy times seven.¹⁴

Yet when Jesus relates a parable to illustrate God's limitless capacity for forgiveness, it culminates rather with the refusal to forgive. The lord who represents God in the parable forgives his servant his debt, but only until the servant himself fails to forgive his debtor. When the servant commits this sin (the first of the seventy-first), the lord demands an eye for an eye and a tooth for a tooth:

> ³²Then his lord, after that he had called him, said unto him, O thou wicked servant, I forgave thee all that debt, because thou desiredst me:
> ³³Shouldest not thou also have had compassion on thy fellow-servant, even as I had pity on thee?
> ³⁴And his lord was wroth, and delivered him to the tormentors, till he should pay all that was due unto him.
> ·³⁵So likewise shall my heavenly Father do also unto you, if ye from your hearts forgive not every one his brother their trespasses.

The biblical text pretends to preach unending forgiveness, yet God himself pays back sins in kind.¹⁵ Thus both Cathy's seemingly destructive commentary on Branderham and Branderham's on Matthew are already contained in the good books they interpret.

The complicated relationship between Lockwood's narrative and the tale of *Wuthering Heights* is rather the reverse of these commentary-text relationships. Whereas both Cathy and Branderham comment destructively on apparently pious texts, Lockwood tries to convert a disturbingly menacing tale into a "good book." He wishes to regard Nelly's tale as benign entertainment. Just as he speaks of his dreams as superstition and uncontrolled imagination (*WH* 32), he repeatedly hints at the merely fictional and formal nature of the story. He speaks of Heathcliff as the "hero" of the narrative, when the actual person stood at his bedside but a short time before (*WH* 80). And although he has actually encountered most of the people in the history he hears, he refers to them as literary "characters" (*WH* 58).

As we have seen, the language of *Wuthering Heights* insists upon irresolvable disjunction, yet for Lockwood Nelly's language functions as the means for uniting people, as a form of sociability:

> I, who had determined to hold myself independent of all social inter-course, and thanked my stars that, at length, I had lighted on a spot where

it was next to impracticable . . . was finally compelled to strike my col-
ours; and, under pretence of gaining information concerning the neces-
sities of my establishment, I desired Mrs. Dean . . . to sit down while
I ate . . . hoping sincerely she would prove a regular gossip. (*WH*
35–36)

Even when Lockwood begins to sense that *Wuthering Heights* is not
quite the unambiguous amusement he sought, he continues to convert
the ominous into the beneficial: "Dree, and dreary! I reflected . . . and
not exactly of the kind which I should have chosen to amuse me. But
never mind! I'll extract wholesome medicines from Mrs. Dean's bitter
herbs" (*WH* 130).

Lockwood makes clear this tendency to extract wholesome medi-
cine from bitter herbs when (in chapter 3) he attempts to protect himself
from the ghost-child of his last dream by throwing up a barrier of texts.
"The fingers relaxed, I snatched mine through the hole, hurriedly piled
the books up in pyramid against it" (*WH* 30). To be sure, these are *good*
books, and Lockwood expects the good text to exorcise an evil that he
perceives as coming from the other side of the windowpane—from
without. He all but forgets that the terrifying figure of the ghost-child
emanates rather from within the margins of those same texts.

Lockwood closes his narration as he began it, by extracting a
benevolent resolution from a text that is at best duplicitous. In his last
journey from Wuthering Heights to Thrushcross Grange, the narrator
makes a diversion in the direction of the kirk, the same path taken in the
second of his dreams. Here he seeks out the graves of Edgar, Cathy, and
Heathcliff. Despite Nelly's report that Heathcliff and Cathy have been
known to "walk" (*WH* 265), Lockwood chooses to imagine peaceful
slumbers for the two lovers: "I lingered round them, under that benign
sky; watched the moths fluttering among the heath and hare-bells;
listened to the soft wind breathing through the grass; and wondered
how any one could ever imagine unquiet slumbers for the sleepers in that
quiet earth" (*WH* 266). Just as he once struggled to free himself from
Cathy's ghost and tried to dispel her specterlike name, so now Lockwood chooses to believe that the menacing supernatural lies at rest. In
this manner the "good book" of *Wuthering Heights* concludes, a tale
enclosed within the covers of Lockwood's reassuring narrative and
therefore mediated by his interpretation.

Yet Lockwood's conclusion ironically echoes an earlier error of an equally mystified narrator—Nelly Dean. On Cathy's death Nelly convinces herself that Cathy has returned peacefully home to heaven:

> Her brow smooth, her lids closed, her lips wearing the expression of a smile. No angel in heaven could be more beautiful than she appeared. . . . My mind was never in a holier frame than while I gazed on that untroubled image of Divine rest. . . . "Whether still on earth or now in heaven, her spirit is at home with God!" (*WH* 137)

The pathetic agony of the ghost-child in Lockwood's dream contradicts Nelly's sentimentalism. And Nelly forgets what Cathy herself has said. The stay in heaven would hardly promise "Divine rest"—rather, a miserable exile from home (*WH* 72). For Cathy, either alternative—heaven or earth—is a banishment from home. Although Lockwood and Nelly both have had evidence of Cathy's restless wandering—Lockwood in his dream and Nelly in her observation of Heathcliff's last days—neither seriously acknowledges the possibility that the endless struggle between polarities must yet continue. The union of Hareton and the second Catherine, their move to Thrushcross Grange, leaves Wuthering Heights to their specter opposites and counterparts, Heathcliff and his Cathy:

> "They are going to the Grange, then?" I said.
> "Yes," answered Mrs. Dean. . . .
> "And who will live here then?"
> "Why, Joseph will take care of the house, and, perhaps, a lad to keep him company. They will live in the kitchen, and the rest will be shut up."
> "For the use of such ghosts as choose to inhabit it," I observed.
> "No, Mr. Lockwood," said Nelly, shaking her head. "I believe the dead are at peace, but it is not right to speak of them with levity." (*WH* 265)

What is in question here is not only a particular ending to the tale of *Wuthering Heights* but the sense of an ending altogether, which is to say, an ending with sense, one that puts to rest all wandering and all generation of contradictory forces. We have already seen Lockwood's determination to fix the boundaries of textuality in his second dream. There the dreamer was able to forgive exactly seven times seventy heads of Branderham's sermon. The first of the seventy-first is the moment of crisis precisely because in exceeding the definitive and literal limits set on the discourse, Branderham's text can no longer be controlled. The "ending" that Lockwood imposes on *Wuthering Heights* is a gesture of the same kind.

However benignly Lockwood closes his interpretative narration of *Wuthering Heights*, the text itself always countercomments his conclusions. Within the good book that Lockwood narrates is the story of the fictional nature of his textual posture, an interpretation of its interpreter. Which, then, is the narrator and which the narrated? As the tale begins in chapter 3 and as it ends in chapter 34, Lockwood desperately tries to keep the menacing text under his control.[16] The excommunication that results from his first struggles with the text is also the result of his last attempts to suppress the supernatural by setting limits to the narrative. Lockwood is once again silenced and displaced as narrator. His position is usurped by a text that, because it is founded on disjunctive self-reading, repeatedly ironizes itself as "good book." Lockwood's conception of literature is one fiction among many that the novel narrates. It creates this fiction in order to excommunicate it, in order to define itself over and against what it is not.

Wuthering Heights is an annunciation of excommunication, both a fabrication in language of the real world—of that which is outside language (ex-communication)—and then again an expulsion of the heretic from its own textuality. The outsider from that "real world" who enters the closed space of Wuthering Heights is peremptorily banished. Yet this excommunication of Lockwood is not simply an expulsion to a position so distant that he no longer threatens what one is tempted to conceive of as the true inside nature of fiction. Excommunication is also incorporation of what the text posits to be its other. Rather than allow Lockwood to separate himself, it holds him in a relationship to itself of violent difference. It risks itself by allowing Lockwood's conception of fiction its apparent victory.[17]

Wuthering Heights is (about) this struggle between fiction and nonfiction. The fictional space is not a home for fiction, securely bound off from the threats of a world that calls itself real. Fiction is always in exile from itself. It involves the elaboration of and repeated struggle with this other realm, a continual marking of the discrepancy between itself and what claims to lie outside. At the same time that fiction defines itself as this disjunction, it renounces the possibility of absolute self-definition, not only because it can "define" itself only through its other but also because no delineating boundary can then be drawn—no limits can be set to the voracious realm of fiction. It is perhaps, after all, not mere superstition that causes Lockwood to struggle against the dream-texts, for as the fictional work marks the discrepancy between itself and that which lies outside, it paradoxically threatens to incorporate all that is within its reach, to assimilate the "real" into its own fiction. Lockwood is genuinely at stake, and this is indicated by the increasingly violent relationship between Lockwood and text in the course of his three dreams. His dreams go through him like wine through water: they write him and his language into their fiction.

The fabrication of Lockwood is the means by which *Wuthering Heights* speaks of its own textuality, and the relationship between Lockwood and the tale of Wuthering Heights is in turn the gap that makes a certain critical language possible—a gap here generated, perhaps, only to close. But what does this alternate generation and closure imply? The implications are critical in several senses. The gesture of generating the disparity between Lockwood as narrator and the narrative fiction, of criticizing Lockwood's naiveté, necessarily falls prey to the very illusions it pretends to disparage. Although Lockwood's conception of language is a fiction created by the novel, from a certain point of view one is forced to take Lockwood literally, to pose at least the imaginative possibility of a language that means what it says and refers to a realm outside the insanity of its own self-reflection. Critical rhetoric depends on temporarily forgetting the madness copresent with the "knowledge" that all is language. This forgetfulness gives free play to a referent that itself, after all, has pretensions to discursive truth. No less than Lockwood's, then, any reading is at stake in the novel's textuality. The enterprise becomes critical in yet another sense of the word—which brings us to the crisis of interpretation in the question of closure. In elaborating a commentary whose theoretical stance implicitly insists on remaining within the enclosure of *Wuthering Heights,* how does such a text fit in? Too well, perhaps. For such supplemental discourse may disrupt the limits of Lockwood's narration, but it is of necessity already accounted for as yet another fiction that the novel itself continues to fabricate.

III
HEINRICH VON KLEIST

4

The Rhetorics of Feminism

I never have known love but as a kiss
In the mid-battle, and a difficult truce
Of oil and water, candles and dark night,
Hillside and hollow, the hot-footed sun
And the cold, sliding, slippery-footed moon—
A brief forgiveness between opposites
That have been hatreds for three times the age
Of this long-'stablished ground.
—Yeats, *On Baile's Strand*

                    the tragedy began
With Homer that was a blind man,
And Helen has all living hearts betrayed.
O may the moon and sunlight seem
One inextricable beam,
For if I triumph I must make men mad.
—Yeats, "The Tower"

If, as the poet says, the tragedy began with Homer and with the yearning of all living hearts for Helen, if the *Iliad* marks, as we who search for points of origin are wont to claim, the beginning of Western literature, marking that origin with a story of love and a story of war, Heinrich von Kleist's *Penthesilea,* in its triumph, "must make men mad." It alters the death of the hero of the epic as predicted by his mother and by Hector's dying words in the *Iliad,* and recounted by Aeneas in Virgil's tale.[1] It denies him that most splendid of funerals described by the ghost of Agamemnon in the *Odyssey* and the grave mound that was both great and perfect.[2] It radically inverts the encounter of Penthesilea and Achilles as told in other texts and legends.[3] But this is not it. Nothing in the theatrical piece is so simple as alteration, betrayal, or even destruction. Penthesilea is about, and goes about, making the ground precarious for the staging of love and war. It questions the principal concepts on which Homer's text and rational thought are based. And if at the very beginning it does so in the voice of Greek reason, if it does so in the figures of those who observe but do not experience a fall into the abyss, at the close of the play it is the voice of the Amazon queen, Penthesilea, that will take those steps.[4]

As the play opens, Odysseus and Antilochus, who have not seen each other since Troy, a context comprehensible to all, now meet at the margins of another field of combat, one that threatens to erase the significance of the first. Still, as Odysseus narrates it, he and Achilles had left behind the walls of Ilium but not the continuity of that struggle. For they had come to set themselves between the son of Priam and Penthesilea, to avert the presumed alliance of Deiphobus with the Amazons.

Nevertheless, the entire action of *Penthesilea* progresses as a carefully placed wedge in the design of Homer's texts. The twenty-four scenes of Kleist's play are predicated in a sense on the completion of the *Iliad*. Penthesilea says as much when she describes the Amazons celebrating the decision to march on Troy.

> In every market-place high songs resounded,
> Celebrating the deeds of the heroes' war
> Of Paris' apple, the rape of Helen,
> Of the squadron-leading sons of Atreus,
> Of the struggle for Briseis, the burning of the ships,
> Also of Patroclus' death, and with what splendor
> You in venging him celebrated the triumph.
>
> (234–35E)

> Auf allen Märkten, hohe Lieder schallen,
> Die des Hero'nkriegs Taten feierten:
> Vom Paris-Apfel, dem Helenenraub,
> Von den geschwaderführenden Atriden,
> Vom Streit um Briseïs, der Schiffe Brand,
> Auch von Patroklus' Tod, und welche Pracht
> Du des Triumphes rächend ihm gefeiert;
>
> (15.2119–25)[5]

She says as much and more when she relates her own reflections on the son of Peleus. For she appears not only as one who has read to the end the twenty-four books of the *Iliad*, who sees the entire world as a patterned weaving of its tales, but also as one who uncannily prefigures

the Penelope of the twenty-four books of the *Odyssey* to come, prefiguring both Penelope and her web, as she reproduces each stitch of those
deeds in the tapestry of her heart, weaving a shroud for the hero even
before his death.

> O son of Peleus!
> Ever my thought when I was awake,
> Ever my dream were you! The whole world
> Lay like a patterned web spread out
> Before me; in every mesh, wide and great,
> One of your deeds was woven in,
> And in my heart, like pure, white silk,
> I burnt in every one with colors of flame.
> Now I beheld you, how you did smite him down,
> Before Ilium, the fleeing son of Priam;
> How you, enflamed by high lust of victory,
> Turned your face as he dragged
> His bloody crown on naked earth
> How Priam, entreating, in thy tent appeared—
> And scalding tears I wept, when I bethought,
> That some feeling, ye inexorable man,
> Runs through thy bosom hard as marble.
>
> (236–37E)

> O Pelide!
> Mein ewiger Gedanke, wenn ich wachte,
> Mein ewger Traum warst du! Die ganze Welt
> Lag wie ein ausgespanntes Musternetz
> Vor mir; in jeder Masche, weit und groß,
> War deiner Taten eine eingeschürzt,
> Und in mein Herz, wie Seide weiß und rein,
> Mit Flammenfarben jede brannt ich ein.
> Bald sah ich dich, wie du ihn niederschlugst,
> Vor Ilium, den flüchtgen Priamiden;
> Wie du, entflammt von hoher Siegerlust,
> Das Antlitz wandtest, während er die Scheitel,
> Die blutigen, auf nackter Erde schleifte;
> Wie Priam flehnd in deinem Zelt erschien—
> Und heiße Tränen weint ich, wenn ich dachte,
> Daß ein Gefühl doch, Unerbittlicher,
> Den marmorharten Busen dir durchzuckt.
>
> (15.2186–2202)

The entire action of *Penthesilea,* then, progresses as a carefully placed
wedge in the cleft and design of Homer's texts. For if, somewhat later in
the scene, Diomede calls upon reason to find the fissure in Achilles'
aberration of mind—

DIOMEDE
Let us united, oh kings, once again,
With composure set reason as wedge
Against his raving resolve.
You will, Odysseus, rich in wiles
Already know to find the cleft he offers.

(173E)

DIOMEDES
Laßt uns vereint, ihr Könige, noch einmal
Vernunft, keilförmig, mit Gelassenheit,
Auf seine rasende Entschließung setzen.
Du wirst, erfindungsreicher Larissäer,
Den Riß schon, den er beut, zu finden wissen.

(1.229–33)

if Diomede would have reason find the potential crack in madness—the
thrust of the play is quite the other way around.

Common sense has it that man is man, and woman woman; which
is to say, a woman like Helen, clear opposite of manly virtues, the passive
object of passion, rape, desire, jealousy, and ultimately war. The madness
of *Penthesilea* is that the (narration of the) Trojan War—so emblematic of
that distinction and many others as well—lies now at stake. Without
Achilles, Pergamon's walls, it is said, will not fall (174E; 2.243), and the
Greeks lie sidetracked in a conflict that makes no sense.

ODYSSEUS
I trust in your good sense, Achilles,
You will follow the wisdom of this command.
For madness would it be, by the Gods,
When the war urgently calls us to Troy
To get embroiled with these maidens,
Before we know *what* they want from us
Or even *whether* they desire something of us?

(185E)

ODYSSEUS
Ich traue deiner Klugheit zu, Pelide,
Du folgst der Weisheit dieser Anordnung.

Denn Wahnsinn wärs, bei den Olympischen,
Da dringend uns der Krieg nach Troja ruft,
Mit diesen Jungfraun hier uns einzulassen,
Bevor wir wissen, *was* sie von uns wollen?
Noch überhaupt nur, *ob* sie uns was wollen?

(4.580–86)

Conflict without cause, without a principle on which to base its opposition, is a struggle that makes the grounds for the Trojan War founder. Quite literally founder, if one is to give weight to the ultimate figure that Achilles offers.

ODYSSEUS
Like one possessed, I asked
If all this struggle for Helen's sake at Troy
Be forgotten, like a dream at dawn?
ACHILLES [*stepping nearer to him*]
Son of Laertes, were the citadel of Troy
To founder, you understand, so that a lake,
A blue one, were to appear in its place;
If hoary fishermen, in the light of the moon,
Made fast their skiff to its weathercocks;
If in the palace of Priam a pike
Should rule, an otter-pair, or rats
Embraced upon the bed of Helen:
It would mean as much to me as now.

(249E)

ODYSSEUS
Wie ein Beseßner fragt ich, ob der ganze
Helenenstreit, vor der Dardanerburg,
Gleich einem Morgentraum, vergessen sei?
ACHILLES [*indem er ihm näher tritt*]
Wenn die Dardanerburg, Laertiade,
Versänke, du verstehst, so daß ein See,
Ein bläulicher, an ihre Stelle träte;
Wenn graue Fischer, bei dem Schein des Monds,
Den Kahn an ihre Wetterhähne knüpften;
Wenn im Palast des Priamus ein Hecht
Regiert', ein Ottern- oder Ratzenpaar
Im Bette sich der Helena umarmten:
So wärs für mich gerad so viel, als jetzt.

(21.2515–26)

It is not simply that Achilles gives up the whole struggle for Helen, not simply that he turns reality to dream, as Odysseus suggests, nor, in Achilles' words, that water might replace land, moonlight daylight, animals humans. The Greek hero does not call for the antithesis or obliteration of Troy any more than for its presence. His is a position of total indifference: "It would mean as much to me as now." Achilles does not wish to convert the heaven of Greek legend to the hell of its inversion, but calls out in the name of a "third place," thus eradicating their unproblematic distinction.

> ODYSSEUS
> By the Styx, Diomede, he is in total earnest!
> ACHILLES
> By the Styx! By the marsh of Lerna! By Hades!
> The entire upper world and underworld
> And that third place. . . .
>
> (249E)

> ODYSSEUS
> Beim Styx! Es ist sein voller Ernst, Tydide!
> ACHILLES
> Beim Styx! Bei dem Lernäersumpf! Beim Hades!
> Der ganzen Oberwelt und Unterwelt,
> Und jedem dritten Ort. . . .
>
> (21.2527–30)

Still, as Odysseus narrates it, he and Achilles had left behind the walls of Ilium but not the continuity of its story nor the sense of its content. They had come to avert the presumed alliance of Priam's son Deiphobus with the Amazons. They are therefore astounded to find these two in furious battle and draw the only conclusions that reason will allow.

> ODYSSEUS
> And we in rapid council decide at once,
> To greet the Amazon princess:
> She, too, halts her triumphant course.
> Was ever counsel simpler or better?
> Had I asked Athena, could she
> More reasonably whisper in my ear?
> She must, by Hades, this maiden, still,
> Who, as from heaven, fit out for battle,
> Suddenly falls to mix in our struggle,

With one of the sides she must join:
And our friend we must think her
Since as enemy to the Trojans, she shows herself.
ANTILOCHUS
What else, by the Styx! Nothing else exists.

(168E)

ODYSSEUS
Und wir, im kurzen Rat beschließen, gleich,
Die Amazonenfürstin zu begrüßen:
Sie auch hat ihren Siegeslauf gehemmt.
War je ein Rat einfältiger und besser?
Hätt ihn Athene, wenn ich sie befragt,
Ins Ohr verständiger mir flüstern können?
Sie muß, beim Hades! diese Jungfrau, doch,
Die wie vom Himmel plötzlich, kampfgerüstet,
In unsern Streit fällt, sich darin zu mischen,
Sie muß zu einer der Partein sich schlagen:
Und uns die Freundin müssen wir sie glauben,
Da sie sich Teukrischen die Feindin zeigt.
ANTILOCHUS
Was sonst, beim Styx! Nichts anders gibts.

(1.44–56)

There is nothing else. Nothing else is thinkable in the logic of the Trojan War, or for that matter any war, where the structure is one of definable opposition. Yet if Penthesilea is foe to the Trojans, she is not friend to the Greeks. She violently refuses to join forces with them both. "The female centaur," as Odysseus calls her, the creature of unthinkable combination, falls upon Trojan and Greek alike.

ODYSSEUS
This much I know, there is in Nature
Only power and its counterforce; there is no third.
That which quenches fire cannot scalding water
Decompose to steam, and conversely. Yet here
A furious foe of both is found
On whose appearance fire does not know
If with the water it should trickle, water,
If with the fire it should heavenwards lick.
Beset by Amazons, the Trojan throws himself
Behind a Grecian shield, the Greek
Delivers him from the maiden who besets him,

And Greek and Trojan must almost now,
Despite the rape of Helen, join
To meet the common foe.
  [*A Greek brings him water*]
Thanks! My tongue is parched.

(170E)

ODYSSEUS
So viel ich weiß, gibt es in der Natur
Kraft bloß und ihren Widerstand, nichts Drittes.
Was glut des Feuers löscht, löst Wasser siedend
Zu Dampf nicht auf und umgekehrt. Doch hier
Zeigt ein ergrimmter Feind von beiden sich,
Bei dessen Eintritt nicht das Feuer weiß,
Obs mit dem Wasser rieseln soll, das Wasser,
Obs mit dem Feuer himmelan soll lecken.
Der Trojer wirft, gedrängt von Amazonen,
Sich hinter eines Griechen Schild, der Grieche
Befreit ihn von der Jungfrau, die ihn drängte,
Und Griech' und Trojer müssen jetzt sich fast,
Dem Raub der Helena zum Trotz, vereinen,
Um dem gemeinen Feinde zu begegnen.
  [*Ein Grieche bringt ihm Wasser*]
Dank! Meine Zunge lechzt.

(1.125–39)

Penthesilea disrupts the relationship between Greek and Trojan as radically as that disruption can take place. Without reversing it. For Greek and Trojan do not join together, only "almost." Penthesilea brings about no simple realignment reestablishing the structure of opposition. She is the third term, the "Drittes," which violates the natural law declaring power and its resistance as the only conceivable forces.

Indeed all this is spoken by a tongue that knows whereof it speaks ("This much I know"), that knows not only what it knows but also both what it desires and what is its opposite. At the close of this speech carried along on metaphors of water and fire, Odysseus is brought the water he asked for from the first (167E; 1.12). "Dank!" he says, "Meine Zunge lechzt" (170E; 1.139). "My tongue desires," or "is parched," as we might say in English. Odysseus's tongue is like the tongues of fire that lick heavenward a few lines earlier (1.132), and it knows to define its opposite, the water that will quench the burning that it feels.

Yet however certain he may be, however knowledgeably he may

speak about his tongue, his tongue, it seems, may not have said, word for word, what he would wish. For even Odysseus, who Homer assures us is unequaled among men for his rhetorical gifts,[6] whose tongue, however deceptive,[7] before this has always stood in loyal service to its master—even Odysseus may not be, as Penthesilea will put it later, "master of the rash lip." Just when he asserts that water cannot act as fire, Odysseus speaks of fire rather than water: "What puts out the glow of fire." Water and fire, it seems, can only be named by way of their opposites—in the very moment of insisting that this is what they are not. Still, although the gesture may be confusing, when the teetertotter of rhetorical substitution stops, one can see that the logic of the statements holds.

And yet when Odysseus, "equal to Jove in council,"[8] goes on to announce the entrance of that third enemy that upsets the fire and water's knowledge of themselves, what one is tempted to call a certain slip of the tongue takes place. But this is not quite it, since it is a question here not of something said in place of another, something different said rather than what was intended, but rather of something different said within the very same place.

Yet here

A furious foe of both is found
On whose appearance fire does not know
If with the water it should trickle, water
If with the fire it should heavenwards lick [*lecken*].

(170E)

Doch hier

Zeigt ein ergrimmter Feind von beiden sich,
Bei dessen Eintritt nicht das Feuer weiß,
Obs mit dem Wasser rieseln soll, das Wasser,
Obs mit dem Feuer himmelan soll lecken.

(1.128–32)

Odysseus intends to speak about a crisis in self-identity, but to speak about it from the distance of his own sure knowledge: "This much I know." Yet *lecken*, declared within the phrase that is to tell with certainty what fire always does, means "trickle" as well as "lick."[9] If at the end of this speech Odysseus's tongue knows with certainty what it is about, that it is on fire ("Meine Zunge lechzt"), the tongue that pronounces the speech and speaks of its knowledge of tongues of fire is no more master of itself than the (implicit tongues of) fire in line 132.

Not that Odysseus feels threatened by or even conscious of this aberration. For Odysseus here, as in Homer's tale, believes in the power of rhetorical persuasion, which is to say, he believes in the power of the speaker to control both what he says and its effect. This is why he repeatedly turns to Antilochus's rhetorical skills to save Achilles from his madness.

ODYSSEUS
Try it, Antilochus, if you will,
And see what your rhetorical art
Can do with him when his lips foam.

(173E)

ODYSSEUS
Versuchs, o Antiloch, wenns dir beliebt,
Und sieh, was deine rednerische Kunst,
Wenn seine Lippe schäumt, bei ihm vermag.

(1.226–28)[10]

The Greeks speak in the name of reason (1.230)[11] or wisdom (4.581) and credit language to be its vehicle. In their own terms, we might say, theirs is an understanding of the "word for word." Thus when Odysseus offers himself as ally to Penthesilea, when Prothoe reminds her that she owes him an answer (an anti-word as a literalization of the German *Antwort* would have it), Penthesilea turns to Odysseus and (as he reports it) replies that

ODYSSEUS
             she is
Penthesilea . . .
Queen of the Amazons, and will
Send me an answer from her quivers.
ANTILOCHUS
So word for word the messenger whom you sent;
Yet in the entire Grecian camp, no one
That understood him.

(169–70E)

ODYSSEUS
             sie sei
Penthesilea . . .
Der Amazonen Königin, und werde
Aus Köchern mir die Antwort übersenden!

ANTILOCHUS
So, Wort für Wort, der Bote, den du sandtest;
Doch keiner in dem ganzen Griechenlager,
Der ihn begriff.

(1.99–105)

How could those who live and speak the "word for word" understand the language of the anti-word? For this is the role that Penthesilea plays, at least for a while. For five hundred lines, as the play opens, the Greeks operate in a realm of reportage, a telling of events as they took place, a telling true to its object and always retellable, a telling that bespeaks all the control of conventional rhetoric. This is not to say that the Amazons function in a linguistic realm that is totally other. For the Amazons do their share of direct narrative, most notably Penthesilea herself in scene 15, in answer to Achilles' desire for the elucidation of so many riddles. Here she instructs her pupil in the history and laws of her people, laws that however counter to those of the patriarchal Greeks nevertheless mirror their structure of authority. Theirs, too, is often a language of objective description, as when Meroe relates Penthesilea's last encounter with Achilles in grim detail.

But Meroe's narration is prefaced by:

THE AMAZON
Here it comes toward us, pale, like a corpse, already
The word of the horror-riddle.

(252E)

DIE AMAZONE
Hier kommt es, bleich, wie eine Leiche, schon
Das Wort des Greuelrätsels uns heran.

(22.2599–2600)

Perhaps this is more to the point. In this play it is not really a question, after all, of Greek reason at odds with Amazonian madness, of fixing the roles of linguistic allegiance to proclaim the death of reason in the body and figure of Achilles. The text forces us to assume this point of view, dependent as we are, in the beginning, on seeing through the eyes of Odysseus's narration. The point is that the body whose approach this play announces is, first and foremost, less the dead body of Achilles than that which would explain the ultimate relationship between Penthesilea and the Greek hero. It promises at least to explain it, for it is heralded as the answer to a riddle, although an answer to a riddle that must at this point be proclaimed horror-ridden. But when the word of the horror-riddle approaches, it is already emptied of its life, "pale, like a corpse," for the answer to the atrocious enigma of just what took place in the battle between Penthesilea and her beloved, of the final resolution between Greek and Amazon, is the word of the riddle itself, the word as riddle rather than explanation.

Perhaps it would be clearer if we left Kleist's formulation in order to say again that it is not a question of opposing Greek literality, an Achaean "word for word," and all that would imply, to an Amazonian force of its refusal. To be sure, the conventions of Amazon law do depend on a structure in which figure is a resistance to the force of denotation. But it is also a duplication of denotation's utter control. The entire enterprise of Amazon violence is to find a substitute for Mars, a "Stellvertreter," he who is both chosen by and will stand clearly in the place of the God.

> PENTHESILEA
> The god shows us, through his priestess,
> A chaste and splendid people that in his place,
> As substitute, should appear to us.
>
> (233E)

> PENTHESILEA
> Der Gott zeigt uns, durch seine Priesterin,
> Ein Volk an, keusch und herrlich, das, statt seiner,
> Als Stellvertreter, uns erscheinen soll.
>
> (15.2051–53)

The interdiction that Penthesilea challenges from the beginning is an interdiction against naming the particular object of desire; once he acquires the proper name Achilles, a third force that is neither simply a proper name nor a simple metaphor disrupts the balance.

> PROTHOE
> Then she named his name to you, Otrere?
> PENTHESILEA
> —She named him, Prothoe, as is fitting
> For a mother in confidence to her daughter.
> ACHILLES
> Why? Wherefore? Does the law forbid it?
> PENTHESILEA
> It is not seemly that a daughter of Mars

Should seek out her opponent. Him should she choose
Whom the god lets appear to her in battle.—

(235E)

PROTHOE
So nannte sie den Namen dir, Otrere?
PENTHESILEA
—Sie nannt ihn, Prothoe, wie's einer Mutter
Wohl ihm Vertraun zu ihrer Tochter ziemt.
ACHILLES
Warum? Weshalb? Verbeut dies das Gesetz?
PENTHESILEA
Es schickt sich nicht, daß eine Tochter Mars'
Sich ihren Gegner sucht, den soll sie wählen,
Den ihr der Gott im Kampf erscheinen läßt.—

(15.2141–47)

If the metaphor is to be rigorously regulated so that the substitute may represent none but Ares, if all risk is to be avoided lest the "Stellvertreter" be taken rather, literally, for himself and overtake the place of the god of war, he must not acquire his own identity. Nothing else could explain the rage and language of the High Priestess in scene 7, where every word she utters is guaranteed by the name and anger of the goddess Diana and where the great multitude of captives is collectively and outrageously named as that for which they stand as metaphor: "Mars," "Ares," "the god."

HIGH PRIESTESS
What matters the son of Peleus to our people?
—Is it seemly for a daughter of Ares, Queen,
To stake her all in battle on one name?
[*To an Amazon*]
Run quickly, Arsinoe, stand before her face,
And tell her in my goddess' name
That Mars has appeared before his brides:
I command her, by the goddess' wrath,
To lead the wreathed god now to our homeland,
Without delay, to Diana's temple,
To begin for him the sacred feast of roses.

(199E)

DIE OBERPRIESTERIN
Was geht dem Volke der Pelide an?

—Ziemts einer Tochter Ares', Königin,
Im Kampf auf einen Namen sich zu stellen?
[*Zu einer Amazone*]
Fleuch gleich, Arsinoe, vor ihr Antlitz hin,
Und sag in meiner Göttin Namen ihr,
Mars habe seinen Bräuten sich gestellt:
Ich forderte, bei ihrem Zorn sie auf,
Den Gott bekränzt zur Heimat jetzt zu führen,
Und unverzüglich ihm, in ihrem Tempel,
Das heilge Fest der Rosen zu eröffnen!

(7.1044–53)

Kleist's text marks no simple antagonism between literality and its other because Penthesilea is the locus of an irresolvable struggle in which a third force prevents them, although they follow close on one another's heels, from meeting on even ground. The text slips unsteadily, for example, between literal and figural uses of the same term. Let us take up once again the metaphorical cleft in Achilles' madness, that small breach through which Diomede hopes reason may enter (like the Trojan horse that might have entered the walls of Pergamon were that history not so utterly torn apart by the tale Kleist prefers to tell). Immediately following Diomede's speech (173E; 1.229–37), we learn of Achilles' fall at the edge of an abyss. Penthesilea, unlike Diomede (as the terms of reason and its lack reverse), is "robbed of judgment." Yet like Diomede, she, too, seeks to find a path to Achilles, a path the text, exactly as in the first passage, also calls a "Riß" (175E; 2.311), but one that has now become totally literal.

To borrow an image from Odysseus's opening lines, we might say that literal and figurative language in this play are like "two enraged wolves" ("zwei erboste Wölfe") (167E; 1.5) "each with its fang in the throat of the other" ("des einen Zahn im Schlund des anderen") (167E; 1.11). Such a sense can account not merely for individual moments of articulation in the text but for the overall thrust of all but the last three scenes.

The problem is quite simply delineated. What Penthesilea speaks as a language of metaphor the Greeks can understand only literally, and, of course, the other way around.[12] Amazon law demands that violence stand as the metaphor for desire.

Is it my fault that on the field of battle,
Fighting, I must woo his love?

What do I wish, then, when I thrust my sword at him?
Do I wish to throw him down to Hades?
Ye eternal Gods, I only wish
To draw him down here to this breast.

(203E)

Ists meine Schuld, daß ich im Feld der Schlacht
Um sein Gefühl mich kämpfend muß bewerben?
Was will ich denn, wenn ich das Schwert ihm zücke?
Will ich ihn denn zum Orkus niederschleudern?
Ich will ihn ja, ihr ewgen Götter, nur
An diese Brust will ich ihn niederziehn!

(9.1187–92)

The Greeks, however, read metaphorical violence only as war.[13] There is a turning point, of course. For when Penthesilea is led to believe that it is she who has taken Achilles, she shifts from the metaphor of battle to the literal lesson we spoke of earlier, in a series of monologues that should set things straight. For the duration of a brief forgiveness between opposites, Achilles understands. But—and here is the catch—the disjunctive that seems to rule their communication is such that for Penthesilea to speak a language that means what it says, Achilles must assume a figural stance. She relates her laws only under the aegis of Achilles' metaphorical surrender.

PROTHOE
    Achilles! She believes me not. Speak thyself!
PENTHESILEA
I took him prisoner?
PROTHOE
        What else? Is it not so?
ACHILLES [*who in the meantime has stepped forward*]
In every more beautiful sense, noble Queen!
My only will, to flutter away my life,
Henceforth fettered by thy glances.

(219E)

PROTHOE
    Achill! Sie glaubt mir nicht. Sprich du!
PENTHESILEA
Er wär gefangen mir?
PROTHOE
        Wie sonst? Ists nicht?

ACHILLES [*der während dessen vorgetreten*]
In jedem schönren Sinn, erhabne Königin!
Gewillt mein ganzes Leben fürderhin
In deiner Blicke Fesseln zu verflattern.

(14.1609–13)

By the time the arrival of Greek and Amazon troops forces the truth of day upon her, Achilles has nevertheless learned enough from what she has taught him to know that he, too, must speak in figures of war to win her.[14]

DIOMEDE
Have you sent the herald to her, son of Peleus?
Is it true? Is it real?
. . . .
ACHILLES
                    Yes. Still a whim to her most holy
Commands that I fall vanquished by her sword in battle;
'Til then she cannot embrace me in love.

(247E)

DIOMEDES
Hast du den Herold ihr gesandt, Pelide?
Ists wahr? Ists wirklich?
. . . .
ACHILLES
                    Ja. Doch eine Grille, die ihr heilig,
Will, daß ich ihrem Schwert im Kampf erliege;
Eh nicht in Liebe kann sie mich umfangen.

(21.2453–54, 2460–62)

Achilles speaks figuratively when he sends his herald so that the hero of the Trojan War may throw himself to the feet of the woman of his passion. He calls Penthesilea forth to a renewed struggle of pure theatricality, for the text is moving through metaphorical speech to total performance. She in turn can respond to him, however, only in a language of literal violence.[15]

And this is where the true madness begins, where both the difficult truce and the difficult battle between hillside and hollow disintegrate, disintegrate into what, after all, approaches the coming together of the literal and the figurative and of lucidity and insanity. In a play whose structure is that of the hunt, a text overburdened with imagery from that endeavor, shot through with images of wolves and hounds and

stags,[16] Penthesilea becomes a bitch who lacerates the breast of her
beloved prey, literally.[17]

THE PRIESTESS
What do you see? Tell! Speak!
THE AMAZON
              Penthesilea,
She lies, companion of her violent hounds,
She whom a human womb did bear, and rends—
The limbs of Achilles she tears to pieces!

(252E)

MEROE
She strikes, tearing the armor from his body,
Strikes her teeth in his white breast,
She and the dogs in rivalry with one another,
Oxus and Sphinx, their teeth in his right side,
She in his left; as I appeared,
Blood dripped from her mouth and hands.

(254E)

DIE PRIESTERINNEN
Was siehst du? Rede! Sprich!
DIE AMAZONE
              Penthesilea,
Sie liegt, den grimmgen Hunden beigesellt,
Sie, die ein Menschenschoß gebar, und reißt,—
Die Glieder des Achills reißt sie in Stücken!

(22.2594–97)

MEROE
Sie schlägt, die Rüstung ihm vom Leibe reißend,
Den Zahn schlägt sie in seine weiße Brust,
Sie und die Hunde, die wetteifernden,
Oxus und Sphinx den Zahn in seine rechte,
In seine linke sie; als ich erschien,
Troff Blut von Mund und Händen ihr herab.

(23.2669–74)

The Amazon queen is here the unnamable embodiment—for we are
repeatedly reminded that she is from now on she whom no name can
name (252E; 23.2607)—of metaphor and literality; the rest of the text is a
dramatic reflection on this juncture. The play began with Odysseus's

meditations on Penthesilea as the unthinkable third that disrupted the clear distinction between warring opposites. But that was quite another scene. For those forces were the object of a knowledge outside—or so it seemed—the medium of thought, and Odysseus was a man who both knew and knew what he knew. The speech of his own tongue may have been invaded by that uncertainty, but not profoundly and not permanently.

As Penthesilea comes to an end, she is the figure not only of a crisis in self-knowledge but also of a crisis in the self-knowledge of language. She returns to the Amazons as a "living corpse" ("lebendge Leich") (256E; 24.2717), with gestures incomprehensible and with face more bleakly expressionless than the desert. In an effort to bring her back to herself, her dearest friend Prothoe suggests that she cleanse herself of her day's handiwork. While the Amazons hope and fear that water may be the element to return her to her senses, it brings the delusion that she is in Elysium, or if among the living, that she has accomplished this time in reality what Achilles' loving metaphors of surrender promised her at their penultimate encounter. For Penthesilea imagines that she has "overcome the Peliden for herself" and, as in scene 14, that she will find him once again behind her back:

PENTHESILEA
I do not have the heart to look around.
PROTHOE
What will you do? What do you think, O Queen?
PENTHESILEA [*looking around*]
Oh Love, you are dissembling.
PROTHOE
                              No, by Zeus,
Eternal god of the world!
PENTHESILEA [*with increasing impatience*]
                              Most holy ladies,
Do disperse!
HIGH PRIESTESS [*pressing close together with the other women*]
                              Dear Queen!
PENTHESILEA [*as she stands up*]
Oh Diana! Why should I not? O Diana!
Once before he stood behind my back.

                                          (262E)

PENTHESILEA
Ich habe nicht das Herz mich umzusehen.
PROTHOE
Was hast du vor? Was denkst du, Königin?
PENTHESILEA [*sich umsehend*]
O Liebe, du verstellst dich.
PROTHOE
                    Nein, beim Zeus,
Dem ewgen Gott der Welt!
PENTHESILEA [*mit immer steigender Ungeduld*]
                    O ihr Hochheiligen,
Zerstreut euch doch!
DIE OBERPRIESTERIN [*sich dicht mit den übrigen Frauen zusammendrängend*]
                    Geliebte Königin!
PENTHESILEA [*indem sie aufsteht*]
O Diana! Warum soll ich nicht? O Diana!
Er stand schon einmal hinterm Rücken mir.

                                        (24.2873–79)

But behind her back something else has taken place. Penthesilea will indeed find Achilles once again, yet still another scene repeats itself here, behind the back, one is tempted to say, of that questionable second reunion. For before Penthesilea's first delusion that Achilles lies, disarmed and at her feet (scenes 14 and 15), a similar sequence of events takes place: moments of utter madness that come to a blank conclusion with the element of water. There at the end of scene 9, as her countrywomen plead with her to flee the oncoming Greeks, Penthesilea wishes to roll the mountain Ida on the Ossa so that she might place herself on top.

MEROE
Supposing now, you had performed this work—?
PROTHOE
Supposing, what would you—
PENTHESILEA
                    Simple one!
By his golden-flaming locks I'd draw
Him down, down to me—
PROTHOE
                    Who?

PENTHESILEA
Helios,
As he soars by above my crown!
[*The princesses regard each other, speechless and with horror*]
HIGH PRIESTESS
Bear her away with force!
PENTHESILEA [*looking down into the stream*]
I, raving mad!
There he lies at my feet! Take me—
[*She wishes to fall into the stream. Prothoe and Meroe hold her back*]
(210E)

MEROE
Gesetzt nun, du vollbrächtest dieses Werk—?
PROTHOE
Gesetzt, was würdest du—?
PENTHESILEA
Blödsinnige!
Bei seinen goldnen Flammenhaaren zög ich
Zu mir hernieder ihn—
PROTHOE
Wen?
PENTHESILEA
Helios,
Wenn er am Scheitel mir vorüberfleucht!
[*Die Fürstinnen sehn sprachlos und mit Entsetzen einander an*]
DIE OBERPRIESTERIN
Reißt mit Gewalt sie fort!
PENTHESILEA [*schaut in den Fluß nieder*]
Ich Rasende!
Da liegt er mir zu Füßen ja! Nimm mich—
[*Sie will in den Fluß sinken, Prothoe und Meroe halten sie*]
(9.1382—88)

The mad conflation of the golden-haired sun god with the Greek hero who had first appeared to her like "a day-star among pale night-stars" ("ein Tagsstern unter bleichen Nachtgestirnen") (237E; 15.2207), the mad conflation of Helios, who she claims lies at her feet, with what must be her own reflected image is, perhaps, not quite without its reason.

It is the last scene of Penthesilea. The water may have cleansed her of the gore of battle, but it has not restored her understanding. For this she must try to find once again the Achilles behind her back. Like the

word of the horror-riddle that entered the stage two scenes earlier, that
"pale . . . corpse," Penthesilea must now confront the riddle of that
other corpse, that now semblance of a corpse, and confront the author of
its loss of life.

PENTHESILEA [*to the Amazons, who carry the body*]
             Stop there!—
What is it you carry? I desire to know it. Stand!
[*She makes her way among the women and pushes through to the body*]
PROTHOE
Oh my queen! Look no further!
. . . .
PENTHESILEA
—'Tis not impossible, I see that.
Sure a swallow's wing I can disable
So that the wing can yet be healed;
The stag I can lure into the park with arrows.
Yet the marksman's art is a betrayer;
And when it is the mastershot into the heart of happiness,
The spiteful gods do guide our hand.
Did I strike too near to where it matters? Speak, is it he?

                                   (262E)

PENTHESILEA [*zu den Amazonen, welche die Leiche tragen*]
             Halt dort!—
Was tragt ihr dort? Ich will es wissen. Steht!
[*Sie macht sich Platz unter den Frauen und dringt bis zur Leiche vor*]
PROTHOE
O meine Königin! Untersuche nicht!
. . . .
PENTHESILEA
—Es ist unmöglich nicht, das seh ich ein.
Zwar einer Schwalbe Flügel kann ich lähmen,
So, daß der Flügel noch zu heilen ist;
Den Hirsch lock ich mit Pfeilen in den Park.
Doch ein Verräter ist die Kunst der Schützen;
Und gilts den Meisterschuß ins Herz des Glückes,
So führen tücksche Götter uns die Hand.
—Traf ich zu nah ihn, wo es gilt? Sprecht, ist ers?

                                   (24.2880–91)

If according to the *Iliad*[18] and in the *Aeneid*[19] it is Apollo who
guides the arrow of Paris to strike the single vulnerable spot, the

legendary heel, Kleist has changed all that. Apollo, who throughout the *Iliad* is friend to the Trojans, must be he who guides the "mastershot" of Penthesilea, a shot that makes her lose all mastery. For Helios usurps Penthesilea's self-mastery here, just as earlier she found him mirrored in the place where her own reflection should by rights have been found. Like Narcissus, infatuated with an appearance that is neither an appropriate object of desire nor an attainable self, Penthesilea sacrifices both self and other. Her missile strikes Achilles "where it matters" ("wo es gilt") (262E; 24.2891), not in the heart so much as in the throat (253E; 23.2649–53). Implicitly here, as elsewhere in mythology more explicitly, Apollo is the great demystifier on the subject of poetry.[20] Achilles and Penthesilea are compelled to learn another form of speech: Achilles the death rattle of disbelief, Penthesilea the language of the deadly bow that makes sheer opposites (life and decay, love and prostitution, as we shall see) come together in a kiss:

> She strains with strength of the madwoman born forthwith
> The bow, so that the ends kiss one another,
>
> (253E)

> Und spannt mit Kraft der Rasenden, sogleich
> Den Bogen an, daß sich die Enden küssen,
>
> (23.2646–47)

But if Penthesilea has learned another manner of speaking, she has not yet mastered the rules of its utterance or learned to recognize her own reflection in this image of Apollo, "God of the silver bow."[21] This new poetry is a language that disintegrates the order of metaphor and literality.

> PENTHESILEA
>   This, however, I would know,
> Who has so godlessly with me competed—
> I do not ask, who struck him down while yet
> He lived . . . .
> Who slew for me the slain, I ask
> . . . .
> Who, o Prothoe, in plundering thus
> The open portal impiously shunned, through all the
> Snowwhite alabaster walls
> Could break, for me, in upon this temple; who this youth—
> The image of the gods—so disfigured,

That life with decay no more disputes
To which of them he belongs; who has shaped him thus
That pity will not weep for him, that love,
The immortal, like a harlot,
Untrue in death, must turn away from him. . . .

(263–64E)

PENTHESILEA
Das aber will ich wissen,
Wer mir so gottlos neben hat gebuhlt!—
Ich frage nicht, wer den Lebendigen
Erschlug . . . .
Wer mir den Toten tötete, frag ich

. . . .
Doch wer, o Prothoe, bei diesem Raube
Die offne Pforte ruchlos mied, durch alle
Schneeweißen Alabasterwände mir
In diesen Tempel brach; wer diesen Jüngling,
Das Ebenbild der Götter, so entstellt,
Daß Leben und Verwesung sich nicht streiten,
Wem er gehört; wer ihn so zugerichtet,
Daß ihn das Mitleid nicht beweint, die Liebe
Sich, die unsterbliche, gleich einer Metze,
Im Tod noch untreu, von ihm wenden muß. . . .

(24.2914–35)

The incomprehensible is not that Achilles' body has lost the spark of life but that the dead man has been killed. It is precisely this outrage of "insulting the senseless clay" that in the *Iliad* causes an uproar on Olympus and brings another Apollo to protect the body of Hector from the cruelty of Achilles' rage:

> But Apollo kept off all pollution from his body, pitying the hero, although dead; and encircled him with the golden aegis, lest that, dragging, he might lacerate him.[22]

Yet in *Penthesilea* Achilles has no golden aegis to protect him. This means that his body can no longer stand as a structure, the alabaster walls of the temple of a subject, image of the (literal) self within; nor can it any longer image forth the gods ("Ebenbild der Götter") of which man's likeness has always been a guarantee. It is no longer a question of the metaphorical and the literal integral enough to be at odds with one another. Can it be insignificant, then, that an earlier version of the play finds Penthesilea kneeling over the fragments of Achilles' lips? For in every imaginable sense, the lips of the Greek hero have been torn apart.[23]

PENTHESILEA
Look, Prothoe, look—the vestige of a lip—
Speak, seems it not as though he smiled?
O by Olympus! He has made his peace with me,
And that other piece, it smiles also.

PENTHESILEA
Sieh, Prothoe, sieh—der Rest von einer Lippe—
Sprich, dünkts dich nicht als ob er lächelte?
O beim Olymp! Er ist mir ausgesöhnt,
Und jener andre Teil er lächelt auch.[24]

If Kleist rejects this passage, it is perhaps that Achilles even now says too much too clearly. For the voice of authority now belongs to the High Priestess, who, although her lips tremble to say it, can give a brutally accurate and literal account of Penthesilea's deadly encounter with Achilles. But if the High Priestess can speak in the name of the goddess, calling on those near her to corroborate her words, she understands nothing of what it means to speak.[25] That is left to Penthesilea, who understands all too well: the god behind *her* back, a quite different one, has been bent on disrupting not only the mastery of the bow (262E; 24.2884–91) but also the mastery of the word and now, it would seem, requires that she contemplate her own reflection. What can we say of Penthesilea's last words, for this is at once her moment of clearest insight and that of utter derangement, where words solve riddles only insofar as they pose them?

PENTHESILEA
    Did I kiss him dead?
FIRST PRIESTESS
                    O Heavens!
PENTHESILEA
No? Did I not kiss him? Torn to pieces, really? Speak?
HIGH PRIESTESS
Woe! Woe! I call to you. Hide thyself!
Let eternal midnight cover thee henceforth!
PENTHESILEA
—Then it was an oversight. Kisses, bites,
That rhymes / makes sense [*das reimt sich*], and whoever loves directly
    from the heart

Can easily grasp [*greifen*] the one for the other.
. . . .
I simply, by Diana, misspoke myself,
Because I am not master of the rash lip.

(265–66E)

PENTHESILEA
    Küßt ich ihn tot?
DIE ERSTE PRIESTERIN
                    O Himmel!
PENTHESILEA
Nicht? Küßt ich nicht? Zerrissen wirklich? sprecht?
DIE OBERPRIESTERIN
Weh! Wehe! ruf ich dir. Verberge dich!
Laß fürder ewge Mitternacht dich decken!
PENTHESILEA
—So war es ein Versehen. Küsse, Bisse,
Das reimt sich, und wer recht von Herzen liebt,
Kann schon das eine für das andre greifen.
. . . .
Ich habe mich, bei Diana, bloß versprochen,
Weil ich der raschen Lippe Herr nicht bin.

(24.2977–87)

Penthesilea has indeed misspoken herself, bound as she was to undo the self with a gesture that is fundamentally linguistic. She, like her victim, might as well be "lipless," for she finds herself disempowered to guide the lips that utter the words that figure reality. What does it mean to confuse *Küsse* and *Bisse* because they rhyme?[26] When the word has become a purely material sound-object such that the two are apparently interchangeable, there is no longer a basis on which to guide the lips to choose their utterance. If this is so, what is lost is not only the individual meaning of the terms but also their ability to stand as metaphor, one in place of the other. The ordered hierarchy that metaphor depends on, that enables the proper distinction between a figure and its true intent, the hierarchy that governed both all the action of the characters and the understanding of the reader throughout the play, is no longer possible once clear difference is thus lost at the surface of language.

There is, however, both rhyme and reason here,[27] a theory of the slip of the tongue that one can readily grasp. But language, it seems, takes with one hand what it gives with the other, or rather takes with one

mouth what it gives with the same. For Penthesilea has another, almost
inverse explanation which is, as she insists, nevertheless, not so mad as it
may seem.

PENTHESILEA
Like many a girl who hangs on the neck of her lover
And says the words—she loves him—oh so much—
That out of love she could eat him up,
And later, when the word is tested, the fool,
Already sated to the point of loathing is she.
Now you, my lover, thus I did not perform,
See here, as *I* upon your neck did hang,
I did it truly word for word,
I was not so mad as it did seem.

(266E)

PENTHESILEA
Wie manche, die am Hals des Freundes hängt,
Sagt wohl das Wort: sie lieb ihn, o so sehr,
Daß sie vor Liebe gleich ihn essen könnte;
Und hinterher, das Wort beprüft, die Närrin!
Gesättigt sein zum Ekel ist sie schon.
Nun, du Geliebter, so verfuhr ich nicht.
Sieh her: als *ich* an deinem Halse hing,
Hab ichs wahrhaftig Wort für Wort getan;
Ich war nicht so verrückt, als es wohl schien.

(24.2991–99)

For the fool who says "she loves [her lover]—oh so much" that she could
devour him out of love, that violent appetite is merely metaphor for her
love. Yet Penthesilea is not so easily sated. For her "word for word,"
unlike that of the Greeks, is no reportage of something outside language,
no verification that keeps its distance from the realm of substance it
depicts. Penthesilea does what she has said: her words give way to pure
deed. If the order of metaphor was upset, according to her first explanation, when the terms of the substitution (*kisses, bites*) became interchangeable at the surface of linguistic materiality, here the usurpation
takes place in bypassing the literal, when the metaphorical is realized in
the depths of utter substance. Once again the impetuous lip, that third
force, becomes master of the self.[28]

It is not that Penthesilea, at the very end, has lost sight or control of the conventional function of the word, both literal and figurative.[29] Everything in the lines that follow testifies to the fact.

> PENTHESILEA
> And—a *word* between ourselves that none must hear:
> Tanais' ashes, scatter them to the winds!
> PROTHOE
> And you my dearest sister-heart?
> PENTHESILEA
> I?
> PROTHOE
>   You!
> PENTHESILEA
>   —I wish to tell you, Prothoe,
> I do renounce our law of women,
> And will follow him, this youth.
>
> (266E, emphasis mine)

> PENTHESILEA
> Und—im Vertraun ein *Wort,* das niemand höre,
> Der Tanaïs Asche, streut sie in die Luft!
> PROTHOE
> Und du, mein teures Schwesterherz?
> PENTHESILEA
> Ich?
> PROTHOE
>   Du!
> PENTHESILEA
>   —Ich will dir sagen, Prothoe,
> Ich sage vom Gesetz der Fraun mich los,
> Und folge diesem Jüngling hier.
>
> (24.3008–13, emphasis mine)

Penthesilea's "word" here could not be simpler, nor more appropriate given what has taken place. It seems to go without saying that the ashes of Tanais might as well be dispersed. For Penthesilea has learnt all too thoroughly the lesson of the corpse, and also of the absolute inefficacy of the law of women. Her renunciation of the Amazon law is no less a denunciation of the patriarchal law of the Greeks, for they are founded on the same principles. No one knows better than Penthesilea—except perhaps Achilles.

Penthesilea can use the literal word with ease (if only to renounce it), but she understands no less that other "word," the figurative, used to represent something other than itself, masking and representing what one really intends. If Penthesilea is here at ease with the conventions not only of literal but also of figurative language, it is because the matter of the text no longer lies within the bounds of either.

PROTHOE
You will—?
HIGH PRIESTESS
       You think—
PENTHESILEA
           What? By all means!
MEROE
                Oh Heavens!
PROTHOE
Then allow me a *word* to you, my sister heart—
[*She tries to take the dagger from her*]
PENTHESILEA
Now then, what?— What do you seek there on my belt?
So, that. Wait, right away! I did not undèrstand.
—Here is the dagger.

                    (266–67E, emphasis mine)

PROTHOE
Du willst—?
DIE OBERPRIESTERIN
       Du denkst—
PENTHESILEA
           Was? Allerdings!
MEROE
                O Himmel!
PROTHOE
So laß mich dir ein *Wort*, mein Schwesterherz—
[*Sie sucht ihr den Dolch wegzunehmen*]
PENTHESILEA
Nun denn, und was?— Was suchst du mir am Gurt?
—Ja, so. Wart, gleich! Verstand ich dich doch nicht.
—Hier ist der Dolch.

                (24.3015–19, emphasis mine)

What need has Penthesilea of this dagger, for if, as she announces, she is to follow the youth at her feet, it was no commonly forged weapon that brought him down. Such corpses arise from a mastershot into the heart of happiness that always misses its mark, striking where it counts, at the origin of the voice (253E; 23.2649), striking the metaphor when the literal is intended, the literal when the metaphorical is the goal, or even the aberrations of language's pure surface or reality's depth, striking always to prove there are no mastershots nor selves to master the trajectory (from self to words, to image, to denotation, to reality).

In a passage, then, that no longer talks *about* language, Penthesilea's language performs. It performs what she promises herself (*sich verspricht*) even as she misspeaks herself (*sich verspricht*).[30] Once again, one might be tempted to say, she loses mastery of the rash lip as she does word for word what she pronounces. And yet this "word for word" is unheard of, as different as possible not only from that of the Greeks but also from the "did it truly word for word" ("wahrhaftig Wort für Wort getan") (266E; 24.2998) a few lines earlier, in which the deed was a fulfillment of words that came before. Here, at least until the final line, there is no temporal or spatial rift between words and deeds.

PENTHESILEA
For now I climb down into my breast,
Like a shaft,[31] and dig forth for myself, cold
Like ore, an annihilating feeling.
This ore, I purify in the fires of woe
Hard, for myself, to steel; steep it then,
With the hot corroding venom of remorse, through and through;
Carry it then to hope's eternal anvil,
And whet and sharpen it for me to a dagger;
And to this dagger now I reach my breast:
Thus! Thus! Thus! Thus! And once more.—Now it is good.
[*She falls and dies*]

(267E)[32]

PENTHESILEA
Denn jetzt steig ich in meinen Busen nieder,
Gleich einem Schacht, und grabe, kalt wie Erz,
Mir ein vernichtendes Gefühl hervor.
Dies Erz, dies läutr' ich in der Glut des Jammers
Hart mir zu Stahl; tränk es mit Gift sodann,
Heißätzendem, der Reue, durch und durch;
Trag es der Hoffnung ewgem Amboß zu,
Und schärf und spitz es mir zu einem Dolch;

Und diesem Dolch jetzt reich ich meine Brust:
So! So! So! So! Und wieder!—Nun ists gut.
[*Sie fällt und stirbt*]

(24.3025—34)

Once before Penthesilea, at the heels of her Achilles, descended
and reascended an abyss—or so the long report of the Greek captain tells
us at the opening of the play (scene 2). But here there is nothing to tell
about, for the telling is the thing. The passage is at once the most daring
of metaphorical conceits and, if we are to judge by the success of her fall
("She falls and dies"), language as its own absolute, immediate realization.[33]

Penthesilea descends into the depths of her bosom. In this hollow
of the heart that is *"like* a shaft," she digs forth a feeling, "cold *like* ore."
Yet when she brings the material to the surface, what she has mined,
what she will work, is not the feeling but rather the simile that stood in
its place, "this ore." The figures of mining that served to image her breast
and emotion, in retrospect assume here an anomalous physical immediacy. The lines that follow forge that metal into an instrument of death.
As if to complete the displacements of the literal and the figurative, it is
the feelings whose position the ore usurped that now serve to shape it—
purified as it is "in the fires of woe," immersed in "the venom of
remorse," sharpened on "hope's eternal anvil."

Gone are the earlier moments of the play when Penthesilea and
Achilles were constrained to speak either figuratively or literally. In a
passage that is about movement and is movement among various levels,
in a passage that both radically produces and conventionally describes
(in a passage where fire and liquid, ironically enough, may finally seem to
know their place), there is nothing to prevent one's slipping and sliding
among figure, denotation, and realization; one can indeed grasp the one
for the other. Penthesilea kills herself with a literalized simile, dug from
the depths of her own feeling, forged in the workshop of language. She
offers her breast to a dagger created from its own hollow, a dagger, then,
destined to dig forth in that breast once again at the moment of her
death and to bring about a repetition of the scene. In a sense she is freed,
after all, of the god behind her back and achieves front on her "mastershot into the heart of happiness."[34] This is because the pitfalls in
language finally take their place unmistakably within her riddled speech
as it performs the obliteration of its master.

5

A Delicate Joke

Like *Penthesilea, Prince Friedrich von Homburg* is about a battle. But unlike the earlier play, which disrupts the texts that came before it, *Prince Friedrich von Homburg* tells, more or less, a true story: there are chronicles to prove it.[1] In June of 1675 the Elector of Brandenburg entrusts Homburg with the entire March cavalry (282E; 1.5.275), poised to continue the struggle with the invading Gustav Karl.[2] Despite explicit orders to the contrary, in an act that openly violates the code of war and warrants the penalty of death, Homburg charges the enemy before receiving the planned signal. Although the battle is more won than lost, his error precludes the decisive routing of the Swedes that might have driven them definitively from Brandenburg soil. For *Prince Friedrich von Homburg* takes place on the *Mark,* the German word for *March,* which is to say, not only on the Brandenburg March but also on the border between the homeland and the foreign, a line that Homburg's incomplete submission to authority may forever have left unclear.

It is not too soon to note that *Prince Friedrich von Homburg* is situated on other boundary lines as well. For in order to recount here the historical events as Kleist's text takes them up, we have left out the beginning and the end, and in doing so we have barely begun to say what Kleist's play is really about. Despite its grounding in historical facts, *Prince Friedrich von Homburg* begins with a play within the play. Like the battle of Fehrbellin, this play is directed by the Elector but is not altogether within his control; it is a play he intends as a jest but whose consequences are grave. Kleist's text ends with a repetition of that scene, rewritten to accommodate and rectify the uncalculated issue of its first performance, but perhaps, nevertheless, with equally unpredictable reverberations.

Moreover, it is questionable whether between these two brief scenes it is the sequence of quasi-historical events to which we have alluded that best makes sense of what is taking place. Or perhaps precisely because they best make sense, they belie by their linearity the inevitable doubleness that so clearly haunts at every stage. For that linearity merely unfolds successively what is always at play throughout, most explicitly, nevertheless, at the beginning and end. And yet it is probably not doubleness after all that definitively determines the structure of the play, that allows us to order it. It is indeed in the name of simple dichotomy that the major characters argue at each crucial juncture of the action—in the name of heart as opposed to orders when Homburg charges precipitately into battle (290E; 2.2.474–76) and of heart and duty when the prince assures himself of the pardon to come, in the name of feeling as opposed to law when Natalie (314E; 4.1.1122–30) and Kottwitz (330–31E; 5.5.1570–1608) plead, in turn, the case of Homburg.[3] Yet when the play opens, the line between the realm of law and that of inner certitude cannot be so easily drawn.

The stage is split, it seems, between the sleeping prince and those who are awake, the Elector, his wife and niece, and most especially Hohenzollern, who are certain of what it means to sleep:

HOHENZOLLERN
    When now the hour strikes,
And the entire cavalry is mounted
The ground outside the city gates trampled down,
Who is missing? the Prince of Homburg, their commander.
With torches and lights and lanterns
The hero is sought and is discovered—where?
    [*He takes a torch out of the hand of a page*]
As a sleepwalker, look, on that bench
Where, in sleep, as you would never wish to believe,
Enticed by the moonlight, busy,
He dreams, like his own posterity,
Weaving his own splendid wreath of glory.
· ·
THE ELECTOR
Sunk in sleep? Impossible!
HOHENZOLLERN
                    Fast asleep!

(272E)

HOHENZOLLERN
        Da nun die Stunde schlägt,
Und aufgesessen schon die ganze Reuterei
Den Acker vor dem Tor zerstampft,
Fehlt—wer? der Prinz von Homburg noch, ihr Führer.
Mit Fackeln wird und Lichtern und Laternen
Der Held gesucht—und aufgefunden, wo?
        [*Er nimmt einem Pagen die Fackel aus der Hand*]
Als ein Nachtwandler, schau, auf jener Bank,
Wohin, im Schlaf, wie du nie glauben wolltest,
Der Mondschein ihn gelockt, beschäftiget,
Sich träumend, seiner eignen Nachwelt gleich,
Den prächtgen Kranz des Ruhmes einzuwinden.

. . . .

DER KURFÜRST
Im Schlaf versenkt? Unmöglich!
HOHENZOLLERN
                        Fest im Schlafe!
                                    (1.1.18–30)

What the torches and lights and lanterns cannot show, and what Kleist's
audience cannot yet perceive (for like Homburg at the end of the play,
they are overwhelmed for the moment with too much light) what
Kleist's audience cannot perceive but every reader must confront, is that
Homburg, according to the first stage directions, "sits with bare head
and open breast, half waking, half sleeping" ("sitzt mit bloßem Haupt
und offner Brust, halb wachend halb schlafend"). From the beginning,
then, the premise on which the text is founded is not the either/or of
rationality and heart ("bare head" *or* "open breast"), reality and fantasy,
but their inextricability. What Kleist calls dream or play can never effect
the eradication of its other. If in the very moment when the curtain rises,
long before the main transgression, Homburg has already challenged an
order of the Elector (here the order to position himself on the field of
battle), it is not because he dreams but because he dreams *and* wakes.
The true enemy of the law is less its opposite than the threat that it might
be impossible to distinguish between the two after all. Homburg is he
who fails to carry out his orders because he lies in trance and he who
through that fantasy has already carried out his orders and won the battle
of Fehrbellin—and both at the same time. In this state (and it is
questionable, despite appearances to the contrary, whether Homburg
ever fully leaves it) Homburg will forever fail to know where he is.

THE PRINCE OF HOMBURG
     Upon my word!
     I don't know where I am.

(276E)

DER PRINZ VON HOMBURG
          Bei meinem Eid!
     Ich weiß nicht, liebster Heinrich, wo ich bin.

(1.4.110–11)

As Homburg dreams and wakes, he weaves for himself a wreath of laurel, whose presence there on march soil, as the Elector is quick to note, signals that the foreign has already taken root.

THE ELECTOR
—Where did he find that in my march sand?
HOHENZOLLERN
Only the just gods would know that.
THE COURTIER
Perhaps in the garden back there where the gardener
Raises yet more of the foreign plants.

(273E)

DER KURFÜRST
—Wo fand er den in meinem märkschen Sand?
HOHENZOLLERN
Das mögen die gerechten Götter wissen!
DER HOFKAVALIER
Vielleicht im Garten hinten, wo der Gärtner
Mehr noch der fremden Pflanzen auferzieht.

(1.1.50–53)

The laurel marks an invasion by the other in a far more crucial sense, however, because as Hohenzollern says, in weaving it the Prince becomes his own posterity. He weaves both the crowning emblem of his heroic deeds and, as Kleist's dedication of the play to Princess Amalie Marie Anne makes almost too evident,[4] the symbol of poetic achievement, for Homburg is throughout no less the figure of the writer than that of the soldier. But what does it mean to become one's own posterity if not to live beyond oneself,[5] to become other enough to write one's own epitaph. And how is one to understand this gesture on the part of Homburg, who finds it so difficult to die—in a play that gives that phrase several turns, as we shall see?

In a sense, one might claim that this scene is like its own posterity, that everything has already taken place here, or perhaps more precisely, that the figure of Homburg encompasses within itself all the possibilities that the text will play out. But on his side too, that other Friedrich, Friedrich Wilhelm, Elector of Brandenburg, soon to play the apologist for inflexible authority, decides to become other and allows himself a joke ("Scherz") (275E; 1.3.83–84). He assumes the role of that posterity and along with his niece, Natalie, offers, or rather retreats from offering, Homburg the wreath.

> [*The Elector takes the wreath from his hand; the Prince reddens and looks at him. The Elector winds his neck-chain around the wreath and gives it to the Princess. The Prince leaps up. The Elector, along with the Princess, who holds up the wreath, withdraws. The Prince follows with arms outstretched*]
>
> THE PRINCE OF HOMBURG [*whispering*]
> Natalie! My maid! My bride!
> THE ELECTOR
> Quickly! Away!
> . . . .
> THE PRINCE OF HOMBURG [*grasping at the wreath*]
> Oh! Dearest! Why withdraw from me? Natalie!
> [*He snatches a glove from the Princess's hand*]
>
> (273–74E)

> [*Der Kurfürst nimmt ihm den Kranz aus der Hand; der Prinz errötet und sieht ihn an. Der Kurfürst schlingt seine Halskette um den Kranz und gibt ihn der Prinzessin; der Prinz steht lebhaft auf. Der Kurfürst weicht mit der Prinzessin, welche den Kranz erhebt, zurück; der Prinz mit ausgestreckten Armen, folgt ihr*]
>
> DER PRINZ VON HOMBURG [*flüsternd*]
> Natalie! Mein Mädchen! Meine Braut!
> DER KURFÜRST
> Geschwind! Hinweg!
> . . . .
> DER PRINZ VON HOMBURG [*nach dem Kranz greifend*]
> O! Liebste! Was entweichst du mir? Natalie!
> [*Er erhascht einen Handschuh von der Prinzessin Hand*]
>
> (1.1.65–70)

But the Elector Friedrich Wilhelm, unlike his namesake, is no poet and knows or thinks he knows well the difference between reality and the nothingness of dreams.

THE ELECTOR
Back into the nothingness with you, Sir Prince of Homburg,
The nothingness, the nothingness! In the battlefield
We'll see each other again, if it pleases you!
In dreams such things cannot be won.

(274E)

DER KURFÜRST
Ins Nichts mit dir zurück, Herr Prinz von Homburg,
Ins Nichts, ins Nichts! In dem Gefild der Schlacht,
Sehn wir, wenns dir gefällig ist, uns wieder!
Im Traum erringt man solche Dinge nicht!

(1.1.74–77)

In dreams one does not win such things, and yet other things can be grasped there. If the Elector sends Homburg back into the nothingness of his dream, it is a nothingness into which the Elector's jest has introduced a pledge. The pledge, in its embodiment, will appear to have entered from that realm we tend to call reality: it is in the nature of the joke, which itself is neither the one nor the other, to bring about uncertainty in distinguishing between the dreamt and the real, nothingness and plenitude. Here, too, changelings are produced. Homburg extends his hand to snatch the wreath and comes away with a glove, the bare mocking form of the hand that would be and would hold substance.[6]

What one can do in dreams far more easily than in the waking world, however, is name the source of that questionable token. For whereas the last syllables of his trance are "Natalie," Homburg gropes hopelessly for that name throughout the fourth scene.[7]

HOHENZOLLERN
—Which lady do you mean?
THE PRINCE OF HOMBURG
                    It's all the same! All the same!
Since I awoke the name has slipped my mind,
And for understanding here, it's all the same.

(277E)

HOHENZOLLERN
—Welch eine Dame meinst du?
DER PRINZ VON HOMBURG
                    Gleichviel! Gleichviel!

Der Nam ist mir, seit ich erwacht, entfallen,
Und gilt zu dem Verständnis hier gleichviel.

(1.4.154—56)

There is indeed good reason why this name is a matter of total indifference to understanding (in a play where the term *gleichviel* ["it's all the same"] repeatedly punctuates the dialogue). It is not so much, as we are led to believe, that the narrative can be easily followed without it; rather, its comprehensibility will be troubled in any case, and even more so when the implications of the name are understood. For the name Natalie suggests the power of the point of origin, of the point of birth, as Homburg himself is quick to suggest.

THE PRINCE OF HOMBURG
The Elector and his Consort and the—third,
—What is her name?
HOHENZOLLERN
                    Who?
THE PRINCE OF HOMBURG [*he seems to search*]
                    The one—I mean!
A mute-born could name her!

(277E)

DER PRINZ VON HOMBURG
Der Kurfürst und die Fürstin und die—dritte,
—Wie heißt sie schon?
HOHENZOLLERN
                    Wer?
DER PRINZ VON HOMBURG [*er scheint zu suchen*]
                    Jene—die ich meine!
Ein Stummgeborner würd sie nennen können!

(1.4.146—48)

Is it simply that the name is so easy to pronounce that even the dumb can find the means to utter it? Or is it not, rather, that pronouncing the name that marks the source of the pledge is coincident with an originary muteness, that Natalie and a coming to terms with the entire scene that she engenders (her offering a wreath of glory that becomes an empty glove in the very moment of Homburg's grasp) performs a fundamental impossibility of naming, grasping, understanding.

As the play continues, that impossibility of uttering the apparently serious origin of what is nevertheless a joke becomes the impossibility of a particular mode of writing. For in the next scene Homburg is called upon to take dictation. Prussian discipline, it would seem, demands adherence not only to the law but also to the form of writing that reflects it. When Homburg enters along with his fellow officers to record the orders of the Elector, the other players in that recently performed piece of theater are grouped at the side of the stage.[8] Just as it comes the Prince's turn to listen to the dictates of the law, Natalie discovers that she has misplaced her glove. Homburg becomes utterly distracted, and wishing to test the authenticity of his prize, he surreptitiously drops the object on which so much turns. It is the Elector himself who recognizes it as the glove in question.

The scenario, then, would seem complex but simple enough to understand: the realm of order and orders on the one hand, that of dream on the other.[9] The Prince, as Hohenzollern explains in act 5, is unable to write because of "this fragment of the dream, that has become embodied for him" ("dies Stück des Traums, das ihm verkörpert ward") (333E; 5.5.1669). His complete absence from himself (334E; 5.5.1704–5) may be ascribed to the joke of the Elector, who created the moment of dream. This is how Hohenzollern reads the scene and the Field Marshal (the Elector is quick to follow suit, although he lays the blame for the play with Hohenzollern).

It clarifies matters to view them so, yet it is Homburg himself who locates the problem elsewhere.

HOHENZOLLERN
—You were distracted. I saw it well.
THE PRINCE OF HOMBURG
Distracted—divided: I don't know what is the matter with me.
Dictation to my plume makes me confused.—

(288E)[10]

HOHENZOLLERN
—Du warst zerstreut. Ich hab es wohl gesehn.
DER PRINZ VON HOMBURG
Zerstreut—geteilt; ich weiß nicht, was mir fehlte,
Diktieren in die Feder macht mich irr.—

(2.2.419–21)

Within the mode of writing that seems to assure reason and unity lies the potential for confusion and madness. Anyone asked to take down

Homburg's orders could see that. For what is it that those orders demand? In a landscape with the single historical name Hackelberg[11] Kleist has invented three others, all based on the prefix *Hackel-*, which according to Grimm means "delicate": *Hackel-berge* ("the delicate mountains"), *Hackel-büsche* ("the delicate thickets"), and *Hackel-witz.*

All the commands of the battle plans "which his Highness, the lord himself, devised" ("den die Durchlaucht des Herrn ersann") (281E; 1.5.249) place the troops in relation to these sites. Homburg's orders, repeated three times and at great length in this critical first writing scene, assign him to take and maintain his place on the plain at Hackelwitz—the locus, then, of a "delicate joke."

FIELD MARSHAL
According to our Lord's express command—
. . . .
Whatever turn the battle may take,
The Prince shall not withdraw from the place assigned him—
. . . .
His Highness, though, so that,
Through misunderstanding, the blow does not fall too soon—
. . . .
Will send an officer from his retinue,
Who will bring the express command, note this well,
For the attack on the enemy.
Not till then should he sound the fanfare.
   [*The Prince stands looking down and dreaming*]
—Do you have it?

(283–85E)

FELDMARSCHALL
Nach unsers Herrn ausdrücklichem Befehl—
. . . .
[Des Prinzen Durchlaucht wird—]
Wie immer auch die Schlacht sich wenden mag,
Vom Platz nicht, der ihm angewiesen, weichen—
. . . .
Doch wird des Fürsten Durchlaucht ihm, damit,
Durch Mißverstand, der Schlag zu früh nicht falle—
. . . .
Ihm einen Offizier, aus seiner Suite, senden,
Der den Befehl, das merkt, ausdrücklich noch

Zum Angriff auf den Feind ihm überbringe.
Eh wird er nicht Fanfare blasen lassen.
[*Der Prinz steht und träumt vor sich nieder*]
—Habt ihr?

(1.5.294—333)

Homburg's transgression, then, on the one hand may consist in a mind
that wanders to the figures of the Elector's initial joke, but the orders
that he fails to note and fails to follow, those orders that throughout the
play seem unambiguously to represent the other side, the serious, the
law, a language based on authority that maintains the possibility of
iterability and enactment, those orders would seem to condemn him to a
similar locus, that of the *Witz*.[12]

Let us forget for a moment that if Homburg had followed the
dictates of the Elector's orders, his place would still be, one way or the
other, that of the joke, forget, as one must to follow the progress of this
play, that in a sense, in Homburg's words, it is all the same ("gleichviel").
The Prince is arrested for his betrayal of the battle plan and condemned
to die. His original transgression is the failure to write; his expiation for
that sin takes place in a second scene of writing.

In a state of utter despair and unheroic terror of the grave,
Homburg leaves his cell to throw himself at the feet of the Elector's wife.
She and Natalie call upon him to compose himself (310E; 3.5.994, 1006),
but nothing can dispel his fear of death and his frenzied yearning for life.
When Natalie consequently pleads her cousin's cause with "Friedrich of
the March" ("Friedrich von der Mark") (313E; 4.1.1078), that figure who
poses on the side of the letter of the law but who never more than here is
on the border, he composes a note to Homburg that promises to set
things straight; or rather it is not exactly *what* he writes that promises,
but his parting words to Natalie. For his letter is less an outright act of
pardon than a call to Homburg to compose a letter of his own in turn.

> THE PRINCE OF HOMBURG [*reads*]
> "My Prince of Homburg, when I had you arrested,
> Because of your untimely charge,
> I thought I but my duty did;
> I counted on your own approval.
> If you believe an injustice has been done to you,
> I beg you tell me with two words—
> And I'll return your sabre right away."

(320—21E)

DER PRINZ VON HOMBURG [*liest*]
"Mein Prinz von Homburg, als ich Euch gefangen setzte,
Um Eures Angriffs, allzufrüh vollbracht,
Da glaubt ich nichts, als meine Pflicht zu tun;
Auf Euren eignen Beifall rechnet ich.
Meint Ihr, ein Unrecht sei Euch widerfahren,
So bitt ich, sagts mir mit zwei Worten—
Und gleich den Degen schick ich Euch zurück."

(4.4.1307–13)

Natalie offers to dictate a response, but Homburg finally chooses to "compose [him]self." This is a gesture that will be communally misread, most especially by the Prince himself,[13] as Homburg's willed commitment to the letter of the law and to the law as a text that can be realized literally.

THE PRINCE OF HOMBURG
Quiet! It is my inflexible wish!
I wish to glorify the sacred code of battle
That I wounded, before the entire army,
Through my voluntary death!

(336E)

DER PRINZ VON HOMBURG
Ruhig! Es ist mein unbeugsamer Wille!
Ich will das heilige Gesetz des Kriegs,
Das ich verletzt', im Angesicht des Heers,
Durch einen freien Tod verherrlichen!

(5.7.1749–52)

Twice in the course of the play the whole order of things is reversed. The pivotal moments of disorientation are the two elaborate scenes in which nothing more significant than a reluctant writing takes place. At these moments the dramatic movement of the text is turned inside out like a glove torn from another's hand. What used to fit the left hand would now fit the right. Despite appearances, however, when Homburg writes, he does not compose himself in the sense the Elector's wife had in mind. He dedicates himself not to the sacred letter of military law but rather to the spirit of the letter: he writes in order to play his role well, to compose or create himself as Prussian hero.[14]

THE PRINCE OF HOMBURG [*as he tears up the letter that he had begun and throws it under the table*]
A dumb beginning.
[*He takes another page*]
. . . .
Bah!—The composition of a rogue, not of a prince.—
I'll think out another turn of phrase.
[*Pause.—He reaches for the Elector's letter, which the princess holds in her hand*]
What did he say exactly in the letter?
. . . .
—I only wish to see how I should compose myself.
. . . .
He calls on me to make the decision!
. . . .
        Quite valiant, in fact, quite noble!
Just the way a great heart should compose itself!

(321–22E)

DER PRINZ VON HOMBURG [*indem er den Brief, den er angefangen hat, zerreißt und unter den Tisch wirft*]
Ein dummer Anfang.
[*Er nimmt ein anderes Blatt*]
. . . .
Pah!—Eines Schuftes Fassung, keines Prinzen.—
Ich denk mir eine andre Wendung aus.
[*Pause.—Er greift nach des Kurfürsten Brief, den die Prinzessin in der Hand hält*]
Was sagt er eigentlich im Briefe denn?
. . . .
Ich will nur sehn, wie ich mich fassen soll.
. . . .
Mich selber ruft er zur Entscheidung auf!
. . . .
        Recht wacker, in der Tat, recht würdig!
Recht, wie ein großes Herz sich fassen muß!

(4.4.1332–44)

In a scene riddled through with questions of composition (*Fassung*)[15] and turn of phrase (*Wendung*) one might well ask along with Homburg whether this turn of events no less than those of the opening scene, whether the whole matter of the letter, is not a dream.

NATALIE
You are pardoned, free; here is a letter
In his hand that confirms it.
THE PRINCE OF HOMBURG
It is not possible! No! It is a dream!

(320E)

NATALIE
Begnadigt seid Ihr, frei; hier ist ein Brief,
Von seiner Hand, der es bekräftiget.
DER PRINZ VON HOMBURG
Es ist nicht möglich! Nein! Es ist ein Traum!

(4.4.1303–5)

Or (also with Homburg) shall we say that after all, here too it is
"gleichviel"[16]—all the same whether one lives or dies, dreams or wakes,
all the same whether one writes literature or according to the dictates of
the law. All the same because in the earlier scene of writing the dictation
of the word as order assigns Homburg to the locus of the joke, and here
the writerly turn of literary phrase commits him to the letter of the law.
The one always implicates the other, however blindly.[17]

All the same as well because despite the Elector's insistence to the
contrary—"In dreams such things cannot be won" ("Im Traum erringt
man solche Dinge nicht!") (274E; 1.1.77)—the realm of dream and the
realm of so-called reality hold precisely the same promise for Homburg,
a promise, whether it is called life or death, with all the plenitude of
life.[18] For what Homburg heroically and before all accepts in the name
of rejecting the dream for reality, law, and death is a life beyond this one,
a life far more glorious, so glorious that the earthly realm must seem as
dark as the grave by comparison.

Thus when the Elector grants Homburg a final boon before his
execution, the Prince replies:

Now see, you have just granted me my life!
Now I shall beseech every blessing
That from the throne of clouds seraphim
Pour down on heroes' heads in jubilation.
Go and do battle, Sire, and overwhelm
The sphere of earth that would oppose you—for you are worthy of it!

(337E)

Nun sieh, jetzt schenktest du das Leben mir!
Nun fleh ich jeden Segen dir herab,
Den, von dem Thron der Wolken, Seraphin
Auf Heldenhäupter jauchzend niederschütten:
Geh und bekrieg, o Herr, und überwinde
Den Weltkreis, der dir trotzt—denn du bists wert!

(5.7.1794–99)

Homburg speaks as the elector of the Elector who encourages his heroic soldier on the eve of war. He calls on his uncle to conquer the worldly sphere; for himself he has another in mind.

THE PRINCE OF HOMBURG
Pinions grow on both my shoulders,
My spirit soars into the silent aether;

(339E)

DER PRINZ VON HOMBURG
Es wachsen Flügel mir an beiden Schultern,
Durch stille Ätherräume schwingt mein Geist;

(5.10.1833–34)

Homburg's place is no longer that of the joke, but Heaven—Homburg who speaks from well beyond, he who speaks at this moment with a blindfold across his eyes and thinks he views the matter well. This particular beyond menaces no invasion of otherness or darkness. For if in the opening lines of the play the Prince weaves laurel from the other side of the "March," at the close of the play, where it is once again a question of plants from without, that foreignness is dispelled.

THE PRINCE OF HOMBURG
Ah, how pleasing fragrant is the dame's violet!
—Do you not smell it?
   [*Stranz comes back to him*]
STRANZ
                    They are gilly flowers and carnations.
THE PRINCE OF HOMBURG
Gilly flowers?—How come they to be here?
STRANZ
                                        I do not know.—
It seems a maiden came to plant them here.
—May I hand you a carnation?

THE PRINCE OF HOMBURG
Dear Friend!—
I wish to put it in some water at home.

(339–40E)

DER PRINZ VON HOMBURG
Ach, wie die Nachtviole lieblich duftet!
—Spürst du es nicht?
[*Stranz kommt wieder zu ihm zurück*]
STRANZ
Es sind Levkojn und Nelken.
DER PRINZ VON HOMBURG
Levkojn?—Wie kommen die hierher?
STRANZ
Ich weiß nicht.—
Es scheint, ein Mädchen hat sie hier gepflanzt.
—Kann ich dir eine Nelke reichen?
DER PRINZ VON HOMBURG
Lieber!—
Ich will zu Hause sie in Wasser setzen.

(5.10.1840–45)

Homburg simply carries it with him to the other side, which has now the fullness of home and ground. Here the carnation, like Homburg, who twice in the course of events has been compared to a flower,[19] can be transplanted, if only into water. It is in the nature of this play to tear up and then, however tentatively, however delicately, to reestablish roots. In an earlier moment, one of far greater despair (and far greater insight) this was all that Homburg wished of life.

THE PRINCE OF HOMBURG
I wish to go to my Rhine estate.
There I wish to cultivate, wish to tear down,
So that the sweat drips down from me, to sow, to harvest,
As though it were for wife and child, to enjoy alone,
And when I've harvested to sow anew,
And round about in this cycle to chase life,
Until it sinks and dies come evening.

(311E)

DER PRINZ VON HOMBURG
Ich will auf meine Güter gehn am Rhein,

Da will ich bauen, will ich niederreißen,
Daß mir der Schweiß herabtrieft, säen, ernten,
Als wärs für Weib und Kind, allein genießen,
Und, wenn ich erntete, von neuem säen,
Und in den Kreis herum das Leben jagen,
Bis es am Abend niedersinkt und stirbt.

(3.5.1030—36)

But in the closing scene Homburg does not quite see it this way, for as he faces the bullets of his heroic destiny, there is no place for "tear[ing] down." The hero's final moment is one of pure light and pure ascendancy.

THE PRINCE OF HOMBURG
Now, oh immortality, you are fully mine!
You shine to me through the bindings of my eyes,
With the gleam of a thousand suns!
Pinions grow on both my shoulders,
My spirit soars into the silent aether;
And as a ship, carried by the breath of wind,
Sees the lively seaport sink,
So all life founders growing dark for me,
Now I still distinguish form and color,
And now all lies beneath me in a mist.

(339E)

DER PRINZ VON HOMBURG
Nun, o Unsterblichkeit, bist du ganz mein!
Du strahlst mir, durch die Binde meiner Augen,
Mir Glanz der tausendfachen Sonne zu!
Es wachsen Flügel mir an beiden Schultern,
Durch stille Ätherräume schwingt mein Geist;
Und wie ein Schiff, vom Hauch des Winds entführt,
Die muntre Hafenstadt versinken sieht,
So geht mir dämmernd alles Leben unter:
Jetzt unterscheid ich Farben noch und Formen,
Und jetzt liegt Nebel alles unter mir.

(5.10.1830—39)

This moment, however, proves Homburg not only blind but also deaf to the reverberations of his own past speech, for what takes place may be an inversion, but is nevertheless a repetition, of his earlier error. The "breath of wind" ("Hauch des Winds") that here beclouds the realm of life, thus assuring his heavenly apotheosis, promised more worldly revelations at the close of act I. There, having reached for wreath and chain, Homburg left his waking trance with glove in hand and found the hand from which it came in the moment when he failed to write. He withdraws from that scene to proclaim his utter certainty of the meaning of that symbol.

> Now then, on your sphere Colossal One,
> You whose veil the breath of wind,
> Billows up like a sail, roll here!
> Already, Fortune, you have touched my locks,
> Tossed down a pledge to me in floating past,
> From your horn of plenty, smiling:
> Today, child of the gods, I seek, elusive one,
> I'll seize you in the field of battle and overturn
> All your abundance at my feet,
> Even were you sevenfold, with iron chains,
> Bound to the Swedes' triumphal car!

(286E)

> Nun denn, auf deiner Kugel, Ungeheures,
> Du, der der Windeshauch den Schleier heut,
> Gleich einem Segel lüftet, roll heran!
> Du hast mir, Glück, die Locken schon gestreift:
> Ein Pfand schon warfst du, im Vorüberschweben,
> Aus deinem Füllhorn lächelnd mir herab:
> Heut, Kind der Götter, such ich, flüchtiges,
> Ich hasche dich im Feld der Schlacht und stürze
> Ganz deinen Segen mir zu Füßen um:
> Wärst du auch siebenfach, mit Eisenketten,
> Am schwedschen Siegeswagen festgebunden!

(1.6.355–65)

The "breath of wind" that in Homburg's last speech carries him off like a ship from the harbor (339E; 5.10.1835), obscuring all worldly immediacy, here fills a very different sail. It raises the veil that the wisdom of iconography places before the figure of Fortune, for Homburg claims to have seen her face on.

If these lines are a celebration of presence, of the presence of Fortune, who has revealed herself, who has touched his locks and given him a pledge in hand, if they are lines that boast of even greater immediacy to come, of seizing Fortune directly in the field of battle to

claim the remaining contents of her cornucopia, they are lines, nevertheless, that have something else in store as well. The passage itself is
something of a horn of plenty, filled as it is with objects of exceptional
significance, each of which refuses, however, to come away in the hand.
For the objects that Hamburg touches on here (the breath of wind, the
sphere [*Kugel*], the chain)—such is the monstrous irony of the passage—
are elsewhere marked with an inverse valence. It is a valence that
disperses them just as "the fragrance that floats over valleys / Disperses
in a fresh breath of wind" ("der Duft, der über Täler schwebt, / Vor eines
Windes frischem Hauch zerstiebt") (278E; 1.4.178–79), making them
recede much like the figures and objects of the original joke.[20]

This, therefore, is not a moment of classical irony, one in which the
naiveté of the desire for immediacy is before or after put in proper
perspective. In *Prince Friedrich von Homburg* there is no ultimate perspective, no distancing possible, only the illusion of absolute heights and
absolute depths. Homburg almost sees this when he calls the coming
moment of his execution a "Schauspiel" (a play but also, literally, a
game of sight)—a scene that passes between an "Überschau[en]" ("com-
manding view of," "comprehending") that naively sees the future as
a fairy realm and an epitaph written from the stony perspective of the
other.[21]

> Look, these eyes that gaze upon you, Aunt,
> They wish to overshadow with darkness,
> To bore through me with murderous bullets [*Kugeln*].
> Already booked, the windows on the market place
> That look down upon the desolate spectacle [*Schauspiel*],
> And he who upon life's pinnacle today
> Looks over [*überschaut*] futurity like a fairyland,
> Lies tomorrow, fragrant between two narrow boards,
> And a stone will tell you of him: he was!
>
> (310E)

> Sieh, diese Augen, Tante, die dich anschaun,
> Will man mit Nacht umschatten, diesen Busen
> Mit mörderischen Kugeln mir durchbohren.
> Bestellt sind auf dem Markte schon die Fenster,
> Die auf das öde Schauspiel niedergehn,
> Und der die Zukunft, auf des Lebens Gipfel,
> Heut, wie ein Feenreich, noch überschaut,

Liegt in zwei engen Brettern duftend morgen,
Und ein Gestein sagt dir von ihm: er war!

(3.5.984–92)

There is no proper perspective possible, only the play of equally power-ful positive and negative ontologies. Homburg's position throughout this play is more or less the same, though to various eyes and hearts there may seem to be a world of difference. For over and over Homburg is torn between what seems to be a choice of opposites in which, chame-leonlike, the one assumes the colors of its other. One waits in vain for orders that might liberate from the locus of this joke, for the scene before one's eyes is the refusal of an exit to an absolute outside itself.

Life, after all—is this not the point?—cannot be defined over against death. Life is not the other of death but a perpetual journey towards what forever seems its loss.

> PRINCE FRIEDRICH OF HOMBURG
> The dervish names this life a journey,
> And a short one. Of course! From two spans
> This side of the earth to two spans beneath.
> I want to lay me down halfway between!
> . . . .
> Aye, a sun, they say, shines there as well,
> And over more brightly colored fields than here:
> I believe it; what a pity then that the eye
> That should regard this magnificence decays.

(320E)

> DER PRINZ VON HOMBURG
> Das Leben nennt der Derwisch eine Reise,
> Und eine kurze. Freilich! Von zwei Spannen
> Diesseits der Erde nach zwei Spannen drunter.
> Ich will auf halbem Weg mich niederlassen!
> . . . .
> Zwar, eine Sonne, sagt man, scheint dort auch,
> Und über buntre Felder noch, als hier:
> Ich glaubs; nur schade, daß das Auge modert,
> Das diese Herrlichkeit erblicken soll.

(4.3.1286–96)

In this passage, appropriately attributed to the voice of the other (to the dervish and to the impersonality of "they"), Homburg is, for a moment at least, not bedazzled by this side or the other. In a rare moment of equilibrium and insight he delineates the impossibility of both. If life is a relentless movement towards death, there is no way to find the line of demarcation between the two, for death must remain a perpetually postponed misperception taking place (or almost) in what we call life. It refuses to be grasped, for it is that which might be taken in hand only with all the naiveté of the taking of Natalie's glove, the glove whose origin only a deaf-mute's powers of language are equal to naming, the object in hand that bespeaks the absence of hand and content. Homburg, after all, despite his own most radiant dreams and plans, cannot become other enough to write his own epitaph.[22] Homburg's writing, like that of Kleist, is always, one way or another, invaded by the joke.[23]

Is this not what the final play within the play is about?[24] At this point, of course, it is just as difficult to find the line of demarcation between the play and the actual, dream and reality, the joke and the serious, as between life and death. The Elector, it seems, has pardoned Homburg's sin of turning from the real world, with its code of orders, to the realm of fantasy, but he enacts that pardon by repeating the originary scene of error and by making certain that the Prince, despite everything, apparently *can* "obtain such things in dreams."

THE PRINCE OF HOMBURG
Dear friend, what radiance spreads around me?
STRANZ [*returns to him*]
My Prince, would you be good enough to rise?
THE PRINCE OF HOMBURG
What is it?
STRANZ
           Nothing that might frighten you!—
I merely wish to open your eyes again.
THE PRINCE OF HOMBURG
Has it struck, my final hour of pain?
STRANZ
           Yes!
Hail to you and blessings, for you are worthy!
[*The Elector hands the wreath on which the chain hangs to the Princess, takes her by the hand, and leads her down the ramp. Lords and ladies follow. The Princess, surrounded by torches, steps up to the Prince, who stands up, astonished. She places the wreath on him, hangs the chain around his neck, and presses his hand to her heart. The Prince faints*]

NATALIE
Heavens! The joy kills him!

(340E)

DER PRINZ VON HOMBURG
Lieber, was für ein Glanz verbreitet sich?
STRANZ [*kehrt zu ihm zurück*]
Mein Prinz, willst du gefällig dich erheben?
DER PRINZ VON HOMBURG
Was gibt es?
STRANZ
            Nichts, das dich erschrecken dürfte!—
Die Augen bloß will ich dir wieder öffnen.
DER PRINZ VON HOMBURG
Schlug meiner Leiden letzte Stunde?
STRANZ
            Ja!—
Heil dir und Segen, denn du bist es wert!
    [*Der Kurfürst gibt den Kranz, an welchem die Kette hängt, der Prinzessin,
    nimmt sie bei der Hand und führt sie die Rampe herab. Herren und Damen
    folgen. Die Prinzessin tritt, umgeben von Fackeln, vor den Prinzen, welcher
    erstaunt aufsteht; setzt ihm den Kranz auf, hängt ihm die Kette um, und
    drückt seine Hand an ihr Herz. Der Prinz fällt in Ohnmacht*]
NATALIE
Himmel! die Freude tötet ihn!

(5.11.1846–52)

What need has Homburg now of chain and laurel, he who had set
his sights on far more heavenly pledges? For the brutality of the Elector's
death sentence has not been erased here but redoubled beyond all
comprehension. Homburg is condemned to life at the point where he
had transvaluated the meanings of life and death, where he had placed all
ontological worth and all sense of reality in the life beyond. He is
condemned to life, but what leaves him momentarily senseless is the
suspicion that there may be nothing else—no ground outside, no heaven
beyond, no "home" in which to place the flower in water—nothing but
the quicksand of the realm of dream that always casts the mirage of the
other within itself. Thus when Homburg asks, half-waking, half-sleep-
ing:

No, say! Is it a dream?

Nein, sagt! Ist es ein Traum?

Kottwitz, whose name confirms the ineluctable presence of the joke, answers:

> A dream, what else?
>
> Ein Traum, was sonst?
>
> (341E; 5.11.1856)

The joke, of course, cannot leave even the realm of dream intact, lest it take on borders that seem to grant it definition and substance. This is why Kottwitz's answer can be read both as the confirmation of the dream and as a delicate irony that might seem to suggest the very opposite. This is also why, after Homburg has been celebrated in the name of dream as the hero of the battle of Fehrbellin, the play reminds us that we are back where we started, with a very real enemy still invading the Brandenburg March:

> KOTTWITZ
> A dream, what else?
> SEVERAL OFFICERS
> To the battlefield! To the battlefield!
> COUNT TRUCHSS
> To battle!
> FIELD MARSHAL
> On to victory! On to victory!
> ALL
> Into the dust with all the foes of Brandenburg!
>
> (341E)

> KOTTWITZ
> Ein Traum, was sonst?
> MEHRERE OFFIZIERE
> Ins Feld! Ins Feld!
> GRAF TRUCHSS
> Zur Schlacht!
> FELDMARSCHALL
> Zum Sieg! Zum Sieg!
> ALLE
> In Staub mit allen Feinden Brandenburgs!
>
> (5.11.1856–58)

Like the first scene and the two scenes of writing, this play within a play is inevitably something of a model for the strategy of Kleist's theater. For what Kleist enacts is the scene of a threshold. It is a threshold that both promises and denies access to a beyond, staging the performance of a disappearing act, a receding in which no place and no-thing can be reached. It is the locus of an endless demarcation between opposites that gives way to a space increasingly "all the same" (the obsessive *gleichviel* of Homburg's rhetoric).[25] It is the strategy of perpetual but never definitive loss, of marking off a stage and homeland for reason and feeling, forever invaded by the enemy of indifference.

6

Soothsaying and Rebellion

If in *Prince Friedrich von Homburg* the Elector of Brandenburg repeatedly places his sovereignty precariously on the line with the gesture of directing a joke, if the figure of authority opens and closes the play by staging a dream in which he himself is implicated, in *Michael Kohlhaas* an altogether different Elector of Brandenburg is at work: he closes the text with a sense of justice far more serious, far more satisfying, and far more prosaic. *Michael Kohlhaas* is above all about that sense of justice, a justice defined, it would seem, despite the outrageous events that are performed in its name, by the scrupulous sense Kohlhaas has for his own profession.

From the outset it is, quite evidently, the profession of trade and exchange that is put into question. Kohlhaas, the horse dealer, passing one day from his home in Brandenburg to the land of Saxony, encounters at the castle of Junker Wenzel von Tronka both a toll bar and the unprecedented demand for a pass. Forced to leave two of his horses as a pledge, he returns to find "instead of his two sleek and well-fed blacks, a pair of scrawny, worn-out nags" ("statt seiner zwei glatten und wohlgenährten Rappen, ein Paar dürre, abgehärmte Mähren") (92E; 13G).[1] The horse dealer, whose sense of judgment, we are told, is itself like the merchant's gold scale (93E; 14G), will seek satisfaction for the wrong done him by weighing equal measure against equal measure. Justice and trade, and with them certain related concepts of language and authority, are guaranteed by such a gesture. Almost consistently throughout the story Kohlhaas asks for nothing more and nothing less than a restoration of precisely that which was taken from him.

> Kohlhaas called out: "Those *are* not my horses, your Lordship! Those are not the *horses* that were worth thirty gold gulden! I want my well-fed and healthy horses back again!" (94E)

138

Kohlhaas rief: "das *sind* nicht meine Pferde, gestrenger Herr! Das sind die *Pferde* nicht, die dreißig Goldgülden wert waren. Ich will meine wohl-genährten und gesunden Pferde wieder haben!"—(15G)

Side by side with this matter of even recompense, indeed anticipat-ing and precipitating the Junker's mistreatment of the blacks, is the insistence on a certain text.

> The Castellan . . . came and asked . . . about the pass [*Paßschein*]. "The pass?"—Kohlhaas asked. He said . . . that as far as he knew he had none, that if somebody would only describe what in the name of the Lord the thing was, he might, perhaps, by some chance, be provided with one. The Castellan . . . replied that without a permit [*Erlaubnisschein*] from the sovereign no dealer would be allowed over the border with horses. (89E)

> Der Burgvogt . . . kam, und fragte . . . nach dem Paßschein.—Kohlhaas fragte: der Paßschein? Er sagte . . . daß er, soviel er wisse, keinen habe; daß man ihm aber nur beschreiben möchte, was dies für ein Ding des Herrn sei: so werde er vielleicht zufälligerweise damit versehen sein. Der Schloßvogt . . . versetzte, daß ohne einen landesherrlichen Erlaubnis-schein kein Roßkamm mit Pferden über die Grenze gelassen würde. (10G)

When Kohlhaas leaves the blacks, they serve as a pledge that he will produce that pass. But the document in question, as the German *Paßschein* suggests, is a mere semblance, a thing so unknowable that one might carry it while remaining totally ignorant of its existence. When Kohlhaas goes to Dresden to seek the paper he appropriately calls (in a more literal translation than that above) "a thing of the Lord," a paper guaranteed by the authority of the sovereign that will allow him to reclaim the blacks and to practice his trade in Saxony, he finds that no such text exists.

> [He] betook . . . himself . . . to the privy chancellery, where he . . . learned just what he had at first believed, that the story about the pass was a fairy tale. Kohlhaas, whom the displeased councilors, on his request, provided with a written certificate [*Schein*] about the groundlessness of that pass, smiled over the joke of the skinny Junker, although he didn't yet understand what he wanted to achieve by it. (91–92E)

> [Er] begab . . . sich . . . auf die Geheimschreiberei, wo er . . . erfuhr, was ihm allerdings sein erster Glaube schon gesagt hatte, daß die Geschichte von dem Paßschein ein Märchen sei. Kohlhaas, dem die mißvergnügten

Räte, auf sein Ansuchen, einen schriftlichen Schein über den Ungrund derselben gaben, lächelte über den Witz des dürren Junkers, obschon er noch nicht recht einsah, was er damit bezwecken mochte. (13G)

The horse dealer learns what he knew already: that the story of the pass is a fairytale, a text without foundation, that no such document guaranteed by the authority of the sovereign exists. Yet if Kohlhaas understands at this particular juncture that it is a question of a joke (*Witz*), a joke, moreover, that has no apparent intention, he has in no way grasped the more general implications. He insists on another semblance (*Schein*), another certificate guaranteed by representatives of the Elector. To be sure, it is furnished at the unpromising site of the privy chancellery, the German term for which, *Geheimschreiberei,* speaks of a writing that is hidden or secret. Moreover, the text he receives speaks only of the groundlessness of that other text that might have assured his right to honest trade. But Kohlhaas has not yet learned to question, and indeed, from beginning to end of this tale there is a part of him that blindly believes in text and law underwritten by the name of authority.

Justice for the horse trader, then, is based on a concept of identity, the possibility of equivalent values evident in his demand for the return of the blacks. This principle in turn is backed by a legal code guaranteed by the power of the Elector's name. But as no reader of Kohlhaas can fail to see, Kleist's story is about aberrations in such a relationship between sovereign authority and text, aberrations that are first staged as a dislocation between the two.

Wherever Kohlhaas turns, whether to Brandenburg or Saxony, the law is mediated. Friends and relatives of the Junker von Tronka interpose themselves between Kohlhaas and the execution of the legal code (101, 103E; 21–23G). When Kohlhaas's attempts to press his claim by way of a lawyer therefore fail, he resolves "to hand my complaint . . . personally to the sovereign of the land himself" ("meine Klage . . . persönlich bei dem Landesherrn selbst, einzureichen") (107E; 27G). "The Sovereign himself, I know, is just; and if I could only manage to get through those who surround him to his own person, I do not doubt that I will get justice for myself" ("Der Herr selbst, weiß ich, ist gerecht; und wenn es mir nur gelingt, durch die, die ihn umringen, bis an seine Person zu kommen, so zweifle ich nicht, ich verschaffe mir Recht") (107E; 27G). But Lisbeth, his wife, convinces him to let her stand in his place, "that it was in a thousand cases easier for a woman to approach him than a man" ("daß es in tausend Fällen einer Frau leichter sei, als einem Mann, ihm zu nahen") (109E; 29G). Moreover, she confesses, she has connections with the castellan of the electoral castle (a figure who will reappear briefly to play a crucial, if elusive, role). This mediation is as inefficacious as those that preceded it, and far more tragic, for Lisbeth presses "forward too boldly toward the sovereign's person" ("zu dreist an die Person des Landesherrn"), a movement towards the ruler countered by a brutal and deadly thrust of the bodyguard's lance (109E; 29G).

It is here, after burying his beloved Lisbeth, that Kohlhaas takes matters into his own hands, into his own hands and his own pen, to lend to justice the immediate authority it has been denied.

> As soon as the mound was raised . . . and the guests . . . dismissed . . . [he] took over the business of revenge. He . . . composed a decree in which, by virtue of the authority inborn in him, he condemned the Junker Wenzel von Tronka to bring the blacks that he had taken from him to Kohlhaasenbrück . . . and in person to fatten them in his stables. (111E)

> Sobald der Hügel geworfen . . . und die Gäste . . . entlassen waren . . . übernahm [er] sodann das Geschäft der Rache. Er . . . verfaßte einen Rechtsschluß, in welchem er den Junker Wenzel von Tronka, kraft der ihm angeborenen Macht, verdammte, die Rappen, die er ihm abgenommen, . . . nach Kohlhaasenbrück zu führen, und in Person in seinen Ställen dick zu füttern. (31G)

Kohlhaas's revenge, as direct and brutal as it may be, is at every stage preceded by such a written proclamation. After sacking the Junker's castle but failing to find the Junker himself, he

> composed a so-called "Kohlhaas Manifesto" in which he summoned the land to give no aid to the Junker Wenzel von Tronka with whom he was engaged in a just war: he required . . . every inhabitant to hand him over . . . on penalty of life and limb. (114E)

> verfaßte ein sogenanntes "Kohlhaasisches Mandat", worin er das Land aufforderte, dem Junker Wenzel von Tronka, mit dem er in einem gerechten Krieg liege, keinen Vorschub zu tun, vielmehr jeden Bewohner . . . verpflichtete, denselben bei Strafe Leibes und des Lebens . . . an ihn auszuliefern. (34G)

The scene repeats itself. Kohlhaas writes; he burns and murders, but the Junker is not to be found.

> So he composed a second manifesto, in which he . . . required "every good Christian," as he expressed himself . . . "to take up his cause against

the Junker von Tronka as the common enemy of all Christians." In another manifesto . . . he called himself "a free lord of the realm and world, subject only to God." (116E)

So verfaßte er ein zweites Mandat, worin er . . . "jeden guten Christen", wie er sich ausdrückte . . . aufforderte "seine Sache gegen den Junker von Tronka, als dem allgemeinen Feind aller Christen, zu ergreifen". In einem anderen Mandat . . . nannte er sich: "einen Reichs- und Weltfreien, Gott allein unterworfenen Herrn." (36G)

Shortly thereafter,

He called himself in the manifesto . . . "a representative of the Archangel Michael who was come to punish with fire and sword for the deceit into which the whole world was sunk all who should take the side of the Junker in this quarrel." There he summoned . . . the people to join with him in setting up a better order of things, and the manifesto was . . . signed: "at the seat of our provisional world government." (121E)

Er nannte sich in dem Mandat . . . "einen Statthalter Michaels, des Erzengels, der gekommen sei, an allen, die in dieser Streitsache des Junkers Partei ergreifen würden, mit Feuer und Schwert, die Arglist, in welcher die ganze Welt versunken sei, zu bestrafen". Dabei rief er . . . das Volk auf, sich zur Errichtung einer besseren Ordnung der Dinge, an ihn anzuschließen; und das Mandat war . . . unterzeichnet: "Gegeben auf dem Sitz unserer provisorischen Weltregierung." (41G)

Although Kohlhaas places his name squarely behind the text he writes, although he fulfills what his manifestoes threaten, although each successive text intensifies both the scope of his audience and his own claim to power, nothing, it seems, can satisfy the fundamental demand for the person of the Junker and his restoration to their original state of the horses. The horse dealer's revenge is tellingly called a "business" ("Geschäft") (111E; 31G), but it can never compel to the appropriate rules of exchange. However great his violence, however apocalyptic the authority he invokes, no act can make good von Tronka's willed dissipation of the value of those black signs for justice.

It is now that he who claims himself beyond the laws of realm and world, "subject only to God," who appears on earth as direct representative of the archangel Michael, hears from another figure who has something to say about mediation. For Martin Luther, here as in the historical chronicle, intervenes to play a critical role. Kohlhaas, who in imitation of the famous doctor is wont to place notices on church doorposts, finds a response in kind. "For Luther [undertakes], by means of the power of appeasing words, supported by the authority that his position in the world gave him, the business of forcing Kohlhaas back into the dam of human order" ("der Doktor Martin Luther [übernahm] das Geschäft, den Kohlhaas, durch die Kraft beschwichtigender Worte, von dem Ansehn, das ihm seine Stellung in der Welt gab, unterstützt, in den Damm der menschlichen Ordnung zurückzudrücken") (122E; 42G). Kohlhaas answers Luther's notice by appearing in person, and together they arrive at a solution that they believe satisfies their shared desire for the immediacy of authority: Luther, who here as in theological matters insists on a direct relationship with the lord, will intercede for Kohlhaas with the Elector of Saxony.

> Luther said: "Look here, what you are demanding . . . is just and had you known . . . how to bring the quarrel before the sovereign himself to decide, I do not doubt that your demands would have been granted, point for point. . . ." Luther said . . . he would like to negotiate for him with the Elector. (127E)

> Luther sagte: schau her, was du forderst . . . ist gerecht; und hättest du den Streit . . . zu des Landesherrn Entscheidung zu bringen gewußt, so wäre dir deine Forderung, zweifle ich nicht, Punkt vor Punkt bewilligt worden. . . . Luther sagte . . . er wolle mit dem Kurfürsten seinethalben in Unterhandlung treten. (47G)

Intercession in the name of immediacy is doomed to the failure that such an obviously ironical juxtaposition implies. The Elector of Saxony offers an amnesty, a forgetting or oblivion of Kohlhaas's disruption of the laws of the land, but the spinning out of events is such that the horse dealer must give up his concept of justice—a justice of equal recompense, a code of law guaranteed by the sacred name of the sovereign. Thus with the deterioration of public opinion, Kohlhaas stands ready in Dresden to accept, not the horses themselves, but "compensation for the horses in money" ("Vergütigung der Pferde in Geld") (144E; 64G). Moreover, the letter of a former confederate inviting Kohlhaas to join his continued pillaging is intercepted and redelivered. It is redelivered to the now imprisoned Kohlhaas by a figure who has come to represent the Elector of Saxony, its authority displaced and in question. Kohlhaas, in turn, writes a response in which, for the very first time, his signature belies the intention behind his words. For Kohlhaas only pretends to accept the offer in order to enlist aid in escaping Saxony.

How can it be insignificant, then, that just when Kohlhaas is about to be condemned for thus breaking the amnesty, "to be pinched with red-hot pincers by knacker's men, drawn and quartered" ("mit glühenden Zangen von Schinderknechten gekniffen, gevierteilt") (157E; 77G), just when text and authority, law and the sovereign's name, have been most radically placed asunder, the blacks themselves are described as "dead: . . . in legal significance dead, since they have no value" ("tot: . . . in staatrechtlicher Bedeutung tot, weil sie keinen Wert haben") (145E; 65G). Like Kohlhaas, they have passed through a long and difficult degradation (from groom to shepherd to swineherd) that leaves them, too, in the hands of the knacker's men. For as has been evident all along, the blacks, as the objects of dispute, are the signs for the empty or full significance of the law.[2]

Thus when everything in the story seems to turn, when the authority of Saxony is displaced by that of Brandenburg and the Holy Roman Empire, when Kohlhaas's sovereign meets him face to face and wins for him an almost exact reparation from the Junker Wenzel von Tronka (if only a little mediated) (181E; 101G) and the representative of the empire exacts a very merciful execution—little enough to pay for the rebel's extensive murder and plunder—when the blacks reappear "shining with well-being" ("von Wohlsein glänzenden") (181E; 101G), does this not mean that all is well with the world and law?[3]

> The Elector spoke accordingly as Kohlhaas . . . came up to him: "Now Kohlhaas, today is the day on which justice is done you! . . . Here I give back to you all that was taken from you with violence at Tronka Castle and which I, as your sovereign, was duty bound to restore: neckerchief, gold gulden, laundry. . . . Are you satisfied with me?" Kohlhaas . . . [read over] the decree handed . . . him with large sparkling eyes and when he found an article in it in which the Junker Wenzel was condemned to two years imprisonment, totally overwhelmed by emotion, . . . he, from afar, knelt down . . . before the Elector. He assured the Archchancellor joyfully . . . that his greatest wish on earth had been fulfilled. . . . The Elector called: "Now Kohlhaas the horsedealer, you to whom in this fashion satisfaction has been done, make yourself ready on your side to give satisfaction for breach of public peace to his majesty, the Emperor, whose attorney stands here!" Kohlhaas . . . said that he was prepared to do so. (181–82E)

Demnach sprach der Kurfürst, als Kohlhaas . . . zu ihm heranschritt:
Nun, Kohlhaas, heut ist der Tag, an dem dir dein Recht geschieht! . . .
Hier liefere ich dir alles, was du auf der Tronkenburg gewaltsamer Weise
eingebüßt, und was ich, als dein Landesherr, dir wieder zu verschaffen,
schuldig war, zurück: Rappen, Halstuch, Reichsgulden, Wäsche. . . . Bist
du mit mir zufrieden? Kohlhaas . . . [überlas] das, ihm . . . eingehändigte
Konklusum, mit großen, funkelnden Augen . . . und da er auch einen
Artikel darin fand, in welchem der Junker Wenzel zu zweijähriger Gefäng-
nisstrafe verurteilt ward: so ließ er sich, aus der Ferne, ganz überwältigt
von Gefühlen . . . vor dem Kurfürsten nieder. Er versicherte freudig dem
Erzkanzler . . . daß sein höchster Wunsch auf Erden erfüllt sei. . . . Der
Kurfürst rief: "nun, Kohlhaas, der Roßhändler, du, dem solchergestalt
Genugtuung geworden, mache dich bereit, kaiserlicher Majestät, deren
Anwalt hier steht, wegen des Bruchs ihres Landfriedens, deinerseits
Genugtuung zu geben!" Kohlhaas . . . sagte: daß er bereit dazu wäre!
(101–2G)

All that we have said so far is more or less evident—little more than
a thematic recapitulation, one might claim, of the plot of *Michael
Kohlhaas*. But in this story of satisfaction and reparation, of fulfilled
equal exchange and sovereign presence, something has been missing.
What the reader discovers, almost at the end of the tale, is that there have
been another plot and another text in question. That plot and that text
have been kept hidden even though at the moment we first hear of them
we find that they had already marked the very beginning of Kohlhaas's
rebellion.[4] That other text and that other plot stand at the critical
crossroads of Kohlhaas's two modes of seeking justice, and yet aptly
enough, the whole matter seems to many critics beside the point.[5]

> *Michael Kohlhaas* calls the political order into question, or rather the
> superb body of the story does; the concluding section, which ostensibly
> resolves the issues of Kohlhaas' "case," only does so formally; it does not
> really answer the radical doubts raised in the course of the narrative, and
> seems . . . , with its fairytale supernaturalism, a good deal less forceful and
> serious. (30E)

Indeed the conversation between the Elector of Saxony and Kohlhaas that first brings up the matter of the text is riddled with a
questioning of the serious. Like so many other pivotal incidents in the
story, the encounter takes place on the border between Saxony and
Brandenburg. The Elector has come here—the irony will soon become
evident—to hunt stags. Kohlhaas is leaving Saxony for his final and just

judgment in the presence of his sovereign, the Elector of Brandenburg. A number of the hunting party, disguised by their hunting attire, "satisfy their curiosity" about Kohlhaas by entering the farmhouse where he is lodged for the night. The Elector, at the suggestion of one of the court ladies, agrees to do the same, as he puts it, in the name of "folly" ("Torheit") (161E; 81G). Wearing a feathered hat and standing behind several of his men, a costume and pose he will reassume in the critical final scene, the Elector finally speaks to Kohlhaas.

> The Elector, who was standing behind the hunters and noticed a small lead capsule hanging . . . from [Kohlhaas's] neck, asked him, since nothing better presented itself for conversation, what this signified and what there was inside? Kohlhaas replied: "Yes . . . this capsule! . . . there are curious circumstances surrounding this capsule! It was about seven months ago, precisely on the day following the burial of my wife and I had set out from Kohlhaasenbrück, as might perhaps be known to you, in order to get hold of Junker von Tronka who has done me a grave injustice." (161–62E)

> Der Kurfürst, der hinter den Jagdjunkern stand, und eine kleine bleierne Kapsel, die ihm . . . vom Hals herabhing, bemerkte, fragte ihn, da sich grade nichts Besseres zur Unterhaltung darbot: was diese zu bedeuten hätte und was darin befindlich wäre? Kohlhaas erwiderte: "ja . . . diese Kapsel! . . . mit dieser Kapsel hat es eine wunderliche Bewandtnis! Sieben Monden mögen es etwa sein, genau am Tage nach dem Begräbnis meiner Frau; und von Kohlhaasenbrück, wie Euch vielleicht bekannt sein wird, war ich aufgebrochen, um des Junkers von Tronka, der mir viel Unrecht zugefügt, habhaft zu werden." (82G)

Curiosity and folly have brought the Elector to see Kohlhaas, and he speaks now only because of a lapse in the conversation, a moment in which language has lost any sense of necessity. The question he poses is that of meaning, and the answer he receives may not after all provide.it. Despite Kohlhaas's lengthy explanation, the Elector cannot entirely satisfy his curiosity.

As Kohlhaas explains it, on the day following the funeral of his wife Lisbeth, and just when he chooses to violate the law, he witnesses and takes part in a scene that is at once, one might claim, both beside the point and the whole point of Kleist's tale, even though for those of us who are curious as to the meaning of the literary text, it may not fully satisfy. In the market square of Jüterbock, on the border, once again, of Brandenburg and Saxony, the two figures of legal sovereignty come together for the sake of a discussion the subject of which remains unknown to Kohlhaas.[6] Kohlhaas's ignorance of their matters is soon to be matched by a certain nonknowledge on their part. The two electors come upon a gypsy fortuneteller and ask her jokingly whether she does not have something pleasing to reveal to them.

> Behind all those people . . . where I stood, I . . . could not make out what the bizarre woman was saying to the two lords, so that when the people . . . pressed forward, less because I was curious really than to make room for the curious, I climbed up on a bench behind me. . . . No sooner had I caught sight from this vantage point . . . of the lords and the old lady, who . . . seemed to be scribbling something, than she suddenly stands up . . . looking around at the people, fixes her eye on me who had never exchanged a word with her nor even in my life desired anything from her kind of knowledge, pushes forward . . . to me and speaks: "There! if the Lord wishes to know it, he may ask you about it!" And with that . . . she handed me . . . this scrap of paper. And when, disconcerted . . . I speak: "Little Mother, what are you giving me?," she answers, after a lot of unintelligible stuff in the middle of which, however, to my great astonishment, I hear my name: "an amulet, Kohlhaas, the horse-dealer. Preserve it well. One day it will save your life!" and vanishes. (162–63E)

> Ich . . . konnte hinter allem Volk . . . wo ich stand, nicht vernehmen, was die wunderliche Frau den Herren sagte; dergestalt, daß, da die Leute . . . sich . . . sehr bedrängten, ich weniger neugierig, in der Tat, als um den Neugierigen Platz zu machen, auf eine Bank stieg, die hinter mir . . . war. Kaum hatte ich von diesem Standpunkt aus . . . die Herrschaften und das Weib, das . . . etwas aufzukritzeln schien, erblickt: da steht sie plötzlich . . . indem sie sich im Volk umsieht, auf; faßt mich, der nie ein Wort mit ihr wechselte, noch ihrer Wissenschaft Zeit seines Lebens begehrte, ins Auge; drängt sich . . . zu mir heran und spricht: "da! wenn es der Herr wissen will, so mag er dich danach fragen!" Und damit . . . reichte sie mir . . . diesen Zettel dar. Und da ich betreten . . . spreche: Mütterchen, was auch verehrst du mir da? antwortet sie, nach vielem unvernehmlichen Zeug, worunter ich jedoch zu meinem großen Befremden meinen Namen höre: "ein Amulett, Kohlhaas, der Roßhändler; verwahr es wohl, es wird dir dereinst das Leben retten!" und verschwindet. (82–83G)

The same scene is later to be related by the Elector of Saxony—from a very different point of view. For if the Elector is soon quite literally dying of curiosity (166E; 86–87G), "more curious than words

can say" ("neugierig . . . mehr als Worte sagen können") (172E; 92G), as
he will put it, Kohlhaas, quite to the contrary, withdraws to a bench
behind him "less because I was curious . . . than to make room for the
curious" ("weniger neugierig . . . als um den Neugierigen Platz zu
machen") (162E; 82G). Here, as in his last encounter with the gypsy
(178E; 98G), he insists that he has never in all his life desired to consult
the art of fortunetelling. Shortly thereafter, the Elector sends a nobleman
to the horse dealer to offer him life and liberty in exchange for the paper
(165E; 85G). But at the moment when Kohlhaas can make the text most
meaningful, when it might fulfill the gypsy's prophecy and save him
from the executioner, he chooses rather to renounce not only his
curiosity about its contents but also its power to signify his own life.

> The horsedealer, who already knew the name and title of the man who had
> fallen into a faint . . . at the sight of the capsule in question and who to top
> off the frenzy . . . needed only to look at the secrets of the scrap of paper
> which he . . . was determined not to open merely out of curiosity, said that
> he wished to hold onto the scrap of paper. To the question of the Junker—
> what caused him to arrive at this strange refusal when nothing less than life
> and liberty were being offered him—Kohlhaas answered. . . . (166E)

> Der Roßhändler, der bereits Rang und Namen dessen, der beim Anblick
> der in Rede stehenden Kapsel . . . in Ohnmacht gefallen war, kannte, und
> der zur Krönung des Taumels . . . nichts bedurfte, als Einsicht in die
> Geheimnisse des Zettels, den er . . . entschlossen war, aus bloßer Neu-
> gierde nicht zu eröffnen: der Roßhändler sagte . . . "daß er den Zettel
> behalten wolle." Auf Frage des Jagdjunkers: was ihn zu dieser sonderbaren
> Weigerung, da man ihm doch nichts Minderes, als Freiheit und Leben
> dafür anbiete veranlasse? antwortete Kohlhaas. . . . (86G)

The horse dealer makes clear his satisfaction both here and with a
similar refusal to give up the paper shortly before his death. In his last
encounter with the fortuneteller he tells her, "Only your certain and
unambiguous demand could separate me, good Mother, from the paper
through which satisfaction has been given me so wonderfully for all that
I have suffered" ("nur deine Forderung, bestimmt und unzweideutig,
trennt mich, gutes Mütterchen, von dem Blatt, durch welches mir für
alles, was ich erlitten, auf so wunderbare Weise Genugtuung geworden
ist") (177E; 98G). The satisfaction Kohlhaas expresses is of another order
than that of which the Elector of Brandenburg speaks in the closing
scene. It is less the satisfaction of exchanging things of equal value

(*Wechseln*) and of the fulfillment of the significance of the law (as authored text) than one of joy in the text as privation of knowledge, satisfaction through negation of meaning, the celebration of a text precisely insofar as it denies the presence of its own authority.[7]

And yet in putting it that way, we have not quite grasped it. For whatever satisfaction Kohlhaas may claim to have from the paper, whatever satisfaction from the decree won for him by Brandenburg and read at the scene of his execution, his hunger for revenge, as we shall see, apparently has not been entirely sated, or at least not in the proper manner. The moment when Kohlhaas receives the paper, let us note it just one more time, coincides with the start of his career as an outlaw. In his conversation with the horse dealer, Luther will claim, nevertheless, that however violently he has challenged its laws, Kohlhaas has never been outside the legal community—and in a sense he is correct. No one has asserted this more persistently than Kohlhaas himself, despite his many manifestoes declaring himself beyond the realm of man, for those same proclamations demand justice very much within the logic of terrestrial law. Moreover, for his own band of brigands and murderers Kohlhaas has created a legal apparatus that mimics the one he pretends to have jettisoned, judging and punishing those who violate its code of morality.[8] All this to say that there is a parallel to be drawn between Kohlhaas's performance as an outlaw and the concept of the text, readable in the figure of that small piece of paper, as privation of knowledge. For if they both turn the models they challenge inside out, they assert, nonetheless, the priority of those models.

As always in Kleist, there are two sides to the story. If the scene in Jüterbock is first described by Kohlhaas, who seems in possession of the text and whose life it may seem to guarantee, it is now narrated by the Elector of Saxony, who in the proximity of the paper is pushed to the verge of madness and death—a narration that clarifies and complicates matters considerably. For the gypsy's soothsaying concerns not only Saxony but also Brandenburg, and the matter in question is not only the particular prediction but the possibility of prediction in general.

> On the third day of our meeting that we were holding in Jüterbock, the Elector of Brandenburg and I encountered a gypsy woman and there the Elector decided, quick-witted as he is by nature, by means of a joke in front of all the people, to destroy the reputation of this woman whose art had been the subject of excessive talk at dinner. Thus he stepped up . . . to her table and demanded a sign from her with respect to the prediction she

was to make for him that could be put to the proof that very day, barring which he would not . . . be able to believe her words. The woman, while measuring us hastily from head to foot, said: the sign would be that the big horned roebock that the gardener's son was raising in the park would come to meet us in the market place where we were, before we should have left it. (170E)

Der Kurfürst von Brandenburg und ich [trafen] am dritten Tage der Zusammenkunft, die wir in Jüterbock hielten, auf eine Zigeunerin; und da der Kurfürst, aufgeweckt wie er von Natur ist, beschloß, den Ruf dieser abenteuerlichen Frau, von deren Kunst, eben bei der Tafel, auf ungebührliche Weise die Rede gewesen war, durch einen Scherz im Angesicht alles Volks zu nichte zu machen: so trat er . . . vor ihren Tisch, und forderte, der Weissagung wegen, die sie ihm machen sollte, ein Zeichen von ihr, das sich noch heute erproben ließe, vorschützend, daß er sonst nicht . . . an ihre Worte glauben könne. Die Frau, indem sie uns flüchtig von Kopf zu Fuß maß, sagte: das Zeichen würde sein, daß uns der große, gehörnte Rehbock, den der Sohn des Gärtners im Park erzog, auf dem Markt, worauf wir uns befanden, bevor wir ihn noch verlassen, entgegenkommen würde. (90–91G)

Brandenburg wishes to destroy the reputation of the fortuneteller by demanding an immediate sign that will stand as proof of the truth of all her predictions. His gesture to empty the significance of her words, his pretension to control with a joke the measure of soothsaying, is met by a glance that measures him in turn. The prediction she offers to test the value of prediction seems excluded from the realm of possibility, for the roebuck (*Rehbock*) that is called upon to meet them in the marketplace of Jüterbock, destined as it is for the Dresden kitchen, is kept bolted and barred in the park nearby. It was

impossible to foresee . . . how the animal according to this strange assertion would come to meet us in the market place where we were standing. The Elector, fearing some hidden knavery, after a short consultation with me, unwaveringly determined, for the fun of it, to dishonor all that she might put forward, sent to the castle and ordered that the roebuck be killed immediately and that it be prepared for dinner on one of the next days. (170–71E)

schlechterdings nicht abzusehen war wie uns das Tier, diesem sonderbaren Vorgeben gemäß, bis auf dem Platz, wo wir standen, entgegen kommen würde; gleichwohl schickte der Kurfürst aus Besorgnis vor einer dahinter steckenden Schelmerei, nach einer kurzen Abrede mit mir, entschlossen, auf unabänderliche Weise, alles was sie noch vorbringen würde, des Spaßes wegen, zu Schanden zu machen, ins Schloß, und befahl, daß der Rehbock augenblicklich getötet, und für die Tafel, an einem der nächsten Tage, zubereitet werden solle. (91G)

It is not altogether clear here why it is Brandenburg who gives orders with respect to what is destined for the Dresden kitchen. The entire scenario is strangely reminiscent of Kohlhaas's unexpected release from his Saxon captors—a release also arranged by Brandenburg and with somewhat similar results, a release that has just taken place when this story within the story is told. For Kohlhaas, too, is liberated from Dresden only to be slaughtered soon thereafter, and what his execution ultimately vouchsafes is something yet to be determined.

The gypsy, unshaken by such orders destined to belie her word, goes on to read the Elector's hand.

> Hereupon, he turned back to the woman in front of whom this matter had been openly handled and said: "Now, come on! What future do you have to reveal to me?" The woman spoke while looking in his hand: "Hail to my Elector and Lord! Your Grace shall rule for many years, the house from which you spring shall endure for a great period of time, and your descendants will be great and glorious and more powerful than all other princes and sovereigns of the earth!" (171E)

> Hierauf wandte er sich zu der Frau, vor welcher diese Sache laut verhandelt worden war, zurück, und sagte: nun wohlan! was hast du mir für die Zukunft zu entdecken? Die Frau, indem sie in seine Hand sah, sprach: Heil meinem Kurfürsten und Herrn! Deine Gnaden wird lange regieren, das Haus, aus dem du stammst, lange bestehen, und deine Nachkommen groß und herrlich werden und zu Macht gelangen, vor allen Fürsten und Herren der Welt! (91G)

As that other Elector of Brandenburg in *Prince Friedrich von Homburg* learns, one cannot direct the scenario of the joke (*Scherz/Spass*) without placing one's own direction on the line. The Elector has presumed to control the validity of the fortuneteller's word by asserting the authority of his own. But the prediction that the gypsy puts forth, a prediction that assures the sovereign of his unshakable authority, carries with it the force of a traditional double bind. The prediction and thus also the authority of which it speaks would seem to be undone precisely insofar as the Elector's word holds the power to have the roebuck slaughtered. But just when both the Elector and the reader have grasped the irony of this contradiction, the stakes will be doubled and doubled again. For it is a question here, after all, less of a traditional double bind, in which the terms of the contradiction are already clearly determined, than of what one is tempted to call a "magic circle" (132E; 51G), a figure of entrapment whose sides seem to multiply endlessly and to enclose all who try to erase it.[9]

The contradiction doubles when, at his tale's end, the Elector of Saxony describes the effect of Brandenburg's orders:

> Now . . . the knight whom the Elector had sent to the castle appeared and informed him . . . that the roebuck had been killed and dragged into the kitchen by two hunters before his eyes. The Elector said: "Now then! So the prophesying was an everyday swindle. . . ." But how great was our astonishment when, still in the course of these words, a shout arose all around the square and all eyes turned toward a large butcher's dog trotting towards us from the castle yard who had seized the roebuck . . . in the kitchen . . . and let the animal fall to the ground three steps from us; so that, in fact, the prophecy of the woman was fulfilled that served as pledge for all that she brought forth, and the roebuck had come to meet us in the market place, although, to be sure, dead. (172–73E)

> Nun trat . . . der Ritter auf, den der Kurfürst ins Schloß geschickt hatte, und meldete ihm . . . daß der Rehbock getötet, und durch zwei Jäger, vor seinen Augen, in die Küche geschleppt worden sei. Der Kurfürst . . . sagte: nun, wohlan! so war die Prophezeiung eine alltägliche Gaunerei. . . ! Aber wie groß war unser Erstaunen, da sich, noch während dieser Worte, ein Geschrei rings auf dem Platze erhob, und aller Augen sich einem großen, vom Schloßhof herantrabenden Schlächterhund zuwandten, der in der Küche den Rehbock . . . erfaßt, und das Tier drei Schritte von uns . . . auf den Boden fallen ließ: dergestalt, daß in der Tat die Prophezeiung des Weibes, zum Unterpfand alles dessen, was sie vorgebracht, erfüllt, und der Rehbock uns bis auf den Markt, obschon allerdings tot, entgegen gekommen war. (92–93G)

What comes to meet the electors in the marketplace is at once the affirmation and the denial of their sovereign authority. For if it is easy enough to read *Michael Kohlhaas,* particularly its closing pages, as a resolution in the name of unmediated authority, as a celebration of Brandenburg's evenhanded dispensation of justice in contradistinction to the maneuvers of Saxony, the story of the gypsy makes that distinction more difficult to maintain.

The appearance of the roebuck reestablishes the authority of Brandenburg's word but only in a sense. If he has had the roebuck killed, it is true that not only was the order effective but its result does not, after all, undermine his destiny of unparalleled power. What it does undermine, however, is the original intention behind his order, for the Elector assumed that the killing of the stag would keep it from the marketplace and destroy its power to stand as pledge for all the gypsy had to say. Brandenburg has had the stag killed, and its death is what makes its appearance possible, an appearance that comes to mean just the opposite of what he had intended.

The whole structure of "standing as a pledge for" (and from the first question of the blacks this is, in a sense, what *Michael Kohlhaas* is about),[10] the whole structure of the pledge, has been turned somewhat inside out. For if from the beginning, by mutual agreement, the stag is to signify something else, the truth of the gypsy's soothsaying, in the end it signifies only by itself becoming totally other, by being emptied of life. In this it is not unlike the "horror-riddle" that enters "pale, like a corpse" at the end of *Penthesilea*. Nor is it unlike the blacks or the paper that Kohlhaas carries with him, a paper that functions until the end insofar as it is *not* read. More precisely, however, what seems to characterize all that concerns the gypsy's mode of signification is less an emptying, necessarily, of what is full than a disruption of control and expectation with regard to those two possibilities, a disruption that could just as well, say, substitute the actual thing for the seemingly empty sign. Thus when the Elector of Saxony sends his chamberlain to attempt once again to retrieve the paper from Kohlhaas, the chamberlain engages an old ragpicker on the streets of Berlin to impersonate the gypsy and, by "the most monstrous blunder," chooses the woman herself.

> Since probability is not always on the side of truth, so it came to pass that something happened here that we indeed report, but we must grant whomever it pleases the liberty to doubt it: the Chamberlain had committed the most monstrous blunder and in the old rag-lady whom he had picked up in the street of Berlin he had hit upon the very gypsy herself whom he wished to have imitated. (175–76E)

> Wie denn die Wahrscheinlichkeit nicht immer auf Seiten der Wahrheit ist, so traf es sich, daß hier etwas geschehen war, das wir zwar berichten: die Freiheit aber, daran zu zweifeln, demjenigen, dem es wohlgefällt, zugestehen müssen: der Kämmerer hatte den ungeheuersten Mißgriff be-

gangen, und in dem alten Trödelweib, das er in den Straßen von Berlin aufgriff, um die Zigeunerin nachzuahmen, die geheimnisreiche Zigeunerin selbst getroffen, die er nachgeahmt wissen wollte. (96G)

What is it, after all, that the scrap of paper so sought after will or could tell? In what way does it function, or fail to function, as a meaningful and useful document? As Saxony continues his tale,

> So! I said confused . . . "from what direction does the danger threaten my house?" Taking up a piece of charcoal and paper, the woman . . . asked whether she should write it down for me; and when I . . . answered "Yes! do that!" she continued: "Very well! I will write down three things for you: the name of the last ruler of your house, the year in which he shall lose his reign, and the name of the man who will . . . seize it for himself." This . . . concluded, she arose. . . . And when I wish to get hold of the scrap of paper, curious . . . more than words can say, she speaks: "By no means, your Highness!" and turns around and raises one of her crutches on high: "From that man there, the one with the feather hat who is standing on the bench behind all the people . . . you can redeem the scrap of paper if you wish!" (171–72E)

> So! sagt ich verwirrt. . . : von welcher Seite her droht meinem Hause Gefahr? Die Frau, indem sie eine Kohle und ein Papier zur Hand nahm . . . fragte: ob sie es mir aufschreiben solle? und da ich . . . antwortete: ja! das tu! so versetzte sie: "wohlan! dreierlei schreib ich dir auf: den Namen des letzten Regenten deines Hauses, die Jahrszahl, da er sein Reich verlieren, und den Namen dessen, der es . . . an sich reißen wird." Dies . . . abgemacht, erhebt sie sich. . . . Und da ich den Zettel, neugierig . . . mehr als Worte sagen können, erfassen will, spricht sie: "mit nichten, Hoheit!" und wendet sich und hebt ihrer Krücken eine empor "von jenem Mann dort, der, mit dem Federhut, auf der Bank steht, hinter allem Volk . . . lösest du, wenn es dir beliebt, den Zettel ein!" (92G)

The instrument of inscription is charcoal, a message passed on to him whose name cannot then be either quite historical[11] or quite incidental. For *Kohlhaas* in German suggests a hatred bound to coal and by the horse dealer's own admission fulfilled by the gypsy's means of writing. But if Kohlhaas finds his hatred satisfied by his possession of the paper, if the failure to possess it repeatedly knocks the locus of electoral power unconscious, bringing him to the point of desperation and death, it is perhaps that neither the Elector nor the horse dealer understands very well the nature of the text in question. For what the gypsy foretells—and history, after all, confirms her prediction—is a future that no foreknowledge can alter. Her soothsaying declares what will take place no matter how (and sometimes because) one goes about manipulating the preceding events. The episode with the stag was about this if nothing else. Her knowledge, it would seem, is absolute, but it gains the knower absolutely nothing. It changes nothing and allows nothing to be changed. A bit like the law of the Holy Roman Empire, her pronouncements stand above and beyond both Brandenburg and Saxony. But unlike the decisions of the Emperor, her words are neither judgments nor appealable—simply the statement of what must be.

Kohlhaas begins to fathom something of this in his last encounter with the soothsayer, shortly before his execution. For no sooner does he exult in the wonderful satisfaction he has had from her bit of writing than he returns to the lack—the rupture in his own understanding—that it has simultaneously produced.

> Kohlhaas repeated his question with respect to the contents of the strange scrap of paper. He wished, as she hastily replied, "that he could certainly open it although it would be mere curiosity," still to receive an explanation about a thousand other things before she left him—who she really was, how she had come by the knowledge she possessed, why she had denied the note to the Elector, for whom it had, after all, been written, and why she had handed the marvelous sheet just to him . . . who had never desired anything from her knowledge. . . . The woman . . . answered: "Goodbye Kohlhaas, until we see one another again! When we meet again, there should be nothing of this that you shall not know!" (177–78E)

> Kohlhaas wiederholte seine Frage, den Inhalt des wunderbaren Zettels betreffend; er wünschte, da sie flüchtig antwortete: "daß er ihn ja eröffnen könne, obschon es eine bloße Neugierde wäre," noch über tausend andere Dinge, bevor sie ihn verließe, Aufschluß zu erhalten; wer sie eigentlich sei, woher sie zu der Wissenschaft, die ihr inwohne, komme, warum sie dem Kurfürsten, für den er doch geschrieben, den Zettel verweigert, und grade ihm . . . der ihrer Wissenschaft nie begehrt, das Wunderblatt überreicht habe. . . ? Das Weib . . . antwortete: "auf Wiedersehen Kohlhaas, auf Wiedersehn! Es soll dir, wenn wir uns wiedertreffen, an Kenntnis über dies alles nicht fehlen!" (98G)

The knowledge that escapes Kohlhaas the reader, too, must forgo, for if the gypsy's knowledge is certain, the source of its authority is utterly unknowable. And despite her last words to the horse dealer, it is not quite the gypsy that Kohlhaas meets again but rather another piece of her writing. The note is carried by that same castellan whose mediation seemed to promise Kohlhaas's wife access to the sovereign.

> Just as he was stepping out . . . the gate of the prison . . . the Castellan of the electoral castle . . . came up to him and gave him a piece of paper that, as he said, had been handed to him for Kohlhaas by an old woman. Kohlhaas, while looking at the man in surprise . . . opened the paper whose seal . . . immediately reminded him of the familiar gypsy. But who can describe the astonishment that gripped him when he found the following communication: "Kohlhaas, the Elector of Saxony is in Berlin; he has already gone on ahead to the place of execution and can . . . be recognized by a hat with blue and white feather plumes. . . . As soon as you are buried he wishes to have the capsule and the paper that is in it opened up.—Your Elisabeth."—Kohlhaas, while turning to the Castellan, thoroughly perplexed, asked him whether he knew the strange woman who had given him the note. But just as the Castellan was answering "Kohlhaas, the woman"—and in the middle of his speech faltered in a bizarre way, Kohlhaas, dragged away by the procession that in this moment started up again, could not hear what the man . . . was saying.— (180E)

> Eben trat er . . . aus dem Tor seines Gefängnisses, als . . . der Kastellan des kurfürstlichen Schlosses . . . zu ihm herantrat, und ihm ein Blatt gab, das ihm, wie er sagte, ein altes Weib für ihn eingehändigt. Kohlhaas, während er den Mann . . . befremdet ansah, eröffnete das Blatt, dessen Siegelring ihn . . . sogleich an die bekannte Zigeunerin erinnerte. Aber wer beschreibt das Erstaunen, das ihn ergriff, als er folgende Nachricht darin fand: "Kohlhaas, der Kurfürst von Sachsen ist in Berlin; auf den Richtplatz schon ist er vorangegangen, und wird . . . an einem Hut, mit blauen und weißen Federbüschen kenntlich sein. . . . Er will die Kapsel, sobald du verscharrt bist, ausgraben, und den Zettel, der darin befindlich ist, eröffnen lassen.—Deine Elisabeth."—Kohlhaas, indem er sich auf das äußerste bestürzt zu dem Kastellan umwandte, fragte ihn: ob er das wunderbare Weib, das ihm den Zettel übergeben, kenne? Doch da der Kastellan antwortete: "Kohlhaas, das Weib"—und in Mitten der Rede auf sonderbare Weise stockte, so konnte er, von dem Zuge, der in diesem Augenblick wieder antrat, fortgerissen, nicht vernehmen, was der Mann . . . vorbrachte.—(100–101G)

The name of the authority behind the text is finally revealed, for like Kohlhaas's wife Lisbeth, the gypsy woman also bears that name. Perhaps this explains what Kohlhaas noticed as she entered his cell, the uncanny resemblance between the two, a similarity in face, hands, and build and, most uncanny of all, a mark on her neck precisely where his wife had borne one. Name, features, gestures, and the mark are yet four more texts the woman bears that signify an undecipherable mode of identity, that refuse the knowledge they seem to suggest—like the unfulfilled promise of meeting again, like the broken sentence of the castellan.

But here on this last occasion Elizabeth sends another paper. Kohlhaas used the first properly, it is true, but he never understood it well. The second comes sealed in a similar fashion. The message is simple and straightforward—anything but the privational knowledge associated with the first. The Elector has come to Kohlhaas's execution wearing a feathered hat, a reversal of Kohlhaas witnessing Saxony's more metaphorical execution in Jüterbock. Perhaps it is a little late, but the man whose rebellion until now has remained within the structure of the laws he challenged seems to have understood. If just before the theologian Jakob Freising, representative of Luther, has favored the condemned man with Holy Communion, Kohlhaas chooses another mode of communion, which might well be just as satisfying.

> The Elector called, "Now, Kohlhaas . . . you to whom in this fashion satisfaction has been done, make yourself ready . . . on your side to give satisfaction to his majesty, the Emperor!" Kohlhaas . . . said that he was prepared to do so. . . . He was just unknotting his neckerchief . . . when, with a hasty glance around the circle formed by the people, he saw a short distance from him, between two knights who half covered him with their bodies, the familiar man with blue and white feather plumes. Kohlhaas . . . while walking right up to him took the capsule from his breast; he took out the paper, unsealed it, read it over, and directing his eyes steadily on the man with blue and white feather plumes, who had already begun to indulge in sweet hopes, he stuck it in his mouth and swallowed it. On seeing this, the man with blue and white plumes became faint and sank down in spasms. Kohlhaas, however, as the disconcerted companions of the man bent over him and raised him from the ground, Kohlhaas turned to the scaffold, where his head fell under the axe of the executioner. Here ends the story of Kohlhaas. (182E)

> Der Kurfürst rief: "nun, Kohlhaas . . . du dem solchergestalt Genugtuung geworden, mache dich bereit, kaiserlicher Majestät . . . deinerseits Genugtuung zu geben!" Kohlhaas . . . sagte: daß er bereit dazu wäre. . . . Eben knüpfte er sich das Tuch vom Hals ab . . . als er, mit einem flüchti-

gen Blick auf den Kreis, den das Volk bildete, in geringer Entfernung von sich, zwischen zwei Rittern, die ihn mit ihren Leibern halb deckten, den wohlbekannten Mann mit blauen und weißen Federbüschen wahrnahm. Kohlhaas löste sich, indem er . . . dicht vor ihn trat, die Kapsel von der Brust; er nahm den Zettel heraus, entsiegelte ihn, und überlas ihn: und das Auge unverwandt auf den Mann mit blauen und weißen Federbüschen gerichtet, der bereits süßen Hoffnungen Raum zu geben anfing, steckte er ihn in den Mund und verschlang ihn. Der Mann mit blauen und weißen Federbüschen sank, bei diesem Anblick, ohnmächtig, in Krämpfen nieder. Kohlhaas aber, während die bestürzten Begleiter desselben sich herabbeugten, und ihn vom Boden aufhoben, wandte sich zu dem Schafott, wo sein Haupt unter dem Beil des Scharfrichters fiel. Hier endigt die Geschichte vom Kohlhaas. (102–3G)

Here also begins and ends the story of Kohlhaas's most radical rebellion. Kohlhaas reads the text that marked his earliest violations of the law and that all along he has refused to use to save his life. He gains the knowledge that Saxony (adorned, as the narrative obsessively insists, with the instruments of writing) so desired. Kohlhaas satisfies his curiosity, perhaps, but as simultaneously as matters permit he also willingly forfeits his head. He knocks the seat of electoral power unconscious, but the same extended gesture affirms the power of the law.[12] For *Michael Kohlhaas,* no less than *Prince Friedrich von Homburg* and despite its ostensible geographical locus of Berlin in the closing scene, is always on the border between Brandenburg and Saxony and all they have come to represent with respect to the question of authority.

7

The Unclosable Wound

"The Duel" comes at the end of Kleist's work, written as it probably was in the summer of 1811, just a few months before his theatrical suicide. It seems to have the final word, if not in our text, for strategic reasons, at least in the sense of conventional literary history. It seems to have the final word in another sense as well, for in rather remarkable fashion it rewrites critical moments of his other works. The result of this gesture of ultimate reassessment gives the appearance of closing uncertainties, resolving struggles, transvaluating the negative.[1]

"The Foundling," as one example among many, opens with a scene of usurpation in which Antonio Piachi sets out on a journey, losing his son in exchange for Nicolo, a monster of illegitimacy, who then proceeds to destroy the family. "The Duel," quite the contrary, begins with the journey of Duke Wilhelm von Breysach, from which he returns with an act of legitimation for his bastard son. By the close of the tale the son's moral right to that elevation is made clear, for Jacob the Redbeard, heir to the throne, has plotted the murder of his brother Wilhelm. To deny his role as fratricide, Redbeard, accepting the challenge of Friedrich von Trota, stands trial in a holy combat before God and there receives the wound that claims his life. In this narration of justice, which ends with the Emperor honoring Friedrich, it is not only the loyal chamberlain who is celebrated but, bizarrely enough, that other Friedrich from the earlier text it plays on and alters. "After the wedding the Emperor hung a chain of honor around Sir Friedrich's neck" ("Der Kaiser aber hing Herrn Friedrich, nach der Trauung, eine Gnadenkette um den Hals") (318E; 261G).[2] With a repetition compulsion that might seem to leave nothing uncanny, "The Duel" cites the crucial scene of *Prince Friedrich von Homburg.*[3] What in the play is twice there as a gesture of irresolvable crisis gives to the tale a sense of closure.

But that is not the whole story. The oblique admonition of "The Duel" is to always read a second time, for both the duchess and her brother-in-law, as we are told repeatedly in rapid succession, read their papers "twice, with great attention" ("zweimal mit Aufmerksamkeit") (290E; 232G). Not that with a second reading one masters the written word in this text—which itself constitutes a second reading of texts that came before. This is a narration whose title and plot are ever insistent on the movement of struggle. This particular struggle compels to interpretation. According to the law of "the sacred verdict of arms which unfailingly would bring truth to the light of day" ("den heiligen Ausspruch der Waffen, der die Wahrheit unfehlbar ans Licht bringen würde") (301E; 244G), the combatants fight before an audience that takes the outcome as an indication of God's judgment. The problem being on this occasion that those who read the judgment of God are forced to read a second time, differently.

If ultimately the figure of righteousness proves to be Friedrich, the immediate outcome of the duel is quite the opposite. Jacob the Redbeard receives only the most trifling of scratches, a "small and apparently insignificant wound" ("dem Anschein nach unbedeutenden Wunde") (312E; 254–55G).

> The two knights . . . lunged at one another. Sir Friedrich wounded the Count with his very first blow, injuring him with the point of his not especially long sword just where, between arm and hand, his armour was linked together; but the Count . . . found . . . it was only that the skin was superficially scratched, and . . . he pressed forward again . . . with renewed vigor, like a perfectly whole man. (303E)

> Beide Ritter . . . gingen auf einander los. Herr Friedrich verwundete gleich auf den ersten Hieb den Grafen; er verletzte ihn mit der Spitze seines, nicht eben langen Schwertes da, wo zwischen Arm und Hand die Gelenke der Rüstung in einander griffen: aber der Graf . . . fand, daß, . . . nur die Haut obenhin geritzt war: dergestalt daß er . . . den Kampf, mit erneuerten Kräften, einem völlig Gesunden gleich, wieder fortsetzte. (245G)

Friedrich, however, is carried from the field of battle with dire and undeniably mortal wounds. The chamberlain is thus declared guilty before he is proven innocent, for it is only with the passage of time that he recovers and his opponent lies moribund. As Friedrich says: "Where lies the obligation of the highest divine wisdom to indicate and utter the truth in the very moment of pious invocation?" ("Wo liegt die Ver-pflichtung der höchsten göttlichen Weisheit, die Wahrheit im Augen-blick der glaubensvollen Anrufung selbst, anzuzeigen und auszu-sprechen?") (311E; 254G). All is well that ends well, one might claim, for if, like Friedrich von Trota, justice seems to endure enormous blows, in the end both the chamberlain and the law of God's truth apparently heal "without suffering any mutilation" ("ohne irgend eine Verstümmlung an seinem Körper zu erleiden") (305E; 248G).

But what of the last lines of "The Duel," lines that one hesitates to call a conclusion, so radically do they question that concept?

> After the wedding the Emperor hung a chain of honor around Sir Friedrich's neck; and . . . as soon as he had again arrived in Worms, he had inserted in all the statutes of the holy and sacred duel—everywhere where it was presupposed that it would result in the guilt coming immediately to the light of day—the words "when/if [wenn] it is the will of God." (318E)

> Der Kaiser aber hing Herrn Friedrich, nach der Trauung, eine Gnaden-kette um den Hals; und sobald er . . . wieder in Worms angekommen war, ließ er in die Statuten des geheiligten göttlichen Zweikampfs, überall wo vorausgesetzt wird, daß die Schuld dadurch unmittelbar ans Tageslicht komme, die Worte einrücken: "wenn es Gottes Wille ist." (261G)

"The Duel" seems to dissolve the disparities of *Prinz Friedrich von Homburg,* replacing the Elector as judge with the more reliable figure of God. On second reading, however, his representative, the Emperor, notes a dislocation in the apparently seamless closure of the text, understanding all too well that there is a small wound in the happy ending. The thrust of "The Duel" would seem to be a celebration of the justice of God and his inevitable proclamation of truth. But "where is the mortal, and were the wisdom of all the ages his, who would dare to interpret the mysterious dictum" uttered in this duel ("wo ist der Sterbliche, und wäre die Weisheit aller Zeiten sein, der es wagen darf, den geheimnisvollen Spruch . . . auszulegen?") (306E; 248G). Where is the mortal—for this is the Emperor's final point—who can read the word of God in any such struggle of warring claims to the figure of truth? For the words that the Emperor inserts, the small rupture he creates in the present text of the law, are "when/if it is the will of God" ("wenn es Gottes Wille ist"). Were it certain that God wishes to make the truth known, the timing would still be in question. As one learns in the case of this duel, God's revelation can be indefinitely deferred. His interpreters can never be sure that they read his signs at the proper moment and thus can never be sure that they read properly.[4] The story that began with an act of legitimation, of making into law, ends with the inverse gesture, with a small but significant hesitation, an apparently trifling scratch in the smooth surface of the word.

One cannot help suspecting, then, that what takes place here is less like the miraculously healed wounds of Friedrich than like the wound of Jacob.

> An extremely decayed condition of his humours prevented . . . the healing of the wound and all the art of the doctors who were called in . . . did not avail to close it. Indeed a corroding . . . pus ate its way cancerlike through the whole system of his hand down to the bone so that . . . it proved necessary to amputate the entire wasted hand, and later—when even this did not put an end to the voracity of the pus—the arm itself. . . . As his entire body gradually decomposed in pus and rot, the doctors explained that there was no way to save him. (312E)

> Ein äußerst verderbter Zustand seiner Säfte verhinderte . . . die Heilung derselben, und die ganze Kunst der Ärzte, die man . . . herbeirief, vermochte nicht, sie zu schließen. Ja, ein ätzender . . . Eiter, fraß auf eine krebsartige Weise, bis auf den Knochen herab im ganzen System seiner Hand um sich, dergestalt, daß man . . . genötigt gewesen war, ihm die ganze schadhafte Hand, und späterhin, da auch hierdurch dem Eiterfraß kein Ziel gesetzt ward, den Arm selbst abzunehmen. . . . Die Ärzte, da sich sein ganzer Körper nach und nach in Eiterung und Fäulnis auflöste, erklärten, daß keine Rettung für ihn sei. (255G)

The small emendation of the law that the Emperor inserts is, after all, not only a change in a text located on the other side of the literary work in the fictional content. It opens as well the apparent closure of the literary text entitled "The Duel," for it will now never be certain that the tale is really over, that the conclusion we read is God's ultimate revelation. It lays open to contention as well, for the infection of uncertainty festers on increasingly larger scales, the legitimacy of those satisfying commentaries on Kleist's other texts that "The Duel" performs.

The matter in question in the law, as the final passage indicates, is immediacy (*Unmittelbarkeit*): "he had inserted . . . everywhere where it was presupposed that it would result in the guilt coming *immediately* to the light of day . . . the words 'when/if . . .'" ("[Er] ließ . . . überall wo vorausgesetzt wird, daß die Schuld dadurch *unmittelbar* ans Tageslicht

komme, die Worte einrücken: 'wenn . . .?' ") (emphasis mine). If in
Michael Kohlhaas there is a strain of longing for immediate presence,
"The Duel" inscribes its naiveté quite pointedly, counterbalancing that
hope with the if and when of God's whims.[5] Indeed nothing in this story
takes place im-mediately, without mediation.

The initial thrust of the plot is to find and arrive at the figure
responsible for taking the life of the monarch. One traces the weapon
that emptied the throne—ironically an object manifestly emblematic of
pointing—from the body of the duke to all parts of Germany, finally to
Strasbourg, where the arrow returns to the chancellor, who gives it to
the duchess, who reluctantly sends it on to Jacob the Redbeard. But in a
verbal sleight of hand that convinces his audience (and, just as likely,
first-time readers) Redbeard both acknowledges and deflects the instrument of indication.

Where the arrow as emblem of direct indication fails, a form quite
its opposite seems to succeed. For even before the arrow circulates, it is a
question of rings, rings given to track devotion and identity and ultimately used to point the finger. To prove his innocence before the
court, Redbeard reveals where he was that fated night. As he himself will
put it, missing an irony that cannot yet be understood, he tells the secret
that should have waited for a more definitive judgment day, the secret of
a night spent with his unlikely lover, Littegarde von Auerstein. Redbeard's accusation, when it reaches her father, is accompanied by the ring
given Littegarde by her husband, stolen by the maid who had played the
role of her mistress in the lover's tryst and passed to Redbeard that Saint
Remigius night. The circulation of this ring back to its owner mismarks
Littegarde as the figure of guilt, but another ring, its counterpart, despite these involutions seems to find its way to the story's villain. For
Redbeard, too, had given his lover a ring, from *his* first spouse. Rosalie,
his lover in the dark of night, takes it in her mistress's stead and later
passes it on to the court in which she has brought suit against Redbeard;
from there it is carried to Basel and delivered to the dying Redbeard. On
receiving the ring, Jacob calls to be carried to the pyre where Friedrich
and Littegarde are to die—punishment for taking false oath before God.
Here Redbeard announces what only the appearance of the ring has
revealed to him, the innocence of Littegarde.

Mediation, it would seem, finds its mark here, reaches an endpoint
from which it need no longer be displaced and deferred. But that, too, is
not quite the end of the story, for in thinking one has arrived at an end,

one far too readily forgets the beginning. In the beginning it was a question of murdering the figure of authority, but the duel, in fact—this is the point—has nothing whatever to do with the question. The Emperor calls upon the duke to appear before his court and to account for two points: "how [his] arrow . . . had come into the hands of the murderer? Also: at which third place he had passed the night of Saint Remigius" ("wie der Pfeil . . . in die Hände des Mörders gekommen? auch: an welchem dritten Ort er sich in der Nacht des heiligen Remigius aufgehalten habe") (292E; 234G).

> Duke Jacob . . . appeared before the bar of the court, and with the passing over of the first, as he alleged, to him completely insoluble question, he spoke as follows, in relation to the second, the one decisive for the matter in contention. (292E)

> Der Graf Jakob der Rotbart . . . [erschien] vor den Schranken des Gerichts . . . und sich daselbst, mit Übergehung der ersten, ihm, wie er vorgab, gänzlich unauflöslichen Frage, in Bezug auf die zweite, welche für den Streitpunkt entscheidend war, folgendermaßen faßte. (234G)

Redbeard passes over the first question, which, despite his claims, is the critical point. He sets the second to mediate in its stead, and with a rhetorical flourish that is as illogical as it is false, he sets it as the force that closes the possibility of mediated action.

> Since you wish to know why it is neither probable nor even possible that I took part—either personally or indirectly [*mittelbar*]—in the murder of my brother, learn that on the night of Saint Remigius . . . I was secretly visiting the beautiful . . . Frau Wittib Littegarde von Auerstein. (293E)

> Weil ihr denn wissen wollt, warum es weder wahrscheinlich, noch auch selbst möglich sei, daß ich an dem Mord meines Bruders, es sei nun persönlich oder mittelbar, Teil genommen, so vernehmt, daß ich in der Nacht des heiligen Remigius . . . heimlich bei der schönen . . . Frau Wittib Littegarde von Auerstein war. (235G)

Redbeard's presence at a third place is irrelevant to the matter of his innocence:[6] as it turns out, while he is at that third place he uses a third person to perform the deed.

That this fact comes to the light of day has nothing to do with the duel, which only concerns whether or not Redbeard spent the night in the arms of Littegarde. For Redbeard has wagered the duel assuming that God would follow the letter of the contest rather than its spirit. If truth is revealed, it is hardly through the word of God. Redbeard chooses to add it as an afterthought, and as an answer to a question directed—how could it be otherwise?—to a third person. In the last paragraph of the story, just as the Emperor is about to lead the now delivered Littegarde off to the imperial palace, he happens to turn to the doctor at his side and ask whether there is any chance of recovery for the miserable Redbeard.

> "No hope!" answered Jacob the Redbeard . . . "and I have deserved the death I am suffering. Since the arm of worldly justice will no longer overtake me, know, then, that I am the murderer of my brother . . . the villain who struck him down with the arrow from my armory was hired by me six weeks before to perform the deed that was to have secured me the crown." (317E)

> "Vergebens!" antwortete Jakob der Rotbart . . . "und ich habe den Tod, den ich erleide, verdient. Denn wißt, weil mich doch der Arm der weltlichen Gerechtigkeit nicht mehr ereilen wird, ich bin der Mörder meines Bruders . . . der Bösewicht, der ihn mit dem Pfeil aus meiner Rüstkammer nieder warf, war sechs Wochen vorher, zu dieser Tat, die mir die Krone verschaffen sollte, von mir gedungen!" (260G)

He who wishes to secure crown and scepter thinks to have mastered the powers of indirection. Redbeard substitutes the question of his love affair for the question of how his arrow found its mark in the body of his brother, whose crown and scepter he so coveted. But Rosalie, his counterpart in guile as well as name, has done him one better, taking the place of her mistress and thus deceiving the would-be master of mediation. The critical issue of the text is less the eradication of a specific figure of authority than the general crisis of authority engendered where the mediate and immediate cannot be distinguished.[7] What one wishes to call truth can never escape this indeterminacy and is thus nowhere to be fixed.

Could this be more evident than in the performance of the duel itself, that Punch-and-Judy show that proves to be so utterly beside the point? The manner of its staging is a commentary on the desire for unmediated presence, made manifest by the audience that observes and inevitably at play as well in the audience that reads Kleist's tale.

Under the light of the midday sun (301E; 243G), as though full light could be shed on the scene, a huge crowd has gathered to witness the sacred verdict of arms. In a sense the battle is over before they know

it, for Sir Friedrich wounds Redbeard with the very first blow. But it is
not only the consequences of that initial scratch that remain hidden to
view.

> Sir Friedrich stood his ground . . . as though he wished to take root there:
> he dug himself into the earth . . . up to his spurs, up to his ankles and
> calves. The fight had already lasted an hour . . . when once again a
> disapproving grumbling arose among the spectators on the platform. This
> time, it would seem, it was aimed, not at Count Jacob who did not lack for
> zeal in pressing the struggle to a conclusion, but at Sir Friedrich's
> entrenching himself in the selfsame spot and his bizarre . . . refraining
> from any attack of his own. Although his tactics may have rested on good
> grounds, Sir Friedrich felt too sensitive not to sacrifice them immediately.
> (303–4E)

> Herr Friedrich stand . . . auf dem Boden, als ob er darin Wurzel fassen
> wollte, da; bis an die Sporen grub er sich, bis an die Knöchel und Waden
> in dem . . . Erdreich ein. . . . Schon hatte der Kampf . . . fast eine Stunde
> gedauert: als sich von neuem ein Murren unter den auf dem Gerüst
> befindlichen Zuschauern erhob. Es schien, es galt diesmal nicht den
> Grafen Jakob, der es an Eifer, den Kampf zu Ende zu bringen, nicht fehlen
> ließ, sondern Herrn Friedrichs Einpfählung auf einem und demselben
> Fleck, und seine seltsame . . . Enthaltung alles eignen Angriffs. Herr Frie-
> drich, obschon sein Verfahren auf guten Gründen beruhen mochte, fühlte
> dennoch zu leise, als daß er es nicht sogleich . . . hätte aufopfern sollen.
> (246G)

What the audience demands is not only a good performance but one that
is quite literally a *Schauspiel,* a play whose action and conclusion take
place before their eyes. Sir Friedrich may have "good grounds" for his
strategy of concealing the ground on which he stands. For until called to
relinquish it, he holds the position that keeps his spurs, ankles, and calves
hidden from view.

That his spurs remain hidden from view would seem to be critical
to holding his own. For no sooner are those spurs (*Sporen*), which in
German, etymologically, speaks of traces (*Spuren*), forced by popular
demand into the light of day than we begin to learn the lesson of their
necessary concealment.

> But already in the first moments of the thus altered combat, Sir Friedrich
> had a mishap that did not quite seem to indicate the presence of higher
> powers ruling over the struggle: entangling his footstep/footprint [*Fuß-
> tritt*] in his spurs, stumbling, he fell, and while he sank to his knees . . .

Count Jacob the Redbeard, in not exactly the most noble and chivalrous manner, thrust his sword into the exposed side. (304E)

Aber schon in den ersten Momenten dieses dergestalt veränderten Kampfs, hatte Herr Friedrich ein Unglück, das die Anwesenheit höherer, über den Kampf waltender Mächte nicht eben anzudeuten schien; er stürzte, den Fußtritt in seinen Sporen verwickelnd, stolpernd abwärts, und während er . . . in die Kniee sank, stieß ihm Graf Jakob der Rotbart, nicht eben auf die edelmütigste und ritterlichste Weise, das Schwert in die dadurch bloßgegebene Seite. (246G)

The audience takes in with its own eyes what it so longed to see, a conclusion to the holy verdict of arms in which truth, as we are told so often in this tale, is unfailingly brought to light (301E; 244G)—never mind that that truth is irrelevant to the larger issue at hand—a conclusion performed only as the result of an insistence on seeing Friedrich's spurs and the ground on which he stands. The problem being that when that ground is laid open to view, in the strange image that Kleist weaves for us, we see footsteps caught in spurs, or footprints enmeshed in traces. What God reveals to the spectators, precisely because they insist on bringing the ultimate foundation of the struggle to the light of day— although we are forewarned that this is not necessarily the sign of a higher power—what God reveals to the spectators, if he reveals anything at all, is not quite "truth" but an entanglement of traces.

"The Duel" functions, then, more as an ironical commentary on the desire to resolve the struggles of Kleist's other texts than as a reassuring transvaluation of their uncertainties. There is, however, one text that his last story reads less to resolve a tale of uncertainty than to unsettle a tale that traditionally has betokened reconciliation with God. In this manner Kleist's narration might be seen to unravel not only the law of the holy combat before God but also, as with *Wuthering Heights,* a passage from that other sacred text, the Bible. There can be no doubt that "The Duel" is an ironical restaging of the scene of Jacob's struggle at Penuel. The Jacob of the Old Testament is folklorically regarded as struggling with an angel, and Jacob's opponent in Kleist's tale is also repeatedly associated with the angels.[8]

The episode in Genesis takes place unexpectedly just as Jacob returns to his homeland after twenty years of exile, an exile imposed on him by his fear of Esau's wrath. For Jacob through that renowned act of deception had put himself in place of his brother, firstborn of the twins and implicitly the rightful heir to the patrilineage of Abraham and Isaac. Jacob claimed his father's blessings with a far greater success in displacing his brother than Jacob the Redbeard. As the biblical usurper returns home, in a passage that immediately precedes his reunion with Esau and disrupts the progression of the narration,[9] Jacob comes to the Jabok, and here a far more formidable version of the rival appears.

> [32.24]And Jacob was left alone; and a man wrestled with him until the breaking of the day. [25]When the man saw that he did not prevail against Jacob, he touched the hollow of his thigh; and Jacob's thigh was put out of joint as he wrestled with him. [26]Then he said, "Let me go, for the day is breaking." But Jacob said, "I will not let you go, unless you bless me." [27]And he said to him, "What is your name?" And he said, "Jacob." [28]Then he said, "Your name shall no more be called Jacob, but Israel, for you have striven with God and with men, and have prevailed." [29]Then Jacob asked him, "Tell me, I pray, your name." But he said, "Why is it that you ask my name?" And there he blessed him. [30]So Jacob called the name of the place Peniel, saying, "For I have seen God face to face, and yet my life is preserved." [31]The sun rose upon him as he passed Penuel, limping because of his thigh. [32]Therefore to this day the Israelites do not eat the sinew of the hip which is upon the hollow of the thigh, because he touched the hollow of Jacob's thigh on the sinew of the hip.[10]

Our folk tradition has it that Jacob struggles with the angel of God and wins his blessing, an answer in a sense to a prayer he had offered up to God shortly before. It takes no great biblical scholar to note, however, that something is out of joint in this reading,[11] for just like Jacob the Redbeard, the future patriarch is crippled by a blow that hardly seems capable of violent effect, a mere touch upon the hollow of his thigh. Even as the text claims victory for Jacob, it has him limp from the scene of triumph.

That victory is openly proclaimed, nevertheless: the "man" saw that he did not prevail against Jacob, and even after delivering the crippling blow, he must beg Jacob to release him and pay the price demanded. What Jacob has won is the blessing of God, but as in the case of the dueling count of Kleist's story, that declaration of blessedness, despite the conventional reading, proves to be somewhat questionable. What Jacob wins, after all, is a new name. He loses the name Jacob, which repeatedly in the Old Testament designates its bearer as a cheat.[12] Gerhard von Rad's commentary tells us that although the original name *yaᶜaqōb* suggested "May God protect," the passage allows a more outrageous etymology to take over, here and elsewhere, deriving the name Jacob from the word *heel* (ʿāqēb).[13] For in a passage immediately prefiguring Jacob's taking of Esau's birthright, the younger twin is said to have come into the world already holding his brother's heel (Gen. 25.26). Jacob's blessing entails, then, losing his name and (if *Jacob* is to betoken *heel*) casting aside his past infamy perhaps but perhaps losing as well a name that bespeaks God's protection.

The entanglement of signs in this passage, which refuses to reveal once and for all the ground they stand on, alongside the implicit desire for a more simplistic and immediate comprehension of their significance, has only begun. For at the same time that Jacob loses a name whose loss can be doubly read, he gains the name of Israel. His opponent explains the meaning of that name: "Your name shall no more be called Jacob, but Israel, for you have striven with God and with men, and have prevailed" (Gen. 32.28). And yet once again—how can it be coincidental?—the original linguistic meaning of that name is quite other, indicating not the triumph of Jacob in his struggle with God and his messenger but rather a call to the continued mastery of God: "May God rule."[14] Jacob's blessing, as the saying goes, is mixed, for if it is said to proclaim his victory over God, the name that victory gains him would seem to proclaim almost the reverse as well.

All this takes place with the asymmetric posing of the same question: "And he said to him 'What is your name?'" (Gen. 32.27). Where Jacob gives a straightforward answer, the angel replies with a question: "Then Jacob asked him, 'Tell me, I pray, your name.' But he [the angel] said, 'Why is it that you ask my name?'" (Gen. 32.29). Why indeed? The knowledge of the name promised, to be sure, a power over the named.[15] This figure, we begin to suspect, throws Jacob out of joint less by an unlikely touch to the thigh than through a series of strange articulations. He is that which cannot be named, not only because he is a (representative of) God but also because he is at once the force of unnaming, renaming, and misnaming. He leaves Jacob, or rather Israel, limping, who now repeats the folly of all his misunderstandings by naming the place of his struggle, or rather misnaming it. For Jacob calls the place Peniel, a pun on the Hebrew word for "face," *panim:*[16] "for I have seen God face to face" (Gen. 32.30), he claims. Jacob would seem bound not only to read the false etymology of the name Israel literally ("for you have striven with God and with men, and have prevailed") but to suppress at the same time the ambiguous double "name" that the angel ascribes to himself (God and man). Like Jacob the Redbeard and the audience of the duel, the future patriarch reads literally and believes that God's presence can be experienced face to face. He represses the possibility that God speaks through a messenger (Angelus), indirectly, and that he might let one message mediate for its opposite. He represses, then, the possibility that God, like Jacob, might be a cheat, something of a wolf in sheep's clothing, pulling one's leg, holding one's heel, and touching one's thigh.

What unravels the biblical passage is a second reading that follows from the rent in Kleist's story. Yet it was always there for any reader who insisted on laying open to view the fundamental ground of those aberrant etymologies over which the struggle takes place. What it opens to view as well is the entanglement that we call criticism, a question of interpretation all along at stake in Kleist, as well as in Brontë and Shelley, a question that reaches its fictional culmination when Kleist tells stories about telling stories in the tales of "Improbable Veracities."

8

The Style of Kleist

Already, no doubt, there has been a misunderstanding. Perhaps it could not be otherwise. For to construe Kleist's *style* in the conventional sense of the word (and in the conventional sense of Kleist criticism), as a "mode of expressing thought in language"[1] or as that which "impressed the stamp of his being,"[2] would be to miss the point. The point on which the anecdote "The Style of God" ["Der Griffel Gottes"] openly insists and which one finds at play throughout Kleist's work as a surreptitious strain is the style he borrows from no less a figure than God—style, that is, in the sense of stylus.

You will wonder why I seem to stress the *instrument* of writing rather than its *form*.[3] It is more a tactical than a definitive gesture. To be sure, the German word *Griffel* signifies "style" only in the first sense—of "implement"—but this explanation is at best convincing and hardly hits the mark. It is not a question of privileging the instrument of inscription as even more immediate to the author than the outward manifestations of his texts. The style (stylus) of Kleist is impossible to get a handle on: in his own words, we find it as elusive as a flash of lightning. It is perhaps most expedient in fact to turn to Kleist's own words, to cite them in entirety, since the anecdotal brevity of "The Style of God" complies with the most radical economies of space.

In Poland there was a countess [*Gräfin*] von P——, an elderly lady who led a very evil life and tormented especially her subordinates, almost to death, by her stinginess and her cruelty. As she was dying, this woman bequeathed her fortune to the convent that had given her absolution, in exchange for which the convent erected in the church-yard a costly gravestone, moulded in bronze, on which, with great pomp, mention was made of these facts. The next day, lightning struck the gravestone, melting

171

the bronze, and left nothing standing but a number of letters which, read together, said: she is condemned! The incident (let the scribes [*Schrift-gelehrten*] clarify it) is established [*gegründet*]; the gravestone still exists, and there are men living in this city who have seen it, together with the aforementioned inscription.

In Polen war eine Gräfin von P. . . . , eine bejahrte Dame, die ein sehr bösartiges Leben führte, und besonders ihre Untergebenen, durch ihren Geiz und ihre Grausamkeit, bis auf das Blut quälte. Diese Dame, als sie starb, vermachte einem Kloster, das ihr die Absolution erteilt hatte, ihr Vermögen; wofür ihr das Kloster, auf dem Gottesacker, einen kostbaren, aus Erz gegossenen, Leichenstein, setzen ließ, auf welchem dieses Um-standes, mit vielem Gepränge, Erwähnung geschehen war. Tags darauf schlug der Blitz, das Erz schmelzend, über den Leichenstein ein, und ließ nichts, als eine Anzahl von Buchstaben stehen, die, zusammen gelesen, also lauteten: *sie ist gerichtet!*—Der Vorfall (die Schriftgelehrten mögen ihn erklären) ist gegründet; der Leichenstein existiert noch, und es leben Männer in dieser Stadt, die ihn samt der besagten Inschrift gesehen. (*KL* 2.263)[4]

In this manner the 1810 reader of the *Berliner Abendblätter* was confronted by a stroke of wit, Kleist's wit and God's. Yet the reader could not fail to be impressed by the moral gravity of the report. God's humor offers above all a serious lesson, the striking immediacy of his communication reminiscent (in more ways than meet the eye) of the Old Testament God as he spoke to Moses on Mount Sinai. His gesture is made in the service of a just sentence; his judgment seems the calculated and appropriate recompense for a life of sin. What could be more clear-cut than the message "she is condemned!"?

Nevertheless, to modify an old saying, God writes in strange ways. His mode of communication here is no less unsettling than it was in "The Duel." His mode of writing, his lightning style, is a violence performed upon another text, and until we note the intentions of the first inscription, we cannot delineate the unprecedented thrust of the one that follows.

That primary inscription, the epitaph of the Countess von P——, is itself a monument to textual sleight of hand. Hardly a simple memorial to perpetuate the actuality of the recently departed, it speaks, we are told, of an elaborate chain of exchanges. Once having received absolution from a cloister, the countess wills it her fortune. In return for this the convent erects a gravestone whose text details the grounds of its own production—the potlatch to the death that obscures the true nature of the noblewoman. If the epitaph thus writes off the original figure it commemorates to display instead the splendor of her gift, this is in complicity with the absolution it also mentions. The memorial functions as a forgetting, just as absolution effects a wiping clean of the slate.

The tablet prefigures, then, its own tabula rasa. Is not this, after all, what the style of God in turn produces: a more complete erasure of the slate, a total de-figuration? Does not the word of God raise the stakes of obliteration, but this time in the name of an even and closed exchange, punishment repaying sin, the moral ground of justice thus ultimately reestablished,[5] the same promise seemingly offered in *Michael Kohlhaas*.

We have only to refer to our most authoritative definition of *style* (the first given in the *Oxford English Dictionary*) to realize that no such simple truth is at work here.

> I. Stylus, pin, stalk.
> 1. *Antiq.* An instrument made of metal, bone, etc., having one end sharp-pointed for incising letters on a wax tablet, and the other flat and broad for smoothing the tablet and erasing what is written : = STYLUS.

The style is no less an instrument of erasure than one of incision, one end fitted out for each of its operations. Only with God's/Kleist's stylus, we never know which end is up: it incises and erases at the same time, incises *by* erasing.

If we wish to understand the meaning of all this, we may be obliged to read between the letters. For the significance of God's gesture hardly finds its truth in the content of the phrase "she is condemned!" but lies rather in the mode of its production. The original epitaph masked the history of its tracing. Its message created the illusion both of a radical return to innocence through absolution and of the significant plenitude of a fortune offered in exchange for the obliteration of the countess's sins. Carried over into textual terms, the tomb inscription, by preparing a pure ground for its text, is able to set itself up as an autonomous and meaningful writing. It establishes its own law and thus affirms power and control of that law's intention. The style of God, however, functions, not by erasing this text in turn, in order to lay a purer ground for another pronouncement, but rather by *partially* obliterating the epitaph it belies. It thus disclaims the autonomy and authority usually carried by the figure of God, for the origin of the inscription is less the speaker-writer than another text in the process of being dis-scribed. How could it be otherwise in an anecdote in which even the overt theme is the death and condemnation of a *Gräfin,* a "writer" in the etymological sense of the word. Nor is the form of God's style as incisive as one might suppose. If it renders questionable authority and content (of the epitaph as well as of its own sentence of condemnation), it does this not by privileging form but rather by way of a gesture of de-formation. Form, content, and authority—each of these categories is both inscribed and erased.

Nothing could be clearer in light of another of Kleist's texts, the 1799 poem "Hymne an die Sonne." The "Hymn to the Sun" is an apparently faithful recasting of Schiller's "Hymn to the Infinite" ("Hymne an den Unendlichen"), in which the twenty-two-year-old pays proper tribute to the master poet. But when Kleist's 1810 anecdote alludes in turn to this youthful endeavor, the pious reverence for the authority, content, and form of the original text has all but vanished: it plays upon the poem in much the same fashion as God's inscription recasts the epitaph. "The Style of God" results from a flash of lightning aimed at the hymn that closes with these lines:

> Look! He rolls it [his wheel of flame] upwards! The nights, how they
> flee—
> Shining, the god writes his name there,
>   Written there
>   With the stylus [*Griffel*] of the ray,
> "Creatures, do you pay homage to me?"
> —Shine forth, Lord! We pay homage to you! (after Schiller)
> July 13, 1799   Heinrich Kleist

> Sieh! Er wälzt es [sein Flammenrad] herauf! Die Nächte,
>   wie sie entfliehn—
> Leuchtend schreibet der Gott seinen Namen dahin,
>   Hingeschrieben
>   Mit dem Griffel des Strahles,
> "Kreaturen, huldigt ihr mir?"
> —Leuchte, Herrscher! wir huldigen dir! (nach Schiller)
> den 13. Juli 1799   Heinrich Kleist

(*KL* 1.44)

The discrepancy between the two texts is more than striking. To be sure, Kleist's signature is appended to the poem as though to assert a continuity of hand, but can it be any less significant, then, that the anecdote of the *Berliner Abendblätter* appeared anonymously? The signature of God has become as illegible in the later work as that of Kleist. However, in the poem, geared to culminate in an autographic epiphany, God is the very figure of readability. He writes his name in the heavens and establishes a thoroughly reassuring communication with man, who answers the inscription with the immediate and symmetrical response, "Shine forth, Lord! we pay homage to you!" Here the style of God is a shining ray (*"Griffel des Strahles"*) summoned and welcomed throughout the hymn as that which will dispel the darkness of night. The lightning style of the anecdote offers no such illumination; it is hardly a light by which to read. The bolt leaves nothing but a "number of letters" to which the only response possible is the questionable task of "read[ing them] together," of writing off the blanks that destroy the continuity of the text. Explanation is relegated to the ironized possibility of the parenthetical quip "let the scribes clarify it." Enlightenment (*Erklärung*), if it is indeed to take place, must be sought outside the dazzling clarity of that momentary flash, for those who have witnessed the incident seem merely to have seen but not understood it. For our explanation we are sent to the scribes, which is to say, to those who not only write but also are learned in the nature of the written text and its interpretation [*Schrift-gelehrten*]. And what sort of illumination will those who write texts offer if not another flash of lightning, an interpretation that tells us that the style of God condemns us to literate illiteracy?

Before we get beyond ourselves and beyond the anecdote, let us note that not only Kleist's juvenilia but the very pillar of German letters is at stake. The bolt of "The Style of God" is directed no less at Goethe's *Faust* than at the "Hymn to the Sun." The stormy relationship between Kleist and Goethe is, of course, very common knowledge, and it has been documented with such scholarly clarity, by Katharina Mommsen in particular,[6] that we cannot claim to be making a radically original mark in that field. "The Style of God," however, sheds a slightly different light on the intertextual struggle.

Like the "Hymn to the Sun," *Faust I* closes with a reassuring word from God. In this, the famous dungeon scene, the final lines are a play between the voice of Mephistopheles and those of moral rectitude, God's voice and Gretchen's. As Gretchen gives herself up to the judgment of God,

MEPHISTOPHELES
   She is condemned!
VOICE [*from above*]
                                    Is saved!
MEPHISTOPHELES [*to Faust*]
                                    Come to me!
   [*Disappears with Faust*]
VOICE [*from within, fading*]
   Heinrich! Heinrich!

MEPHISTOPHELES
   Sie ist gerichtet!
STIMME [*von oben*]
                                    Ist gerettet!
MEPHISTOPHELES [*zu Faust*]
                                    Her zu mir!
   [*Verschwindet mit Faust*]
STIMME [*von innen, verhallend*]
   Heinrich! Heinrich!⁷

If Goethe's stage directions give priority to an alliance of the voice "from above" and "from within," Kleist disorients this scenario such that the stylus from above destroys all sanctity of the coherent internal voice. As God writes, he disrupts the text that promises salvation, indeed speaks in the voice and plays the role of Goethe's Mephistopheles, citing his lines and belying the word of Goethe's God. The cohort of the Mephistophelean voice (I indicate the point, well recognizing its lack of *intentional significance*) is, here as there, a certain Heinrich.

Elsewhere in Kleist we find another cohort of the devil who is singularly less adept at riddling the context of this intertextual play. In the short story "The Foundling" ("Der Findling"), the construct of which is so encumbered with locked passageways, with secrets and their obscured solutions, it is the logograph of his own name that appears to open all doors for Nicolo, to provide him with the ultimate password. While playing with the ivory letters of his name, *Nicolo* transposes them to read *Colino:* "Nicolo thought he had discovered the key"⁸ ("so glaubte Nicolo den Schlüssel . . . gefunden zu haben" [*KL* 2.211]). In this moment of self-naming, he thinks to discover evidence that his passionate desire for his adoptive mother is reciprocated, for in *Colino* he recognizes the name he has heard Elvire whisper with such adoration.

The reader knows better. Early in the story Colino is identified as the young Genoan who sacrificed his life to save Elvire fifteen years before. Nevertheless, an uncanny likeness binds Nicolo to his anagrammatic double. Nicolo so resembles a painting of the knightly hero that, appropriately masqueraded, he twice throws Elvire into a sudden faint. This likeness is first revealed by the voice of childhood innocence and clarity, by Klara, the little daughter of Nicolo's lover Xaviera.

> But how stunned Nicolo was when little Klara (as the daughter was called), as soon as he had raised the curtain, exclaimed, "God my father! Signor Nicolo, who else is it but you?" Xaviera was dumbfounded. The picture, in fact, the more she looked at it, the more striking seemed its likeness to Nicolo, especially when she imagined him . . . in the knight's costume he had worn . . . when he had secretly been with her at the carnival. (*TMO* 240)

> Doch wie betroffen war Nicolo, als die kleine Klara (so hieß die Tochter), sobald er nur den Vorhang erhoben hatte, ausrief: "Gott, mein Vater! Signor Nicolo, wer ist das anders, al Sie?"—Xaviera verstummte. Das Bild, in der Tat, je länger sie es ansah, hatte eine auffallende Ähnlichkeit mit ihm: besonders wenn sie sich ihn . . . in dem ritterlichen Aufzug dachte, in welchem er . . . heimlich mit ihr auf dem Karneval gewesen war. (*KL* 2.208)

But are we to believe the voice of clarity? For if the reader "knows better," it is not because he or she knows clearly or knows more; it is certainly not because he or she hears the voice of truth and reason. What is it exactly that the reader knows? The whole question is peculiarly veiled, perhaps doubly so. Klara announces the identity of Nicolo and Colino as soon as the curtain is raised, but that same curtain rises once again, this time on a slightly different scene. Nicolo has dressed himself once again in garments "exactly like those the image wore" ("genau so, wie sie das Bild trug") (*TMO* 244; *KL* 2.212) and attempts now to replace that image.

> He slipped into Elvire's bedroom, covered the picture in the niche with a black cloth, and . . . striking the very same pose as that in which the young patrician was portrayed, awaited Elvire's adoration. . . . He had calculated quite correctly; for a few minutes later Elvire entered the room, undressed in placid silence, and drew back, as she was accustomed to do, the silk curtain covering the niche—which no sooner had she done and perceived him standing there than she cried, "Colino, my love!" and fell in a dead faint to the floor. Nicolo emerged from the niche; he paused for a moment . . . but, as there was no time to lose, he picked her up in his arms

and, while pulling down the black cloth from the painting, carried her over to the bed. (*TMO* 244–45)

[Er] schlich . . . sich . . . in Elvirens Zimmer, hing ein schwarzes Tuch über das in der Niche stehende Bild, und wartete . . . ganz in der Stellung des gemalten jungen Patriziers, Elvirens Vergötterung ab. Er hatte auch, im Scharfsinn seiner schändlichen Leidenschaft, ganz richtig gerechnet; denn kaum hatte Elvire, die bald darauf eintrat, nach einer stillen und ruhigen Entkleidung, wie sie gewöhnlich zu tun pflegte, den seidnen Vorhang, der die Nische bedeckte, eröffnet und ihn erblickt: als sie schon: Colino! Mein Geliebter! rief und ohnmächtig auf das Getäfel des Bodens niedersank. Nicolo trat aus der Nische hervor; er stand einen Augenblick . . . hob sie aber bald, da keine Zeit zu verlieren war, in seinen Armen auf, und trug sie, indem er das schwarze Tuch von dem Bild herabriß, auf das . . . Bett. (*KL* 2.212)

If Nicolo has miscalculated, can we simply ascribe it to the unexpected return of Elvire's husband, an event that soon takes place with all the overwhelming force for which Kleist's descriptions are renowned? This would seem to be the only explanation, and yet it ignores a small detail of the text, almost lost in the rapid succession of more meaningful actions. Why does Nicolo tear the black cloth from the painting, having so carefully placed it there just a few lines earlier, especially when, as we are told, "there was no time to lose"? There is no logical reason for him to do so, nor is it clear that he acts intentionally. If Nicolo's calculations go awry, it is less because his father rushes into the picture than because the picture (of Colino) reasserts itself to disown Nicolo as its offspring.[9] It appears on the scene, shedding its second veil, not in order to reveal a secret but to reestablish the enigma that governs the relationship between Colino and Nicolo (an enigma, not unsimilar perhaps, to that of Lisbeth-Elisabeth in *Michael Kohlhaas*). The game is that of the logogriph, and Nicolo's plans to imitate, coincide with, and usurp his double simply are not in the rules.

What are the rules of logogriphic play? For all its apparent centrality in Kleist's text, there is little we can say definitively about it. The logogriph operates as a word riddle, as a puzzle about words in which a certain word is to be formed from the transposed letters of another. It operates quite literally (and etymologically) as a word riddle (*logos griphos*), as a sifter of words in which—but here is the catch: in this cradle of words nothing is caught, for the logogriph breaks the integrity of the word, passing it on as mere letters that ultimately elude the grasp.

Unless, of course, there is a solution, as one would always like to suppose there is. Yet the solution to the riddle is always its dissolution. This is what Nicolo cannot grasp. The solution to the logograph, Nicolo, is not and can never be identical with him. No black cloth will remain to permanently veil the other. Moreover, while *Colino* may be the logogriphic answer to the enigma *Nicolo,* it offers no ultimate unriddling. That answer is in turn the question, the puzzle whose solution could be *Nicolo,* riddle and solution perpetually producing one another, with no word more the one than the other.

This is precisely how the logograph functions in the particular context of our story, for no sooner do we see *Colino* as the solution to the riddle *Nicolo* than we are faced with the new and unanswerable riddle of their relationship. What did it mean, then, to insist that the reader "knows better" than Nicolo? Perhaps little better than nothing. If he or she knows that Nicolo and Colino are not identical, there is, nevertheless, no conclusive explanation for their similarity. Why the anagrammatic correlation of the two, and why is this compounded by the uncanny physical resemblance between the painting and the foundling? Here the narrative remains silent, and the silence and secrecy are obstinately maintained to the very last line of the narrative, taking place, as it does, "completely in silence" ("ganz in der Stille") (*KL* 2.215, my translation).

If "The Foundling," no less than "The Style of God," remains silent on this question of intertextual enlightenment, I might tell of a third story where this enigma of the relations among texts that succeed and resemble one another is explicitly stressed: "Improbable Veracities" ("Unwahrscheinliche Wahrhaftigkeiten").[10] I should warn my readers in advance, at the risk of rendering them overly self-conscious, that despite appearances, this is not the relation of three improbable anecdotes but rather the story of someone who tells three stories.

Kleist never lets us forget it, however carried away we may be by the trajectories of the stories. For the narrative is repeatedly disrupted by reflections on the incredibility of its material. Let us attempt, nevertheless, to veil its brokenness, to restore a certain order, to create a sense of unity, in order to fulfill our critical obligations. "To be sure the entire task [is] calculated more as a deception than as an actual restoration of the bridge" that links the three together.[11] But I am sure the reader will understand.

The first story takes place in the Rhine campaign of 1792. The narrator tells of a soldier who continues to march in rank and file despite a bullet wound through the chest. His fellow soldiers cannot believe their eyes, for they see "the hole in front . . . where the bullet had entered, and another in back . . . where it had left" ("das Loch vorn . . . wo die Kugel eingeschlagen hatte, und hinten ein anderes . . . wo sie wieder herausgegangen war") (*KL* 2.278). That evening an army surgeon explains the deceptive wound. He finds "that the bullet, having ricocheted [*zurückgeprellt*] from the breastbone, which it had lacked the force to penetrate, had slid between the ribs and skin . . . around the entire body, and in back, since it ultimately hit against the backbone, had gone back to its original perpendicular direction and had once again broken through the skin" ("daß die Kugel vom Brustknochen, den sie nicht Kraft genug gehabt, zu durchschlagen, zurückgeprellt, zwischen der Ribbe und der Haut . . . um den ganzen Leib herumgeglitscht, und hinten, da sie sich am Ende des Rückgrats gestoßen, zu ihrer ersten senkrechten Richtung zurückgekehrt, und aus der Haut wieder hervorgebrochen war") (*KL* 2.278).

So much takes place (or fails to take place) in this narrative that one is at a loss to locate its central point except, perhaps, by telling the second story. It is the story of an enormous block of stone at a quarry several hundred feet above the river Elbe, poised to fall. The narrator and his friend, like many other inhabitants of the city, come daily to the spot in the hopes of catching the moment of the stone's descent. But this story, like the first, opens with the historical parameters of time (1803) and place (Königstein) only to speak of a moment missed and of a displacement. Like the officers in the first story, who witness only the result of the shot, so here the moment of force is closed to the perceiver, and only its "result" may be recounted. The effect of the fall is felt by a barge, laden with wood, in the river below. Deflected from its course, the barge is stranded on the opposite shore, where the narrator himself has witnessed the efforts to put it back on course. This, indeed, is the only content of his eyewitness report. This effect, like that of the ricochet, is a certain indirection, for the stone upsets all expectations by falling on the narrow strip of land between the wall of rock and the river, rather than in the water. "An Elbe barge . . . that was the result of this fall, was, by means of the pressure of the air that was thus produced, an Elbe barge was placed on dry land" ("Ein Elbkahn . . . das war die Wirkung dieses Falls gewesen, war, durch den Druck der Luft, der dadurch verursacht worden, aufs Trockne gesetzt worden") (*KL* 2.279).

Our third story also tells of an unexpected deflection across the river, and of a simultaneous lapse in perception. And once again that lapse in the powers of the eye is marked by a violence that fails to take its proper place. Just as the gunshot fails to enter the core of the soldier's body, just as the stone fails to hit the barge directly, so here an explosion produces its remarkable effect upon a cadet officer without hitting its mark. The scene is the historically renowned 1585 siege of Antwerp by the Duke of Parma, who had blocked access to the city with a bridge of ships stretched across the Schelde. The Antwerpian forces attempted to break the blockade by sending fire ships to explode the bridge.

> "In that moment, gentlemen, in which the vessels float down the Schelde to the bridge, there stands, observe well, a cadet officer on the left bank of the Schelde right next to the Duke of Parma: now, you understand, now the explosion takes place, and the cadet, complete with flag and pack and without the slightest thing happening to him on this journey, stands on the right bank. And the Schelde is here, as you will know, a small cannon shot wide."
>
> "Did you understand?"

> "In dem Augenblick, meine Herren, da die Fahrzeuge die Schelde herab, gegen die Brücke, anschwimmen, steht, das merken Sie wohl, ein Fahnen-junker, auf dem linken Ufer der Schelde, dicht neben dem Herzog von Parma; jetzt, verstehen Sie, jetzt geschieht die Explosion: und der Junker, Haut und Haar, samt Fahne und Gepäck, und ohne daß ihm das mindeste auf dieser Reise zugestoßen, steht auf dem rechten. Und die Schelde ist hier, wie Sie wissen werden, einen kleinen Kanonenschuß breit."
>
> "Haben Sie verstanden?" (*KL* 2.280)

Can one really survive this trip without the least thing happening? In this, the only tale from a remote historical past, the account is reduced to two moments in the narrative present. Like the prestidigitator who chants "Now you see it, now you don't," our narrator calls upon us to see ("observe well") the cadet now on this side of the Schelde, now on the other, to make the passage with him in a manner of speaking. Despite this insistence on our perceptive understanding ("now, you under-stand") and knowledge ("as you will know"), we are, of course, bound to miss the connection. For if the listeners venture to answer yes to the query "Did you understand?" it is only insofar as they admit the lapse.

You will have remarked, no doubt, that the text has surreptitiously shifted its locus. What had previously diverted the listeners is suddenly diverted to the listeners. More than ever, they have become the subject matter of the text. For the first time, the officer incorporates the audience's reaction into the actual telling of his tale. If the auditors were stunned by the first story and skeptical about the second, we know of this only by way of an impersonal third-person commentator. Why should this shift take place here? It is no longer a question of the (absent) presence of the officer at the scene, of a would-be witness, who mediates between reality and the audience. The distance between the two figures has, in a sense, collapsed. This is because of the sudden deflection from the improbable realm of storytelling to the surer ground of fact, or so it would seem. The narrating officer no longer maintains a privileged position with respect to the event: both he and his audience have become listeners, interpreters of a more authenticated text, the text of history.

If the perceiver of the first two tales, as well as the listener, has suffered from the internal rupture of disbelief, history appears at the end of Kleist's text to close the wound. It is here, where all possibility of immediate perception, of "catching the moment," is lost, that, paradoxically, the "irreproachability of the sources" is guaranteed.[12] It is not the storytelling officer, of course, who sets things straight, for he has abruptly jumped the scene, you understand.

> "Did you understand?"
> Go to the Devil! shouted the country gentleman.
> I have spoken! said the officer, took his walking stick and hat and left.
> Captain! called the others laughing—Captain!—They wanted at least to know the source of this fantastic story that he claimed to be true.
> Let him go, said a member of the gathering: the story [*Geschichte*] is in the appendix to Schiller's History of the Revolt of the United Netherlands, and the author notes expressly that a poet should not make use of this fact; the history writer [*Geschichtschreiber*], however, because of the irreproachable nature [*Unverwerflichkeit*] of the sources and the agreement of the witnesses is compelled to take it up.

> "Haben Sie verstanden?"
> Himmel, Tod und Teufel! rief der Landedelmann.
> Dixi! sprach der Offizier, nahm Stock und Hut und ging weg.
> Herr Hauptmann! riefen die andern lachend: Herr Hauptmann!—Sie wollten wenigstens die Quelle dieser abenteuerlichen Geschichte, die er für wahr ausgab, wissen.
> Lassen Sie ihn, sprach ein Mitglied der Gesellschaft; die Geschichte

steht in dem Anhang zu Schillers Geschichte vom Abfall der vereinigten Niederlande; und der Verfasser bemerkt ausdrücklich, daß ein Dichter von diesem Faktum keinen Gebrauch machen könne, der Geschichtschreiber aber, wegen der Unverwerflichkeit der Quellen und der Übereinstimmung der Zeugnisse, genötigt sei, dasselbe aufzunehmen. (*KL* 2.280–81)

Who is this "member of the gathering," the auditor who suddenly speaks in place of the storyteller, and is the effect simply a reassuring shift of ground from the voice of fictional narrative to that of history? Truth to tell, we are hard put to say just where we stand. This intervention establishes the bridge to history and thus guarantees the historical veracity of Kleist's story while in the same breath announcing the poet's inevitable abuse of that text. As readers of what seems, then, neither history nor story and yet somehow both, we might well feel compelled to take up Schiller's historical text "because of the irreproachable nature of the sources."

This source is rather disconcerting, for in its account of the explosive journey across the Schelde there is a slight deviation from the officer's tale.[13] "A whirlwind seized a young man from the Duke's bodyguard on the bridge near the Flemish coast and flung him over the entire stream to the Brabantian shore without his receiving any other injury but a small wound on the shoulder as he fell" ("Einen jungen Menschen von des Herzogs Leibwache ergriff auf der Brücke, nahe an der Flandrischen Küste, ein Wirbel, und schleuderte ihn über den ganzen Strom auf das Brabantische Ufer, ohne daß er eine andere Beschädigung als eine kleine Verletzung an der Schulter beim Herabfallen erhielt") (*SCH* 290). Kleist effaces the scar of that small wound. This should not astonish us, since all three anecdotes are about a violence that does not take place, making this small erasure understandable in the interest of good fiction. But the fiction of violence that fails to leave its mark is all the better when one considers the context in Schiller's history. There the effects of the explosion are nothing short of apocalyptic.

> He has just traversed the bridge . . . when the mine ship hits the bridge and flies up with a terrible grinding explosion as though heaven and earth were being hurled down. The mighty river is stirred up to its very ground and surges furiously over its bank. . . .
>
> What a horrible theater offered itself to him here! . . . So terrible beyond all description was the devastation of the explosion. Never since the discovery of gun powder had comparable forces of it been reported.

> Kaum hat er die Brücke zurückgelegt, . . . da stößt das Minenschiff an die
> Brücke, und fliegt mit einem entsetzlichen zermalmenden Knall auf, als
> stürzten Himmel und Erde zusammen. Der Mächtige Strom wird bis auf
> den Grund aufgewühlt, und tritt zürnend über seine Ufer heraus. . . .
> Welch ein entsetzliches Schauspiel bot sich ihm hier dar! . . . So über
> alle Beschreibung schrecklich war die Verwüstung der Explosion. Nie
> hatte man seit Erfindung des Pulvers von ähnlichen Wirkungen desselben
> gehört. (*SCH* 287–88)

Even this omission is not, perhaps, in and of itself significant.
Giving meaning to a lapse is in any case problematic throughout
"Improbable Veracities." Critical for our understanding, however, are
the events that follow, for the attempt is made to repair the damage, or at
least to pretend to repair it.

> Hardly has he [the Duke of Parma] recovered from his first stupefaction
> when he orders Georg Basta . . . to prepare the bridge, the bulwarks and
> all the sentries on the bank, to reestablish order, . . . and since still no
> enemy appears, he decides forthwith to reconstruct the bridge. . . . With a
> dreadful noise of drums and trumpets, in order to drown out the din of
> those working, the debris is taken away and in the very same night the
> opening in the bridge is . . . closed again. To be sure, the entire task was
> calculated more as a deception than as an actual restoration of the bridge.

> Kaum hat er [der Herzog von Parma] sich von der ersten Betäubung
> erholt, so befiehlt er Georg Basta . . . die Brücke, die Schanzen und alle
> Posten am Ufer zu bereiten, die Ordnung wieder herzustellen . . . und da
> noch immer kein Feind erscheint, beschließt er, ungesäumt die beschä-
> digte Brücke wieder herzustellen. . . . Unter einem furchtbaren Geräusch
> von Trommeln und Trompeten, um das Getöse der Arbeitenden zu
> übertönen, werden die Trümmer fortgeschafft, und noch in derselben
> Nacht wird die Oeffnung in der Brücke . . . verschlossen. Freilich war
> diese ganze Arbeit mehr auf eine Täuschung als auf eine wirkliche Wieder-
> herstellung der Brücke berechnet. (*SCH* 291–92)

Much is at stake, since the restoration that takes place here is parallel not
only to the masking of the shoulder wound but also to the gesture that
closes the anecdotes, the construction of a bridge to historical sources in
order to repair the rupture occasioned by disbelief. On this point the
commentary of the historical text is nothing short of devastating. It
discloses those final lines as a din to drown out the turmoil in which the
debris created by the text is surreptitiously removed. Thus these lines
lend credence to the third story and implicitly to the first two, but like

the Duke of Parma's second bridge, this is calculated more as a deception than as a true reconstruction.

This feint was expected, however, since Schiller's text warns explicitly that if the writer of history is compelled to take up this fact because of the irrepudiability of the sources, a poet is bound to misuse it. The call to history, then, has been something of a disaster for storytelling. For when we return to the "source," we find that history refuses to be misappropriated, that it denounces the story's deceptive camouflage of epistemological violence as a misuse. What we seem to witness is the triumph of history. It establishes itself as the ultimate interpretation of fabulation and thus proves itself ethically and philosophically superior. A more significant repair of epistemological uncertainty is thus brought about in the name of history (*Geschichte*) precisely insofar as it can distinguish itself from the story (*Geschichte*). (The reader will, no doubt, perceive the difference.)

But this gesture of distinction, cited so precisely within Kleist's text as the words of the historian, is but a further fabulation: "and the author notes expressly that a poet should not make use of this fact; the history writer, however, because of the irreproachable nature of the sources . . . is compelled to take it up" (*KL* 2.281). Nowhere in the account of the fall of Antwerp do we find such a statement, although a similar reassurance about history's factual basis for reasoning does indeed appear: "As story-like and unbelievable as that seems, history gives us, nevertheless, sufficient explanation of this enigmatic event" ("So fabelhaft und unglaublich das scheint, gibt uns doch die Geschichte hinreichende Aufschlüsse über den Zusmmenhang dieses räthselhaften Ereignisses") (*SCH* 292).[14] Yet what is it that the historian finds so "story-like and unbelievable"? Not the events themselves but the "total ignorance (*Unwissenheit*) of that which had taken place at the bridge," the ignorance both of its destruction and of the illusory nature of its reconstruction.

Whether we turn to the (fictional) historical text cited within the story or to that alluded to outside it, we are reminded that the restorable integrity of the bridge (all the more so since it is metaphorical for the bridge to Schiller's text, a bridge that would ground fiction in history and repair the rupture to truth) is a calculated deception, both "story-like and unbelievable."[15] A naive insistence on the possibility of such reconstruction would be tantamount to explaining away the deflections of bullet, barge, and man, to recuperating the lost moment of perception for the onlooker, to eliminating the lapses of disbelief in the listener, to repairing all ruptures between cause and effect.

It was here we began in a sense, for the crux of our critical ordering of the stories was their common concern with a deflection and a lapse in the understanding that marked an unexpected discontinuity between cause and effect. The question of cause and effect is also Kant's, in another context, in *The Critique of Pure Reason*. This is not to raise the issue of sources, to ask along with others before us whether Kleist actually read the *Kritik*.[16] "Improbable Veracities" is, notwithstanding, a rewriting of certain moments of that text. Not that it hits its mark directly; let us just say that it throws it temporarily off course. Nor is this to repeat the tedious banalities of Kleist's Kant crisis. One is tempted, rather, to call this confrontation Kant's Kleist crisis—at the risk of disrupting our conventional concept of time-order.[17] In any case, Kleist's text does not necessarily follow from Kant's, although it might be heard as a kind of repetition, an echo of the voice of philosophy, with results that are incalculable.

If Kleist's text is about anything, it is about an incalculability in the sequence of events. A bullet that enters a man's chest and exits from his back does not wound him, an enormous block of stone falls towards the river below without hitting a passing barge, a blast of apocalyptic proportions carries a soldier to the other side of the river without a trace of violence. Yet Kant's text insists on the rule that links cause with effect.

> But it [the appearance] can acquire this determinate position in this relation of time only in so far as something is presupposed in the preceding state upon which it follows invariably, that is, in accordance with a rule. From this there results a twofold consequence. In the first place, I cannot reverse the series, placing that which happens prior to that upon which it follows. And secondly, if the state which precedes is posited, this determinate event follows inevitably and necessarily. (Smith 225)

> Aber ihre bestimmte Zeitstelle in diesem Verhältnisse kann sie nur dadurch bekommen, daß im vorhergehenden Zustande etwas vorausgesetzt wird, worauf es jederzeit, d. i. nach einer Regel, folgt: woraus sich denn ergibt, daß ich erstlich nicht die Reihe umkehren, und das, was geschieht, demjenigen voransetzen kann, worauf es folgt: zweitens daß, wenn der Zustand, der vorhergeht, gesetzt wird, diese bestimmte Begebenheit unausbleiblich und notwendig folge. (*Kritik* 249)[18]

Kant's obsessive insistence on this rule is understandable, for the consequences of being without it are devastating.

We should then have only a play of representations, relating to no object.

The experience of an event . . . is itself possible only on this assumption.

The principle of the causal relation in the sequence of appearances is therefore also valid of all objects of experience . . . as being itself the ground of the possibility of such experience.

Understanding is required for all experience and for its possibility. Its primary contribution [consists] in making the representation of an object possible at all. This it does by carrying the time-order over into the appearances and their existence. (Smith 222–27)

Wir würden auf solche Weise nur ein Spiel der Vorstellungen haben, das sich auf gar kein Objekt bezöge.

Nur lediglich unter dieser Voraussetzung allein, ist selbst die Erfahrung von etwas, was geschieht, möglich.

Der Grundsatz des Kausalverhältnisses in der Folge der Erscheinungen gilt daher auch vor allen Gegenständen der Erfahrung . . . , weil er selbst der Grund der Möglichkeit einer solchen Erfahrung ist.

Zu aller Erfahrung und deren Möglichkeit gehört Verstand, und das erste, was er dazu tut, ist . . . daß er die Vorstellung eines Gegenstandes überhaupt möglich macht. Dieses geschieht nun dadurch, daß er die Zeitordnung auf die Erscheinungen und deren Dasein überträgt. (*Kritik* 246–52)

Objectivity, experience, the possibility of representation, and the primary function of the understanding are at stake.

Why does this "carrying the time-order over into the appearances" fail to take place in "Improbable Veracities"? If we are unable to restore these continuities, we might nevertheless ask about the forces that make such restoration impossible. No answer can be ventured, of course, for the scene of immediate perception. If we are discomposed by these stories, it is not that our experience simply mirrors that of the eyewitness. As co-auditors of the officer, however, we have much to trace in the text of his narration. The force of deflection in the first tale is that of the ricochet shot (*Prellschusses*), for we are told that the bullet had ricocheted back (*zurückgeprellt*) from the breastbone to make the unbelievable journey around the soldier's body, leaving it intact. If the onlookers could not believe their eyes, the auditors cannot believe their ears: "What? asked several members of the gathering, stunned, and they thought they had not heard correctly" ("Wie? fragten einige Mitglieder der Gesellschaft betroffen, und glaubten, sie hätten nicht recht gehört") (*KL* 2.278). The listener is not only "betroffen" ("stunned") but also *getroffen* ("hit") in a way that the soldier seems not to be, and this precisely because of a "Prellschuss" ("ricochet shot") that finds its mark in his ears. If the soldier is spared by the doubling back of the bullet, the *Prellschuss* inevitably injures the listener's sense of hearing, for *prellen* means not only "to rebound" but also "to bruise," a wounding that is bound to take place despite and because of the refusal of physical violence. Need it be added that this wound in the significance of *prellen* is further aggravated, for it doubles back on itself once again in the third sense of the term, "to deceive."

What throws the listener off course in the first story is a deceptive and uncontrollable reverberation in the language of the narrator. The force of deflection in the second is even more foreign to the ear of the listener, even more difficult to calculate. The moment of the block's fall is, in the words of the officer, "remarkable, because of the thunder that reverberates [*widerhallenden*] strangely in the mountains and many other phenomena that arise from the shock to the earth that cannot be calculated" ("wegen des sonderbar im Gebirge widerhallenden Donners, und mancher andern, aus der Erschütterung des Erdreichs hervorgehender Erscheinungen, die man nicht berechnen kann, merkwürdig") (*KL* 2.279). What is the cause of this strange moment? It is anything but the kind of force we see at work at the end of the anecdote. There the narrator makes much of what he has seen with his own eyes: "These eyes saw it in the sand—what am I saying? The next day they even saw the workers who were laboring with levers and cylinders to get it afloat once again" ("diese Augen haben ihn im Sande—was sag ich? sie haben, am anderen Tage, noch die Arbeiter gesehen, welche mit Hebbeln und Walzen, bemüht waren, ihn wieder flott zu machen") (*KL* 2.279–80). What is open to the narrator's perception is the use of levers and cylinders to return the barge to its correct course. What escapes his gaze, however, is a force that makes far less sense than that of predictable, practical tools: "The workers tend, in the case of large blocks, when they can no longer get to it with tools, to throw solid objects, especially pipe stems, into the fissure, and they leave the business of fully separating the block from the cliff to the wedge-shaped [*keilförmig*] working force of these small objects" ("Die Arbeiter pflegen, bei großen Blöcken, wenn sie mit Werkzeugen nicht mehr hinzu kommen können, feste Körper, besonders Pfeifenstiele, in den Riß zu werfen, und überlassen der, keilförmig wirkenden, Gewalt dieser kleinen Körper das Geschäft, den Block völlig von dem Felsen abzulösen") (*KL* 2.279). If we cannot fathom why pipe stems in the fissure are what moves this enormous weight, we are nevertheless told that this is a "wedge-shaped [*keilförmig*] working force." These wedge-shaped bodies may seem to function similarly to the levers used on the barge, but they serve to disorder the path of progress rather than to set it straight. Moreover, the human agent is no longer a factor, and their minute size seems bizarrely inadequate to the king of stones.

How can their enormous power be explained? As in the first anecdote, the listener might well believe he has not heard correctly. What takes place is the incalculable reverberation of "keilförmig," which marks the invasion of a language made foreign to itself, a *Keilschrift* ("cuneiform writing") that repeatedly escapes human apprehension, a cuneiform force that echoes in the small fissure of the text to split assunder what seemed unmovable, with shocking results.[19]

If a predictable law of causality fails to operate in the events of each anecdote, that breakdown has its crucial point, as we have just seen, in the language of its telling. This is not solely due to a semantic disarray in the terms describing the force of deflection between cause and effect. For if we look to "Improbable Veracities" as a whole, there is a certain necessity that orders the succession of stories, although it is not that of causality. The first story does not determine those that follow. Nor is there a historical, autobiographical progression, for the personal experiences of 1792 and 1803 are followed by the 1585 siege of Antwerp. This is not to say that we are left, as Kant would have it, with "a merely subjective play of my [or Kleist's] fancy" ("nur . . . ein subjektives Spiel meiner Einbildungen" [Smith 227; *Kritik* 252]). It is a question of another order.

Any critical investigation of this text must inevitably be struck by the fact that these stories are somehow the same story. Perhaps this explains the progressive outrage of the officer's audience. The elements of the first and second—the military encounter, the woundless blasting of a man, the missed moment of perception, the journey across the river—are all at play in the last anecdote. It takes them up as if they were the miraculously preserved fragments of a great explosion, fragments, however, that are never joined together as an organic whole. This is not due to any lack of eloquent coherence in the last narrative but rather to the manner in which it echoes those that precede it. For it is not only the elements of the plot that reappear in the anecdotes but also the way in which the assembled parts transmit, or fail to transmit, order to one another.

The story of the errant bullet opens with its mark "erect, with gun and pack, in rank and file" ("stramm, mit Gewehr und Gepäck, in Reih und Glied") and ends only a few days later with a perfect restoration of order: "he once again stood in rank and file" ("so stand er wieder in Reih und Glied"). The bullet itself ricochets only for the short journey around the body of a man, then returns "to its original . . . direction" ("zu ihrer ersten senkrechten Richtung") (*KL* 2.278). The second anecdote also moves from order to disorder to order, but with somewhat less reassuring precision, for the fall of the enormous block leaves the barge stranded, and the narrator is witness only to the efforts to set it back on course, never to their success. The third narration seems to omit the gesture of recuperation altogether, for shortly after the cadet makes his journey, "complete with flag and pack" ("samt Fahne und Gepäck"), across the Schelde, the narrating officer "took his walking stick and hat and left" ("nahm Stock und Hut und ging weg") (*KL* 2.280). In a sense the commentary offered by one of the auditors might be interpreted as a gesture of this kind. At least it attempts to reinstate the narrative within the order of history, but it reveals, as we have seen, an apocalyptic disaster far greater than any previously intimated.

If time as a medium of continuity is tossed aside with deliberation in both the content and the form of "Improbable Veracities," this is not to discount the role of temporality. We are confronted in the course of the anecdotes with a discontinuous intensification of disorder, for rather than cause and effect, the driving thrust of the text is a contra-repetition. It is the force of a *Widerhallen* ("contrary-echoing") rather than a *Wiederholung* ("catching again") in their literal senses, a force that might well be said to lead nowhere, to be the refusal of narrative completion as the story becomes increasingly truncated in its repetition.

This is all the more evident if we consider yet another of the relentless lessons of history. Schiller's *History of the Revolt of the United Netherlands* is called upon as the ultimate cause of the officer's third anecdote, as the "source of this fantastic story" ("die Quelle dieser abenteuerlichen Geschichte") (*KL* 2.280). The single citation we are offered from this source, however, is not, by way of verification, about the siege but about the way in which stories and histories differ in their relationship to their sources: "that a poet should not make use of this fact; the history writer, however, because of the irreproachable nature of the sources and the agreement of the witnesses is compelled to take it up" ("daß ein Dichter von diesem Faktum keinen Gebrauch machen könne, der Geschichtschreiber aber, wegen der Unverwerflichkeit der Quellen und der Übereinstimmung der Zeugnisse, genötigt sei, dasselbe aufzunehmen") (*KL* 2.281). Let us forget for a moment that this citation is nowhere to be found in Schiller; we will remember it soon enough. What defines history is that its relationship to its sources is *unverwerflich* ("irrefutable"); they are literally incapable of being dislocated. The text of history is founded upon an "agreement of the witnesses" to which it simply adds its voice by way of corroboration. History's repetition of its sources verifies their authenticity, as though they were the necessary cause of history, but with the writer's repetition of the text of history all that is shot to pieces. What better proof do we have of this than the passage cited above, which misrepresents its historical source? For Schiller's history, as we have seen, preaches not the valorization of historical truth but the naiveté of believing possible a repair of the rupture his history has just described.

One suspects then that no *Geschichte* can escape its own disruptive repetition from history to story, and perhaps this means that it is impossible to have such a text that does not thereby ultimately become *critical* in the Kantian sense of the word (reason undertaking the task of self-knowledge [Smith 9]) and critical even beyond the limits of sense.[20] We have witnessed the uncontainable movement implicit in Kleist's text from historical sources to history, from history to its misrepresentation in story, and the self-reflection that arises from this maneuver. If in this movement Kleist's text necessarily generates a critical self-commentary, that commentary is never adequate to the object of its reflection.

Friedrich Schlegel, while citing the Kantian concept of critical philosophy as his point of departure, like Kleist, though far more explicitly, also speaks of a poesy that becomes self-critical, endlessly producing a self-commentary that exceeds its object.

> Just as one would not set great value on a transcendental philosophy that was not critical, that did not present the producer along with the product

and contain at the same time within the system of transcendental thoughts a description of transcendental thinking, so too this poesy should unite the . . . transcendental materials and exercises preparatory to a poetic theory of the poetical faculty with the artistic reflection and beautiful self-mirroring . . . and in all its presentations this poetry should present itself, and always be, at once, poesy and poesy of poesy.

So wie man aber wenig Wert auf eine Transzendentalphilosophie legen würde, die nicht kritisch wäre, nicht auch das Produzierende mit dem Produkt darstellte und im System der transzendentalen Gedanken zugleich eine Charakteristik des transzendentalen Denkens enthielte: so sollte wohl auch jene Poesie, die . . . transzendentalen Materialien und Vorübungen zu einer poetischen Theorie des Dichtungsvermögens mit der künstlerischen Reflexion und schönen Selbstbespiegelung . . . vereinigen und in jeder ihrer Darstellungen sich selbst mit darstellen, und überall zugleich Poesie und Poesie der Poesie sein. (53)[21]

Poesy of poesy may introduce "artistic reflection and . . . self-mirroring" into poesy, but this cannot be understood as a fixed philosophy of literature. Another of Schlegel's fragments shows the thrust of this maneuver to be rather philosophically disconcerting. "The entire history of modern poesy is a running [*fortlaufender*] commentary on the short text of philosophy; all art should become science and all science art; poesy and philosophy should be united" (Lyceum fragment 115) ("Die ganze Geschichte der modernen Poesie ist ein fortlaufender Kommentar zu dem kurzen Text der Philosophie: Alle Kunst soll Wissenschaft, und alle Wissenschaft soll Kunst werden; Poesie und Philosophie sollen vereinigt sein" [22]). This is not to say that poesy and philosophy, art and science, should simply be united. The "short text of philosophy" may make this optimistic proposal, but, Schlegel tells us, modern literature is a continual commentary on this short text of philosophy[22] and an ironic one at that, one that literally runs away (*fortlaufender*) from its object.

And yet it [Romantic poesy] can, better than any other, hover in the middle between the presented [*Dargestellten*] and the presenter, free of all real and ideal interest, on the wings of poetic reflection and can raise that reflection to a higher power again and again, can multiply it as in an endless succession of mirrors. . . . Romantic poetry is still becoming; indeed, that is its actual essence, that it, eternally, can only become and can never be perfected. No theory can exhaust it. . . . Romantic poetry is the only one that is more than a type, and is, as it were, the art of poetry itself, for in a certain sense all poesy is or should be Romantic. (Athenaeum fragment 116)

Und doch kann auch sie am meisten zwischen dem Dargestellten und dem Darstellenden, frei von allem realen und idealen Interesse, auf den Flügeln der poetischen Reflexion in der Mitte schweben, diese Reflexion immer wieder potenzieren und wie in einer endlosen Reihe von Spiegeln vervielfachen. . . . Die romantische Dichtart ist noch im Werden; ja das ist ihr eigentliches Wesen, daß sie ewig nur werden, nie vollendet sein kann. Sie kann durch keine Theorie erschöpft werden. . . . Die romantische Dichtart ist die einzige, die mehr als Art und gleichsam die Dichtkunst selbst ist: denn in einem gewissen Sinn ist oder soll alle Poesie romantisch sein. (39)

In this manner, Schlegel, like Kleist, jumps the limits of the Kantian sense of reason. If modern poetry is a running commentary on the naive proposal of simply uniting fiction and philosophy, this is because "in a certain sense . . . all poesy" produces its own theory only to transgress it; theory of poesy endlessly produced to become poesy of poesy. It is this production and transgression that is at work throughout this volume, most explicitly in the readings of Shelley's "Medusa" and Brontë's *Wuthering Heights*.

It is no coincidence that Paul de Man uses this last passage cited from Schlegel to elaborate the trope of irony.[23] As a critical reading not only of certain texts of Schlegel but also of "The Rhetoric of Temporality" would show, criticism and irony have a startling affinity.[24] What can it mean to pronounce criticism and irony in the same breath, however ironically? Criticism would no longer perform its traditional task of adequation, grounding the literary text in its past, be it a historical, literary, psychological, or sociological source. Criticism would, rather, be a refusal of recapitulation, its relationship to its object guaranteed by no necessity, most certainly not that of cause and effect. It would serve at once as the telos of all texts and as a deflection from the path of their progress or totalization. The critical text would put into play a disruptive repetition, the intensification of disorder that implodes all belief in narrative content by redefining the relationship of text to source. This "critical text" is the force at play within and without the literary text, a perpetual distancing between itself and the object of its reflection. It is neither fiction nor truth, unless, perhaps, both the truth of fiction and the fiction of truth.

At this point in the history of criticism this symmetrical turn of phrase may seem an empty commonplace that leaves the role of criticism ambiguous. And yet its paradox is exact. There are those, no doubt, who would prefer to eradicate that ambiguity, to situate criticism, to locate its place, to demonstrate, if possible, its determinate and necessary limits— and to do this without reverting to a criticism of adequation. Kleist's text makes this possible because, in the context of "Improbable Veracities," criticism operates with the same duplicity as *Geschichte*. Our story became history, you remember, at the height of its auditors' disbelief, and the moment when its narrator chose to jump the scene. History appeared then in the guise of a verification that could establish the story's source and thereby its authenticity. A similar if equally questionable reward is offered for doubling the notion of criticism, for demarcating the boundaries of Kleist's text, by shifting from that endlessly self-ironizing, critical voice within the text to another outside it. Displacing criticism to the authority and stylus of another, this other critical irony would then indicate a distance between criticism and its object that enables the voice of the former to calculate and reiterate the echoings of the latter. That same nameless "member of the gathering," however, who privileges history only to have it (as the result of a certain style) melt back into the story is also the figure of the external commentator, whose truth of fiction inevitably becomes the fiction of his own truth.

Geschichte-Geschichte-Kritik-Kritik: one might be tempted to read this as the ultimate story or perhaps as the ultimate interpretation, to read it as a narrative that begins in history, that becomes transfigured first to story, then to ironic self-criticism, and finally to a criticism that displaces itself outside the literary text, ironizes, deforms, dismantles, and thereby controls it. One is tempted to read it in this way because it would place us on a line of time with magnitude (however infinite), direction (however negative), and sense. For whether we read this vector away from the origin as possibly positing the horizon of a fulfillment (Friedrich Schlegel as read by the young Benjamin)[25] or as the endless displacement from its point of departure, the orientation, however negatively, is still towards the origin. Walter Benjamin's angel of history could be read as such a figure.

A Klee painting named "Angelus Novus" shows an angel looking as though he is about to move away from something he is fixedly contemplating. His eyes are staring, his mouth is open, his wings are spread. This is how one pictures the angel of history. His face is turned toward the past. Where we perceive a chain of events, he sees one single catastrophe which keeps piling wreckage upon wreckage and hurls it in front of his feet. The angel would like to stay, awaken the dead, and make whole what has been smashed. But a storm is blowing from Paradise; it has got caught in his wings with such violence that the angel can no longer close them. This storm irresistibly propels him into the future to which his back is turned, while the pile of debris before him grows skyward. This storm is what we call progress.

Es gibt ein Bild von Klee, das Angelus Novus heißt. Ein Engel ist darauf dargestellt, der aussieht, als wäre er im Begriff, sich von etwas zu entfernen, worauf er starrt. Seine Augen sind aufgerissen, sein Mund steht offen, und seine Flügel sind ausgespannt. Der Engel der Geschichte muß so aussehen. Er hat das Antlitz der Vergangenheit zugewendet. Wo eine Kette von Begebenheiten vor uns erscheint, da sieht er eine einzige Katastrophe, die unablässig Trümmer auf Trümmer häuft und sie ihm vor die Füße schleudert. Er möchte wohl verweilen, die Toten wecken und das Zerschlagene zusammenfügen. Aber ein Sturm weht vom Paradiese her, der sich in seinen Flügeln verfangen hat und so stark ist, daß der Engel sie nicht mehr schließen kann. Dieser Sturm treibt ihn unaufhaltsam in die Zukunft, der er den Rücken kehrt, während der Trümmerhaufen vor ihm zum Himmel wächst. Das, was wir den Fortschritt nennen, ist dieser Sturm.[26]

But the disposition of *Geschichte-Geschichte-Kritik-Kritik* in "Improbable Veracities" does not permit catastrophe and progress to be thus uttered in the same breath. We have seen the temporally linear and therefore satisfying schema end tragically in Kleist's text, since the narrative appendix constructs a bridge both to history and to external commentary that is doomed to disintegrate. Yet Kleist's irony is more shattering than tragic.

Although one could rightly argue that the temptations of history and external criticism are implicit throughout the narrative, they become explicit only in the text's last paragraph. One begins, then, not at the beginning but *in medias res,* with the story and its self-reflection. History and a criticism placed in the voice of the other arise only at the point where a certain ricochet (*Prellen*) within the stories sets into play an incalculable echoing that upsets the rules of causality and logic. The remedy offered by the member of the gathering is first of all the attempt to establish a linear concept of time. The "history" of his afterword not only functions as the attempt to ground the story in a prior reality but is also akin to any commentary that seeks a text's past as the resting ground for its explication.

If a return to the past through a criticism of adequation offers no escape from the maelstrom of the text, one might run on to the future, thrusting the text into a position of anteriority and inferiority in relation to a critique of differentiation, taking it apart and putting it back together in a solution as satisfying as Nicolo's rearrangement of the letters *C O L I N O.* The dilemma being, of course, that—for this is where we began—"Improbable Veracities" engulfs both these gestures. It poses, then, a *Geschichte-Kritik* whose untenable circumstances drive its claustrophobic reader-auditor to the past and then to the future in the hopes of escaping the text through another sort of *Geschichte* and another sort of *Kritik,* only to find them already included and ironized within the text. That being realized, nothing prevents—in fact all encourages—an ever more daring repetition of escape and circumscription. The result, however, for our limited reader could only be a transformation of textual claustrophobia to agoraphobia—not that there is the least thing to be afraid of—as the confines of the text endlessly expand, inevitably approaching a critical mass.

Appendix: "Improbable Veracities"

A Translation of "Unwahrscheinliche Wahrhaftigkeiten,"
by Heinrich von Kleist

"Three stories," said an old officer at a gathering, "are of the type that, although I myself completely believe them, were I to tell them, I would run the risk, nevertheless, of being taken for a windbag. For people demand of truth, as its primary requirement, that it be probable. And yet probability, as experience teaches us, is not always on the side of truth."

Tell them, called several members of the gathering, tell them!—for the officer was known as a bright and esteemed man who was never guilty of lies.

The officer said, laughing, that he wanted to oblige the company, but he explained once again beforehand that in this particular case he made no claim for their belief.

The company in return promised him their belief in advance: they simply exhorted him to speak and listened.

"On a march in the Rhine campaign," began the officer, "I noticed, after a battle we had had with the enemy, a soldier who walked erect, with gun and pack, in rank and file, although he had a shot through the middle of his chest: at least one saw the hole in front of the strap of his ammunition pocket, where the bullet had entered, and another in back, in his jacket, where it had left. The officers, who couldn't believe their eyes at this strange sight, ordered him repeatedly to go behind the front lines and get his wounds dressed; but the man assured them that he had no pain whatsoever and asked that they not separate him from his regiment for the sake of a ricochet shot [*Prellschusses*], as he called it. That evening, when we had returned to the camp, the surgeon who had been called in examined his wounds and found that the bullet, having ricocheted [*zurückgeprellt*] from the breastbone, which it had lacked the

197

force to penetrate, had slid between the ribs and skin, which stretched in an elastic manner, around the entire body, and in back, since it ultimately hit against the backbone, had gone back to its original perpendicular direction and had once again broken through the skin. Moreover, this small flesh wound gave the sick man nothing but a wound-fever, and when a few days had passed, he once again stood in rank and file."

What? asked several members of the gathering, stunned, and they thought they had not heard correctly.

The bullet? Around the entire body? In a circle?—The company had difficulty repressing their laughter.

"That was the first story," said the officer, as he took a pinch of snuff and became silent.

Good heavens! a country gentleman burst out—there you are right. This story is the kind that cannot be believed.

"Eleven years later," said the officer, "in the year 1803, I found myself with a friend in the town of Königstein in Sachsen, near to which, as is well known, about a half-hour away, at the edge of an extremely steep, perhaps three-hundred-foot-high bank of the river Elbe, there is an important stone quarry. The workers tend, in the case of large blocks, when they can no longer get to it with tools, to throw solid objects, especially pipe stems, into the fissure, and they leave the business of fully separating the block from the cliff to the wedge-shaped [*keilförmig*] working force of these small objects. It so happened that just at this time an enormous block measuring several thousand cubic feet was ready at the quarry for its fall to the surface at the bank of the Elbe. And since this moment is so remarkable, because of the thunder that reverberates [*widerhallenden*] strangely in the mountains and many other phenomena that arise from the shock to the earth that cannot be calculated, we, my friend and I, along with many other inhabitants of the city, betook ourselves every day, evenings, to the quarry, in order to catch the moment when the block would fall. The block fell, however, in the noon hour, as we were sitting at the table in the Königstein inn, and it was only at five o'clock towards evening that we had time to walk out there and to make inquiries about the circumstances under which it had fallen. But what had been the result of this fall? First of all you have to know that between the rock wall of the quarry and the bed of the Elbe was located a considerable strip of land, taking up about fifty feet in width, such that the block (which is here the important thing) fell, not directly into the water of the Elbe, but rather onto the sandy area of this strip of land. An Elbe barge, gentlemen, that was the result of this fall, was, by means of the pressure of the air that was thus produced, an Elbe barge was placed on dry land—a barge that was about sixty feet long and thirty wide, heavily laden with wood, lay on the other, opposite bank of the Elbe. These eyes saw it in the sand—what am I saying? The next day they even saw the workers who were laboring with levers and cylinders to get it afloat once again and to get it down from the bank and back into the water. It is probable that the whole Elbe (the surface of it) overflowed for a moment, spilled over the other flat bank, and left the barge there, it being a solid object, just as a piece of wood remains on the edge of a flat vessel when the water on which it drifts is shaken."

And the block, asked the company, did not fall into the water of the Elbe?

The officer repeated: no!

Strange cried the company.

The country gentleman was of the opinion that he knew how to choose well those stories that would verify his proposition.

"The third story," the officer continued, "took place in the war of independence of the Netherlands, at the siege of Antwerp by the Duke of Parma. The duke had blocked the Schelde river by means of a bridge of ships, and the Antwerpers were working on their side, under the leadership of a talented Italian, to explode the bridge by means of fire boats which they launched against it. In that moment, gentlemen, in which the vessels float down the Schelde to the bridge, there stands, observe well, a cadet officer on the left bank of the Schelde right next to the Duke of Parma: now, you understand, now the explosion takes place, and the cadet, complete with flag and pack and without the slightest thing happening to him on this journey, stands on the right bank. And the Schelde is here, as you will know, a small cannon shot wide."

"Did you understand?"

Go to the Devil! shouted the country gentleman.

I have spoken! said the officer, took his walking stick and hat and left.

Captain! called the others laughing—Captain!—They wanted at least to know the source of this fantastic story that he claimed to be true.

Let him go, said a member of the gathering: the story [*Geschichte*] is in the appendix to Schiller's History of the Revolt of the United

Netherlands, and the author notes expressly that a poet should not make use of this fact; the history writer [*Geschichtschreiber*], however, because of the irreproachable nature [*Unverwerflichkeit*] of the sources and the agreement of the witnesses is compelled to take it up.

—Berliner Abendblätter, 10 January 1811

Notes

Preface: The Dagger of Language

1. See the preface to Paul de Man's *The Rhetoric of Romanticism* (New York: Columbia University Press, 1986); the introduction to Cynthia Chase's *Decomposing Figures* (Baltimore: Johns Hopkins University Press, 1986); the first chapter of Thomas Weiskel's *The Romantic Sublime* (Baltimore: Johns Hopkins University Press, 1976); and Philippe Lacoue-Labarthe and Jean-Luc Nancy's *The Literary Absolute,* trans. Philip Barnard and Cheryl Lester (Albany: State University of New York Press, 1988).

Chapter 1. On Looking at Shelley's Medusa

1. Stanzas 1–5 are taken from Percy Bysshe Shelley, *The Complete Poetical Works of Percy Bysshe Shelley,* ed. Thomas Hutchinson (Oxford: Clarendon Press, 1904), 646–47. The "Additional Stanza" is from a transcript by Mary Shelley, *Bod. MS Shelley adds. d.,* 97, 100.

2. The poem appears in full in Percy Bysshe Shelley, *Selected Poetry,* ed. Neville Rogers (London: Oxford University Press, 1968), 357–58.

3. Irvin Kroese, *The Beauty and the Terror* (Salzburg: University of Salzburg, 1976).

4. Mario Praz, *The Romantic Agony* (New York: Meridian, 1956), 25. For a rebuttal of Praz's argument see Jerome McGann, "The Beauty of the Medusa," *Studies in Romanticism* 11 (1972): 3–25.

5. Two contemporary critics have written with exceptional insight on the problematics of this text, although, strangely enough, in order to do so they fix their critical glances on quite another object. It is a question, to begin with, of the figure under whose aegis a version of this essay was first published (*Yale French Studies* 69 [1985], *The Lesson of Paul de Man,* 163–79). To publish under the aegis of Paul de Man, however—perhaps this goes without saying—is not to write under his protection or patronage. Nor will an erasure of the dictionary definition in favor of the mythical origin of the term set things straight. The aegis was the singularly adorned shield borne by Pallas Athene. To be sure, she was

also the provider of that very different shield whose brazen glare allowed Perseus to contemplate the Medusa while escaping the powers of its gaze. Nowhere in de Man's work does he make such a gesture. He may offer us a mirror of sorts, but his writings, more like that other shield borne by the goddess herself, are an aegis to which the head of the Medusa is affixed and which we contemplate at our own risk. One aspect of those writings, especially in de Man's later criticism, is a rhetoric of temporality in which a complex temporal strategy drives the critical enterprise. It is the metaphor of time that opens a reflective space, enables a semblance of knowledge, and, coincidentally, elaborates a theory of figural language while ironizing all sense of theoretical progress (see my essay "Allegories of Reading de Man" in *Reading de Man Reading*, ed. Lindsay Waters and Wlad Godzich [Minneapolis: University of Minnesota Press, 1988]). What takes place in Shelley's poem might be called a rhetoric of spatialization, for "On the Medusa of Leonardo da Vinci" does with the space what de Man performs with time. If that places this essay under de Man's critical aegis, it places it under the aegis of his irony. Also of considerable critical significance is Louis Marin's *Détruire la peinture* ([Paris: Galilée, 1977], 117–80), in which he offers a remarkable analysis of what it means to observe Caravaggio's painting *The Head of the Medusa* and at the same time, of necessity, comments on that other Medusa at the Uffizi.

6. Neville Rogers, "Shelley and the Visual Arts," *Keats-Shelley Memorial Bulletin* 12 (1961): 16–17. Rogers was the first to publish the sixth stanza and also the first to give the text well-warranted critical attention.

7. If so, we could then attribute to the literary text, in Shelley's terms, a fundamental "wisdom," for in "Adonais" Shelley speaks of "wisdom the mirrored shield" (line 240). To be sure, he speaks of Keats, and perhaps all exemplary poets, failing to wield it.

8. See Rogers, "Shelley and the Visual Arts," 13.

9. See also lines 9, 33, 38, and 46.

10. Charles Baudelaire, "Une Mort héroïque," in *Oeuvres complètes* (Paris: Pleiade, 1964), 269–73.

11. "A Defence of Poetry," in Percy Bysshe Shelley, *Shelley's Poetry and Prose,* ed. Donald P. Reiman and Sharon B. Powers (New York: Norton, 1977), 505.

12. The word *strain* appears quite often in Shelley's poetry, most often with the sense of a strain of poetry or music. For a reading counter to this one see McGann, "The Beauty of the Medusa," 7. McGann reads the poem rather as "an allegory about the prophetic office of the poet and the humanizing power of poetry." Daniel Hughes also sees here the hope of the poet that the " 'melodious hue of beauty' might 'humanize and harmonize the strain.' " It makes sense, then, that he goes on to read Shelley's position as that of a "reverse Perseus" who could escape the threat of transformation to stone, mastering the Medusa as he brings "under his own submission this now 'identified' monster of thought" ("Shelley, Leonardo, and the Monsters of Thought," *Criticism* 12 [1970]: 204–5).

13. The poem imitates or describes the painting, but within the poem the image of another mode of reflection also takes place.

14. See Paul de Man, *Blindness and Insight* (Minneapolis: University of Minnesota Press, 1983), 285–86.

15. The first stanza of the "Hymn to Intellectual Beauty," for example, is an attempt to define that elusive poetic force through a long series of similes whose terms of comparison seem peculiarly at odds with one another. Thus the "awful shadow" is compared to "moonbeams," floating to creeping, "hues of evening" to the colorless "clouds in starlight," "harmonies" to "memory of music fled." Like the figures in the "Medusa," those of the hymn mark the refusal of language to define by affirming an identity. Intellectual beauty, its inconstancy, is nothing if not this refusal, a denial, then, of those conventional concepts of language as naming or invocation, the "frail spells" and "poisonous names" of the later lines. On related questions in the "Hymn to Intellectual Beauty" see Jonathan Baldo, "A Semiotic Approach to Prospection in Shelley," *Semiotica* 64 (1987): 279–96. An extended study of such gestures in Shelley would have to confront the figure of Demogorgon in *Prometheus Unbound*.

16. This critical moment of figurative language as uncreation pivots, ironically enough, around the verb *grow*. Ironically enough because it upsets, of course, all that the concept of growth would seem to guarantee, a linear progression with a sense of origin. As the involutions of stanza 5 will show, figural language upsets as well that particular temporal and spatial ordering implicit in the title of the poem—Medusa : painter : painting : poet : poem : reader.

17. In these same lines the rock becomes watery, while shortly thereafter the air becomes solid. The poem is riddled with such unpredictable reifications and unshapings.

18. On the question of an implicit double reading throughout Shelley's work see J. Hillis Miller's fine essay "The Critic as Host," in Harold Bloom et al., *Deconstruction and Criticism* (New York: Seabury Press, 1979), 217–53.

19. Bk. 7 of *The Republic*.

20. Plato, *The Republic,* trans. Benjamin Jowett (New York: Vintage, 1955), 257.

21. The poem is a parody only of a literal reading of that text, since Shelley's "Medusa" might well be viewed as an enlightened allegory of all that takes place in Plato's passage. Just as Shelley's Medusa repeats the scene within the cave, so Plato echoes that scene in the voice of Socrates. For the philosopher, in narrating his parable, as one cannot fail to note, repeats the structure he denounces. He stands, as it were, behind Glaucon and asks him to "Behold" "in a figure how far our nature is enlightened or unenlightened" (253). One might argue that Glaucon and Socrates are, nevertheless, at least one level of reflection beyond that of those they observe; the same might be said for the Medusa, as we shall see.

22. Rogers, "Shelley and the Visual Arts," 16.

23. Intermittently because the entire poem functions like the vaporous mirror, ever shifting between a mimetic concept of reproduction (stanzas 1, 4, 6) and another that has yet to be traced. Those seemingly simple descriptive moments, therefore, are, from the very beginning, *images* of the mimetic.

24. *The Compact Edition of the Oxford English Dictionary.*

25. On the question of fragmentation in relation to self-knowledge and mirroring see Paul de Man, "Shelley Disfigured," in Bloom et al., *Deconstruction and Criticism,* 40, 45, and 55.

26. Daniel Hughes makes the link between "kindling" and the poetic act in Shelley's poetry in "Kindling and Dwindling: The Poetic Process in Shelley," *Keats-Shelley Journal* 13 (1964): 13–28.

27. See *Prometheus Unbound* 2.4.72: "He gave man speech, and speech created thought."

28. "Defence," 480. All future references to this text will simply be noted as page numbers within the text proper.

29. On the more general question of the relationship of metaphor and power in Shelley, and for a thorough review of the secondary literature, see Jerrold Hogle's superb essay, "Shelley's Poetics: The Power as Metaphor," *Keats-Shelley Journal* 31 (1982): 159–97.

30. The passage refers to the works of Francis Bacon.

Chapter 2. Unbinding Words

1. Unless otherwise indicated, references to *Prometheus Unbound* are to act, scene, and line. All citations are from *Shelley's Poetry and Prose,* ed. Donald H. Reiman and Sharon B. Powers (New York: Norton, 1977).

2. See also 1.405–7.

3. Quite understandably, almost all of Shelley's readers insist on the teleological structure of the drama, though many have been struck by the difficulties of locating the action. To name just two typical examples: Milton Wilson, *Shelley's Later Poetry* (New York: Columbia University Press, 1957), 42, 50, 56; and Carlos Baker, who reads the first act as containing the complete "moral reformation of Prometheus" (98) and therefore "the hour of the world's redemption" (92) (*Shelley's Major Poetry* [New York: Russell and Russell, 1961]).

4. Percy Bysshe Shelley, "Passages from Faust," in *The Complete Works of Percy Bysshe Shelley,* ed. Roger Ingpen and Walter E. Peck, 10 vols. (New York: Gordian, 1965), 7:277–78.

5. Johann Wolfgang Goethe, *Goethes Faust* (Hamburg: Christian Wegner, 1963); translations are my own.

> It stands written: "In the beginning was the *Word!*"
> Here I already falter! Who will help me to go on?
> Impossible for me to value the word so highly,
> I must translate it differently,
> If I am indeed enlightened by the spirit.
> It stands written: In the beginning was the *sense.*
> Ponder well the first line,
> Lest your plume rush on too fast!
> Is it the *sense* that effects and creates everything?
> It should read: In the beginning was the *force!*
> But even as I write this down,

Already something warns me that I will not stick with it.
The spirit will help me! Suddenly I find counsel
And solaced write: In the beginning was the *deed!*

(1.1224–37, emphasis mine)

6. See, e.g., Peter Butter, *Shelley's Idols of the Cave* (Edinburgh: Edinburgh University Press, 1954), 175; Earl Wasserman, *Shelley: A Critical Reading* (Baltimore: Johns Hopkins Press, 1971), 259; and Meyer Abrams, *Natural Supernaturalism* (New York: Norton, 1971), 302.

7. *Prometheus Unbound,* perhaps more than any of Shelley's texts that display a similar theme of liberation or revolution, compels its reader to search for the necessity of its dramatic development or temporal sequence. Thus Shelley's interpreters have often sought to show, if not the inevitability of each element on the path, at least the undeniable logic of its place in the progression (see, e.g., Baker, *Shelley's Major Poetry,* 92, 102, 109; Wilson, *Shelley's Later Poetry,* 101; Butter, *Shelley's Idols,* 175–76; and Wasserman, *Shelley,* 277, 289, 298. For Wasserman, however, Shelley's doctrine of Necessity is one of causality, but it is not teleological [313–15]).

8. Most of Shelley's readers see this as the crucial moment (see, e.g., Baker, *Shelley's Major Poetry,* 92, 98; Butter, *Shelley's Idols,* 173; and Abrams, *Natural Supernaturalism,* 303. See also Lawrence Zillman's gloss of early readings with a similar bent; *Shelley's "Prometheus Unbound,"* ed. Lawrence Zillman [Seattle: University of Washington Press, 1959], 350–51, 400). For readings counter to this sense of an early ending see Frederick A. Pottle, "The Role of Asia in the Dramatic Action of Shelley's *Prometheus Unbound,*" in *Shelley: A Collection of Critical Essays,* ed. George M. Ridenour (Englewood Cliffs, N.J.: Prentice-Hall, 1965), 133–43, who reads Asia's action in act 2 as efficacious, a reading that we will shortly question; and also Stuart M. Sperry, "Necessity and the Role of the Hero in Shelley's *Prometheus Unbound,*" *PMLA* 96 (January 1981): 243–44. Sperry also gives a partial gloss of the literature on the question, as does Susan Hawk Brisman. The latter, in a fine essay on the question of voice, points out that what is at stake here is larger problems of language ("'Unsaying His High Language': The Problem of Voice in *Prometheus Unbound,*" *Studies in Romanticism* 16, no. 1 [1977]: 51–52).

9. See Brisman, "'Unsaying,'" 61. William Hildebrand ("Naming-Day in Asia's Vale," *Keats-Shelley Journal* 32 [1983]: 190–203) sees no problem of logic or language here, but "the spiritual economy of the drama" whereby Prometheus must suffer the passion of the grief his words have brought about. In fact, what has been revoked, according to Hildebrand, is "the tyranny of phenomena that results from the mind's 'misuse of words and signs'" (192).

10. Butter, *Shelley's Idols,* 173, in conjunction with the interventions in *Times Literary Supplement,* 16 December 1955, 6, 20 January 1957, and 15 February 1957.

11. *The Compact Edition of the Oxford English Dictionary.*

12. Brisman, "'Unsaying,'" 60.

13. Ibid., 74–75.

14. See Dana Polan, "The Ruin of a Poetics: The Political Practice of *Pro-*

metheus Unbound," *Enclitic* 7 (1983): 38–39. Polan briefly recognizes the implications of the pun *recall* but sees *Prometheus Unbound* as a text that "moves from stasis to stasis." The full complexity of the play of *recall,* however, involves a refusal of any possibility of stasis.

15. Generated by Prometheus's desire to hear his own voice is a crisis in the possibility of communication. For a hundred lines in the interchange between Earth and her son, Prometheus complains of the inarticulate voice he hears:

PROMETHEUS
Who dares? for I would hear that curse again. . . .
Ha, what an awful whisper rises up!
'Tis scarce like sound. . . .

(1.131–33)

Obscurely through my brain like shadows dim
Sweep awful thoughts, rapid and thick,—I feel
Faint . . .

(1.146–48)

Earth nevertheless insists on the necessity of speaking a language incomprehensible to the gods, the language of the dead.

THE EARTH
                         How canst thou hear
Who knowest not the language of the dead?
PROMETHEUS
Thou art a living spirit—speak as they.
THE EARTH
I dare not speak like life, lest Heaven's fell King
Should hear, and link me to some wheel of pain
. . . .
THE EARTH
                         No thou canst not hear:
Thou art immortal, and this tongue is known
Only to those who die . . .

(1.137–51)

Yet just when Prometheus so eloquently bemoans the voice that makes him faint with uncertainty, he nevertheless gives evidence of perfect comprehension. The crisis becomes, then, not that of Prometheus alone, whose attention to his mother's speech is alternately punctuated by perplexity and apparent understanding, but also that of Shelley's readers, who, with good reason, have found it impossible to define the tenor and the logic of this exchange. (For a summary of some of the earlier critical response see Zillman, *Shelley's "Prometheus Unbound,"* 354–55.) If the gods cannot understand the language of the dead, how does Prometheus understand his mother's speech, and why does she, in turn, assume that Jupiter, himself a god, on hearing the language of the dead will comprehend enough to take revenge on the shade who speaks? (1.209–18).

The necessity of this interchange is to empty language of its fullness—one way or the other. Earth claims to speak, and Prometheus to hear, a language that cannot be properly articulated. For we who understand, who hear—or at least read—the words with little trouble, the logic between what is said about the words and what is said by the words is disruptive. For very different readings of this predicament see Wilson, *Shelley's Later Poetry*, 61; Wasserman, *Shelley*, 266; and for a far more optimistic vision, Norman Thurston, "The Second Language of *Prometheus Unbound*," *Philological Quarterly* 55 (1976): 126–32.

16. Wasserman reads this passage as Prometheus facing his former moral self (*Shelley*, 260). In a sense this is certainly true, but the confrontation is also between two modes of language, or, more accurately, between Prometheus's desire for a confirmation of self-identity through language and the figure's refusal.

17. Tilottama Rajan ("Deconstruction or Reconstruction: Reading Shelley's *Prometheus Unbound*," *Studies in Romanticism* 23, no. 2 [1984]) reads this moment as one in which "Asia discovers the right method of reading," a "process of moving beyond the linguistic sign to the language of the eyes" (324, 325). In the tale that she tells of successful interpersonal communication serving as "a model for the dialogue intended to occur between the author and the actual reader," it is quite telling that Rajan reads neither the narration of Panthea's dream nor Ione's reaction to it. Rajan's article is admirable for its careful attention to detail in key moments of the text. One has difficulty, however, in following an argument that uses the term *deconstruction* in a manner that differs so pointedly from that of Derrida.

18. This echoes the structures of open-endedness (hope, love, doubt, and desire) brought about by Prometheus and of which the Furies speak in act 1, lines 542–45.

19. Hildebrand sees this as quite the opposite ("Naming-Day," 197–98).

20. Robert Graves, *The Greek Myths*, 2 vols. (Aylesbury: Penguin, 1955), 1:78–79.

21. Ovid's version is that Hyacinthus catches the missile thrown by his lover—as though to mark the danger of catching that thrown by the god of poetry.

22. The second dream displaces the shape in Panthea's eyes (2.1.131–33).

23. Baker ascribes to Asia the fullest powers of interpretation based on her encounter with Panthea (*Shelley's Major Poetry*, 104). Her dialogue with Demogorgon, however, would seem to belie this.

24. See Wasserman, *Shelley*, 322.

25. See Tilottama Rajan, *Dark Interpreter* (Ithaca: Cornell University Press, 1980), 89–90.

26. In "A Defence of Poetry," in *Shelley's Poetry and Prose*, 505.

27. Given the exchange between Asia and Demogorgon, Demogorgon's commentary on "the deep truth" can hardly be read as a simple defeat for Shelley (see Richard Harter Fogle, "The Abstractness of Shelley," in Ridenour, *Shelley*, 170, 176; see also Ross Grieg Woodman, *The Apocalyptic Vision in the Poetry of Shelley* [Toronto: University of Toronto Press, 1964], 136).

28. See above, chap. 1.

29. The weaving of harmonies here recalls another, suppressed interweaving earlier in the text. In act 1, Earth talks of the "two worlds of life and death" (line

195). An earlier version had added "Which thou henceforth art doomed to interweave" (Zillman, *Shelley's "Prometheus Unbound,"* 143). Just how these realms of life and death relate to the cave, we will soon explore.

30. In a sense the human world and its mutability invade the apparent enclosure of Prometheus's cave even before this, if only in the form of a denial. "What can hide man from Mutability?—" (3.3.25) is interjected, out of order it seems, and disrupts the logic of insistence on the changelessness of the cave.

31. "Mont Blanc," lines 30–48, in Reiman and Powers, *Shelley's Poetry and Prose. Prometheus Unbound* echoes in a sense, and most especially in this, the third act, the situation of "Mont Blanc." However, what in the earlier poem is problematized as a crisis of epistemology and rhetoric is here dramatized as a struggle for political power.

"Mont Blanc" opens with a series of questions never made explicit: how to understand "the everlasting universe of things," "the mind," and "the source of human thought"—how to think, then, the relationship among the phenomenal world of nature, a mind that exceeds the human mind, and the poet's "own separate phantasy" (line 36), those same three realms at play in the description of Prometheus's cave.

The answer to the dilemma is at once given and refused by the series of similes that govern the first nineteen lines. For in order to better specify how the "source of human thought" brings its tribute to the flow of the "universe of things" through "the mind," the text proposes a figure. (Never mind that one remains, after all, quite uncertain as to what the simile delineates, whether it is indeed a likeness of the movement of human thought or of the universe of things, for in the problematic glitter and gloom of those opening lines one tumbles ceaselessly trying to find such footholds of stability.)

> —with a sound but half its own.
> Such as a feeble brook will oft assume
> In the wild woods, among the mountains lone,
> Where waterfalls around it leap for ever,
> Where woods and winds contend, and a vast river
> Over its rocks ceaselessly bursts and raves.
>   II
> Thus thou, Ravine of Arve—dark, deep Ravine—
> Thou many-coloured, many-voiced vale,
> . . . .
> . . . . awful scene,
> Where Power in likeness of the Arve comes down
> From the ice gulphs that gird his secret throne,

(lines 6–17)

To understand how human thought flows through "the mind" with a sound but half its own, we are given an image from nature. The source of human thought is like a feeble brook in contention with waterfalls, woods, winds, and the vast river that bursts over its rocks—like a natural brook overwhelmed by other forces of nature, doubled by a river that passes over and obliterates its path. Appropriately enough, the river that vies with the brook for its own bedrock is said to "rave." Within the simile borrowed from the natural scene, a voice proffered to explain the flow of human thought, we are thrown back to the realm of man's mind. Yet this is the sound of insane human articulation, of the mind gone mad, as well it might here. In the relationship among human thought, "the mind," and nature, as in Prometheus's cave, no sooner does one provide the ground for the other, lend it an identity, than it destabilizes it as well.

This dizzying search for definition through figures grounded in other realms continues into the second stanza. For we are told that the "many-voiced" (line 13) Ravine of Arve, that presumably real vale whose name echoes the raving of line 11, is like that which came before. Is it, then, like the "everlasting universe of things" flowing through "the mind," or like the "source of human thought" bringing its tribute from secret springs, or perhaps like the "feeble brook" burst over by a raving river? Moreover, the Ravine of Arve, so uncertainly located by the "thus," is the locus for the descent, not of the Arve river itself, but of "Power" in likeness of the Arve (line 16), which uses the Arve as its guise. The mode of images seems inescapable.

We are lulled, nevertheless, by the comparative simplicity of the lines that follow, convinced by the abundance of natural imagery that we have at last found our way to echoes purely of "the Arve's commotion, / A loud, lone sound no other sound can tame" (lines 30–31), as though echoes could ever do away with a sense of otherness. We seem to find our place in a scene unthreatened by "the mind" or human thought, and yet we are returned at the close of stanza 2 to the poet's "separate phantasy," his "own," his "human mind" (lines 36–37).

> Dizzy Ravine! and when I gaze on thee
> I seem as in a trance sublime and strange
> To muse on my own separate phantasy,
> My own, my human mind, which passively
> Now renders and receives fast influencings,
> Holding an unremitting interchange
> With the clear universe of things around;
> One legion of wild thoughts, whose wandering wings
> Now float above thy darkness, and now rest
> Where that or thou art no unbidden guest,
> In the still cave of the witch Poesy,
> Seeking among the shadows that pass by
> Ghosts of all things that are, some shade of thee,
> Some phantom, some faint image; till the breast
> From which they fled recalls them, thou art there!
>
> (lines 34–48)

All this takes place under the influence of a "strange sleep" (line 27) that takes over when the "voices of the desart fail" (line 28), when the echoes of "the Arve's commotion" bring the poet to what seems to be a self-reflective "trance sublime." But this "separate phantasy" cannot maintain itself as separate. It holds an "unremitting interchange / With the clear universe of things," although one is never sure whether things are things in Shelley. This soon proves to be a musing on a "legion of wild thoughts" that seek, from within the cave of Poesy, the

·

"Ghosts of all things that are." And these ghosts in turn will be a shade of the ravine, as both source and image of the human mind. In a sense, then, one might claim, from the beginning, all has been written from the perspective of the cave, of a poesy that seeks an image for the source of its own phantasy. As in stanza 1, where the ravine appeared as image of "the mind," to which "human thought" and the "universe of [natural] things" had a ceaselessly changing relationship, so at the close of stanza 2, human phantasy (and poesy), with a more encompassing task of "recall" possibly to come, slips among the "universe of things," the ghosts of things, its own thoughts, and its own image. As with the activity in Prometheus's final abode (and despite the non-equivalence of the two caves), there is no pretension to establishing a center that can hold, only a wandering of voices, an unremitting echo.

32. "Mont Blanc," lines 41, 33.

33. Ovid, *Metamorphoses,* trans. Rolfe Humphries (Bloomington: Indiana University Press, 1955), 122.

34. Earl Wasserman writes: "When Prometheus enters his cave with Asia the possibility of narrative has ended because he has passed beyond the limits of imagery and language" (*Shelley,* 360). But it would seem that in the description both of the interior of the cave and of its relation to the human realm there is the insistence that although Prometheus may no longer be a subject for narrative, he cannot pass beyond such limits.

35. This relationship between ineffability and Love runs counter to that suggested by Stuart Peterfreund in "The Two Languages and the Ineffable in Shelley's Major Poetry," in *Ineffability: Naming the Unnamable from Dante to Beckett,* ed. Peter S. Hawkins (New York: AMS Press, 1984), 123–29.

36. I would agree with Daniel Hughes ("Prometheus Made Capable Poet in Act I of *Prometheus Unbound,*" *Studies in Romanticism* 17, no. 1 [1978]: 3–11), therefore, as he, along with others, reads act 1 as the moment in which Prometheus gives up a mystified mode of language. But Hughes sees the ultimate horizon of Prometheus's understanding as "language [as] a perpetual Orphic song," a position, it would seem, perpetually ironized.

37. The danger in Shelley (which is as much the comfort) is taking any one statement on the nature of language as the final word. Thus neither Asia's description of Prometheus's relation to language in act 2, scene 4, nor Earth's insistence on man's orphic song, nor, for that matter, ironically, the last ironical words of Demogorgon should be given the weight of their literal statements— out of context (see, e.g., the opening pages of Frederick Burwick's "The Language of Causality in *Prometheus Unbound,*" *Keats-Shelley Journal* 31 [1982]: 136–37; or Brisman's concept of the Promethean principle in "'Unsaying,'" 58, 61).

38. See Rajan's fine reading of this in *Dark Interpreter,* 91.

39. Percy Bysshe Shelley, "The Necessity of Atheism," in Ingpen and Peck, *Complete Works,* 5:208.

40. In this regard see the interpretation of D. J. Hughes, "Potentiality in *Prometheus Unbound,*" *Studies in Romanticism* 2, no. 2 (1963): 125–26; and Wasserman, *Shelley,* 306, 361. In contrast, Wasserman also writes, "Shelley's

serpent is not the supernatural power of evil but the hieroglyphic serpent of temporal change" (292).

Chapter 3. At the Threshold of Interpretation

1. *Wuthering Heights* (New York: Norton, 1963), 17, 32, hereafter cited as *WH*.

2. The phrase is Edgar F. Shannon's in "Lockwood's Dreams and the Exegesis of *Wuthering Heights,*" *Nineteenth Century Fiction* 14 (September 1959): 99. Shannon's essay assumes Lockwood's reasoning in its insistence on the causal relationship between "reality" and dream: "Mrs. [Dorothy] Van Ghent bases her case for the symbolism of the nightmare upon a supposed inadequacy of determinants for it and for Lockwood's cruelty to the dream child. But, to gain the reader's acceptance, Emily Brontë prepares consistently for this culmination to Lockwood's initial experiences at Wuthering Heights. In addition to the obvious contributions of his reading of Cathy's books . . . and the insistent branch—the chief representative and presentative elements of both dreams— there is ample "stuff" for the "Manifest content" of the nightmare" (97).

3. This question of the text, which forms the crux of this chapter, plays the central role in Robert McKibben's article "The Image of the Book in *Wuthering Heights,*" ibid. 15 (September 1960): 159–69. McKibben reads the novel literally in search for books. At the Grange books are misused to "reflect a shrinking from reality" (162); at the Heights they are equally misused, for they are subordinated to the creation of reality (162). But at the novel's conclusion they function as the stabilizing force that resolves the apparently insurmountable tension between these two alternatives. "In this new life founded upon acceptance, operating as reconciliation, the book fulfills its proper duty" (168). In order to restore the misused book to its "proper duty," McKibben must dance rather gingerly over the texts in Lockwood's dream (161). And what is the use of missing this scene if not McKibben's apprehension that it would cast him in the role of Lockwood, who also restores texts to their "proper" place?

4. This is the limited thrust, for example, of Ronald E. Fine's reading, "Lockwood's Dreams and the Key to *Wuthering Heights,*" ibid. 24 (June 1969): 16–30. Fine reads the dreams as "the template for the narrative which they introduce. First they contain elements which recur throughout the novel. . . . Second, the actions of the dreams are archetypes for crucial narrative actions" (21). In this context see also William A. Madden's *"Wuthering Heights:* The Binding of Passion," ibid. 27 (September 1972): 127–54.

5. Frank Kermode, "A Modern Way with the Classic," *New Literary History* 5 (Spring 1974): 415–34, hereafter cited as *MW.*

6. No one understands the implications of this reading better than Kermode himself. In his long meditation *The Sense of an Ending* (London: Oxford University Press, 1966) he repeatedly concludes: "Men, like poets, 'rush into the middest,' *in medias res,* when they are born; they also die *in mediis rebus,* and to make sense of their span they need fictive concords with origins and ends, such as give meaning to lives and poems" (7). Such are the comforting end and meaning that Kermode assigns to *Wuthering Heights.* And yet they are "the unconsciously

false" (40), both in Kermode's text and in the novel. It is the conscious falsity that Kermode fails to confront in its complexity, although he himself writes: "'making sense' . . . is something that literature achieves only so long as we remember the status of fictions" (41). *Wuthering Heights* remembers its status as fiction and only plays at its forgetting.

7. In addition to the varied pairing of the name *Catherine* with *Earnshaw, Heathcliff,* and *Linton,* Isabella is first a Linton and then a Heathcliff, and her son is named Linton Heathcliff.

8. Inga-Stina Ewbank, in *Their Proper Sphere: A Study of the Brontë Sisters as Early-Victorian Female Novelists* (Cambridge: Harvard University Press, 1966), admirably outlines the functioning of repetition with a difference as a structural device in the plot of the novel.

9. The desire for possession as such paradoxically comes into play only well after the moment of usurpation. It operates as the foredoomed struggle to close the gap between property and possessor, to render the one present to the other, to establish a definitive mastery. Hindley's method is gambling, the attempt to perpetually increase his property. But as Catherine says, "what he grasps with one hand, he flings away with the other" (*WH* 87), and the gesture intended to render present is precisely that which spends. Heathcliff, on the other hand, would close the gap between himself and his property by demolishing it, a measure that would indeed put an end to the chain of inheritance. But he cannot bring himself to do so, and the space remains open for new usurpers:

> "It is a poor conclusion, is it not," he observed, having brooded a while on the scene he had just witnessed. "An absurd termination to my violent exertions? I get levers and mattocks to demolish the two houses, and train myself to be capable of working like Hercules, and when everything is ready, and in my power, I find the will to lift a slate off either roof has vanished! My old enemies have not beaten me; now would be the precise time to revenge myself on their representatives: I could do it; and none could hinder me. But where is the use? I don't care for striking, I can't take the trouble to raise my hand!" (*WH* 254–55)

10. Despite the literal completion of Lockwood's difficult journey to the Grange, it cannot be said to close the gap between Wuthering Heights and home. Rather, Lockwood's arrival at Thrushcross Grange marks yet another excommunication, as already suggested. This excommunication silences Lockwood as narrator and places him out of direct communication not only with the reader but also, of course, with Wuthering Heights as both narrative and locality.

11. See J. Hillis Miller's subtle elaboration of this paradox of passion, *The Disappearance of God* (Cambridge: Harvard University Press, 1963), 173–76.

12. The pause between the two phrases is, of course, also the juncture at which Heathcliff leaves Wuthering Heights, the critical severance of Cathy and Heathcliff.

13. See Vereen M. Bell, "*Wuthering Heights* and the Unforgivable Sin," *Nineteenth Century Fiction* 17 (September 1962): 188–91: "and of course what Jesus is urging is perpetual forgiveness, perpetual charity, *only he phrases it in finite terms*" (189, emphasis mine). As might be expected, Bell extends this

interpretation of the Bible to an interpretation of Lockwood's unforgivable sin as the absence of forgiveness.

14. *The New Testament* (Philadelphia: Griffith and Simon, 1846), 36–37.

15. This is precisely what takes place in Lockwood's dream. Jabes reads an apparently interminable list of forgivable sins, yet just when Lockwood refuses to forgive, Jabes, like the lord in the parable, refuses to forgive Lockwood.

16. It is at this juncture that I can best delineate what separates this reading from that of Dorothy Van Ghent in *The English Novel: Form and Function* (New York: Rinehart, 1953), 153–70. To be sure, her interpretation prefigures certain strategies in my own, but these are here incorporated into a text that Van Ghent would consider fundamentally "other" to hers. Van Ghent's essay proceeds from an incisive and promising declaration that *Wuthering Heights* is "of all English novels, the most treacherous for the analytical understanding" (153). And she develops a cogent argument throughout her essay for placing this treachery on one side of an axis that defines *Wuthering Heights* variously as a tension between mythical imagination and civilization, between excess and limitation, between outside and inside, between otherness and consciousness. Although Van Ghent sees these "two kinds of reality" intersecting in each of the characters, she is unwilling to extend this "breaking-through of a separating medium" to the final outcome of the novel (165). On the contrary: she undermines the radicality first by reinscribing the text under the protective aegis of Lockwood's reassuring "dream-rejecting reason" (155) and lastly, in her closing passage, by maintaining that this boundary between excess and limitation was never actually violated. Here this violation takes place such that limitation is inscribed within excess.

17. Lockwood seeks to maintain Wuthering Heights in one of two comfortable proximities—either as totally foreign to his reality or as totally coincident with it, either as a mere formal fiction with a hero and heroine or as a simple, actual history unmenaced by the supernatural. It is the perilous struggle between these two alternatives that he longs to escape.

Chapter 4. The Rhetorics of Feminism

1. *The Iliad of Homer,* trans. Theodore Alois Buckley, Bohn's Classical Library (London: Henry G. Bohn, 1857), 21.392, 22.412; all references to the *Iliad* are to book and page. See also *The Aeneid of Virgil,* trans. Rolfe Humphries (New York: Charles Scribner's Sons, 1951), bk. 6, 145.

2. *The Odyssey of Homer,* trans. Richard Lattimore (New York: Harper, 1965), 346–47.

3. The text usually considered to be Kleist's most likely source of reference is Benjamin Hederich, *Gründliches Mythologisches Lexicon* (Darmstadt: Wissenschaftliche Buchgesellschaft, 1967), in which none of the many versions of the tale of Penthesilea coincides with Kleist's.

4. In her last monologue of the closing scene.

5. All citations to *Penthesilea* are taken from Heinrich von Kleist, *Sämtliche Werke und Briefe,* ed. Helmut Sembdner, 3d expanded and revised ed., vol. 1 (Munich: Carl Hanser Verlag, 1964); and from the English edition of *Plays,* ed.

Walter Hinderer (New York: Continuum, 1982). References to the German edition are to scene and line; references to the English edition are to page, followed by an *E*. The translations are reworkings, sometimes radical, of the Continuum edition.

6. *Iliad* 2.41, 3.56.

7. In the *Iliad* Odysseus is repeatedly described by such epithets as "crafty" (e.g., 4.169), "much contriving" (e.g., 8.138), "much scheming" (9.159), "wise [and] skilled in strategems" and "of many wiles" (23.438).

8. *Iliad* 2.41; see also 3.56: "But when he did send forth the mighty voice from his breast, and words like unto wintry flakes of snow, no longer then would another mortal contend with Ulysses."

9. The etymology of *lechzen* points to *lecken* as *tröpfeln*, "to let water run through or drip" (*Duden Etymologie Herkunftswörterbuch der deutschen Sprache* [Mannheim: Dudenverlag, 1963], 392).

10. See also:

ODYSSEUS
And so try, then,
Now your rhetorical arts, O Antilochus!

(186E)

ODYSSEUS
Nun, so versuch doch
Jetzt deine Rednerkunst, o Antiloch!

(4.622–23)

11. See Walter Müller-Seidel, "'Penthesilea' im Kontext der deutschen Klassik," in *Kleists Dramen: Neue Interpretationen*, ed. Walter Hinderer (Stuttgart: Reclam, 1981).

12. Certain readers of *Penthesilea* have mentioned the inability of Penthesilea and Achilles to understand each other's metaphors: Walter Müller-Seidel, *Versehen und Erkennen* (Cologne: Böhlau, 1961), 140–41; and Hans Heinz Holz, *Macht und Ohnmacht der Sprache* (Frankfurt: Athenäum, 1962), 60. Holz makes the interesting comment that Achilles understands Penthesilea's violence as metaphorical for love at one point but that that love is for him, once again, metaphorical for violence (60).

13. Thus when Achilles enters in scene 11 to take the queen who fell to him in battle, the Amazons speak a language of menace that is empty of genuine intent. Yet almost in the same breath of jovial disbelief in their threats ("I cannot believe it, sweet, like the ringing of silver / Your voice punishes the lies of your speech" ["Ich kanns nicht glauben: süß, wie Silberklang, / Straft eure Stimme eure Reden Lügen"] [212E; 11.1428–29]), Achilles has his soldiers respond to them with all too deadly blows.

14. Bernard Böchenstein intelligently notes the movement forth and back between metaphors and reality in the play ("Ambivalenz und Dissoziation in Kleists Werk," in *Die Gegenwärtigkeit Kleists*, ed. Wieland Schmidt [Berlin: Erich Schmidt Verlag, 1980], 51, 54).

15. Her will to literal understanding of the herald's message is mocked by a

phrase whose irony reverberates more and more intensely as the play progresses. Penthesilea to Prothoe: "You must repeat it to me word for word" ("—Du mußt es Wort für Wort mir wiederholen") (244E; 20.2375).

16. See lines 5, 163, 213–18, 384, and 530, among other examples.

17. That earlier metaphors become realized in *Penthesilea* has been noted by many of Kleist's readers; see, e.g., Böchenstein, "Ambivalenz," 50.

18. *Iliad* 14.367, 21.392, 23.412.

19. *Aeneid*, bk. 6, 145. For other mythological references to this scene see Hederich, *Mythologisches Lexicon*, 37.

20. One might think, for example, of the myth of Hyacinth (see chap. 2) or of the myth of Marsyas. It cannot be insignificant, then, that Kleist named his journal *Phöbus*.

21. *Iliad* 24.445.

22. *Iliad* 24.444, 23.423. Throughout the *Iliad* there is an obsession with saving and preserving bodies. Linda Hoff-Purviance notes the connection between violence to Hector's body in the *Iliad* and violence to Achilles' in *Penthesilea* ("The Form of Kleist's *Penthesilea* and the *Iliad*," *German Quarterly* 55, no. 1 [1982]: 43–44).

23. In every literal sense as well, from the beginning, for *Achilles* in Greek means "lipless," a reference to the myth of his infancy, for it was said that he did not put his lips to the breast of his mother (Hederich, *Mythologisches Lexicon*, 31).

24. Heinrich von Kleist, *Dramen, Zweiter Teil* (Munich: Deutscher Taschenbuch Verlag, 1965), 285.

25. Indeed Penthesilea, even more so in the closing scene than in the moment of her act of violence, is the most radical threat imaginable to the function of the priestess. For this is a function that depends on accurately representing, in words, the will of the gods Mars and Diana (cf. scene 15). This explains why the priestess continually wants to obliterate the queen ("veil," "hide" her, "pile mountains" on the evidence of her crime).

26. The confusion in terms of Penthesilea, as mad as it might seem elsewhere, makes perfect sense, but in point of fact, of course, *Küsse* and *Bisse* do not rhyme (except perhaps in the particular pronunciation of a dialect of the time). Helmut Arntzen is one of the few readers of Kleist who attempts to deal with this passage and that which follows it ("Gewalt und Sprache," in Schmidt, *Die Gegenwärtigkeit Kleists*, 76; see also Heiner Weidmann, *Heinrich von Kleist: Glück und Aufbegehren* [Bonn: Bouvier, 1984], 154–55).

27. There is rhyme and reason here in more ways than one. For how are we to explain that just when Penthesilea's argument speaks of the purely physical aspect of language, her phrases ring double such that "das reimt sich" can mean not only "it rhymes" but also "it makes sense," can at once mark the purely nonsignifying materiality of language and also assert meaning? Or that *greifen*, like the English *grasp*, performs in much the same way, implying a taking ahold bodily and also an understanding of the one for the other?

28. This passage is hardly Penthesilea's attempt to veil the monstrousness of her deed as Jakob Spälti insists (*Interpretationen zu Heinrich von Kleists Verhältnis zur Sprache* [Bern: Lang, 1975], 79). The monstrousness of the text appears,

rather, openly for the first time, as Penthesilea tries to come to terms with the implications of her language, which is almost tantamount to saying with the implications of what it means to be queen of the Amazons.

29. Even, then, after the most radical moments of seeming linguistic aberrations, what takes place is less a fall into meaninglessness than a reflection that will bring about another kind of fall. Such a reading would run counter to that of Ursula Mahlendorf, who sees the play as one in which the characters "regress to preverbal states of human development, a regression which is reflected stylistically in their literalness and tendency to reify in their lapses into confusion, hallucination, and silence" ("The Wounded Self: Kleist's *Penthesilea*," *German Quarterly* 52, no. 2 [1979]: 253). It also runs counter to those who, on the other hand, read the closing scene as an unambiguous triumph of meaning (see, e.g., Elmar Hoffmeister, *Täuschung und Wirklichkeit bei Heinrich von Kleist* [Bonn: Bouvier, 1968], 36).

30. Kleist himself plays openly on this double take of *sich versprechen* in an epigram entitled "Das Sprachversehen," in *Sämtliche Werke und Briefe* 1:23.

31. This bosom is marked by the absence of the other, for the Amazons, or "breastless ones," rip the right breast from their sides to assume their mastery over the bow. Here, then, where all the feelings have found refuge (231E; 25.2015), Penthesilea descends, into a passage indeed marked by the absence of the other, for even the remaining breast is "like a shaft."

32. If not a parody, this passage is at least a counterimage of the forging of Achilles' armor by Vulcan at the end of book 17 of the *Iliad*. Vulcan is bent on creating an object of protection, and he covers it with allegorical figures that are incidental to its function. Penthesilea creates not merely a weapon but one she intends to use for self-destruction. The allegory in Penthesilea's production is the forming of the dagger itself through a process of figuralization.

33. This would be at odds, then, with the eloquent reading of Ilse Graham: "This is the end of the drama, when she 'falls' into consciousness, when, in a breathlessly rapid process of maturation, she comes to understand the difference between material signs and their significances and rises to full human stature, forging for herself a symbol strong enough to kill" (*Heinrich von Kleist: Word into Flesh* [Berlin: Walter de Gruyter, 1977], 110). Is it really a question of "understanding the difference"? As Robert Labhardt (one of the few readers to ponder the rhetoric of *Penthesilea* at length and whose study contributes to an overall sense of Kleist's use of metaphor) points out, this is the moment when iron and heart come together (*Metapher und Geschichte* [Kronberg: Scriptor Verlag, 1976], 264). Earlier in the play, Penthesilea perhaps understood that the iron weapon was a controlled metaphor for the feelings of the heart it signified. This reading is at odds as well with the many readings that do not take the linguistic thrust into account, a recent example among many being Barbara Belhalfaoui, "Kleists *Penthesilea* in heilsgeschichtlicher Sicht: Eine Interpretation," *Études germaniques* 40, no. 2 (1985): 193-94.

34. Belhalfaoui, "Kleist's *Penthesilea*," emphasizing the Christian imagery of the passage, reads this moment as a "Verklärung" and "Vergöttlichung" through earthly suffering. It is as though one might repress in the name of literalization of

name and a reassuring apotheosis the outrageous manner in which it all takes place. Only thus can one assert the thrust of that which is inevitably upset by the implications of the passage's language. Belhalfaoui's essay is only an extreme example of the tendency of many other readings to find some form of transcendence. Robert Labhardt, as a case in point, reads this moment as the culmination in which "Das Subjektive bemächtigt sich des Objektiven" (*Metapher und Geschichte*, 241). Surely the question of mastery remains considerably more complicated.

Chapter 5. A Delicate Joke

1. The historical information and documents relevant to this play are presented in Richard Samuel's superb edition, Heinrich von Kleist, *Prinz Friedrich von Homburg*, ed. Richard Samuel (Berlin: Erich Schmidt Verlag, 1964); and also in Klaus Kanzog, ed., *Heinrich von Kleist, "Prinz Friedrich von Homburg": Text, Kontexte, Kommentar* (Munich: Carl Hanser Verlag, 1977).

2. All citations are from Heinrich von Kleist, *Sämtliche Werke und Briefe*, ed. Helmut Sembdner, 3d expanded and revised ed., vol. 1 (Munich: Carl Hanser Verlag, 1964), and from the English edition: *Plays*, ed. Walter Hinderer (New York: Continuum, 1982). Unless otherwise noted, references to the German edition are to act, scene, and line; references to the English edition are to page, followed by an *E*. The translations are sometimes reworkings of the Continuum edition.

3. Much of Kleist criticism has devoted itself, quite understandably, to the duality of dream and reality. In a recent essay Roland Heine gives a thorough gloss of those works as well as a subtle interpretation of his own ("'Ein Traum, was sonst?' Zum Verhältnis von Traum und Wirklichkeit in Kleists *Prinz Friedrich von Homburg*," in *Literaturwissenschaft und Geistesgeschichte: Festschrift für Richard Brinkmann*, ed. Jürgen Brummack [Tübingen: Niemeyer, 1981], 287–88). For an intelligent critique of the approach to the text through the structure of dualisms see John M. Ellis, *Heinrich von Kleist: Studies in the Character and Meaning of His Writings* (Chapel Hill: University of North Carolina Press, 1979), 89–115. Ellis himself reads the play as an initial contrast between the Prince and the Elector that gives way to questioning the difference between them (*Kleist's "Prinz Friedrich von Homburg": A Critical Study* [Berkeley: University of California Press, 1970], 12, 14).

4. The dedication to the princess Amalie Marie Anne makes the parallel between the Prince and the author obvious:

But [there is] one, he thinks, in the circle of the crowd,
To whom the feelings of the breast dedicate themselves.
In her hands she holds the prize that falls to him,
And if she crowns him, then all will crown him.

Doch eine denkt er in dem Kreis der Menge,
Der die Gefühle seiner Brust sich weihn;

Sie hält den Preis in Händen, der ihm falle,
Und krönt ihn die, so krönen sie ihn alle.

(Kleist, *Sämtliche Werke,* 629)

5. See Werner Hamacher, "'Disgregation of the Will': Nietzsche on the Individual and Individuality," in *Friedrich Nietzsche,* ed. Harold Bloom (New York: Chelsea House, 1987), 163–92.

6. The glove does not function, therefore, simply as an indication of the real as Gerhard Fricke suggests ("Kleists *Prinz Friedrich von Homburg,*" *Germanisch-Romanische Monatsschrift,* n.s. 2 [1952]: 192). See also Heine, "'Ein Traum, was sonst?'" 295.

7. Although most of the names in the play are either historical or taken from figures that surrounded Kleist, *Natalie* appears to have been an invention of Kleist's (Samuel, *Prinz Friedrich von Homburg,* 173).

8. Ibid., 179–80.

9. Helmut Arntzen, among others, notes that the split is not quite so simple (see "'Prinz Friedrich von Homburg'—Drama der Bewußtseinsstufen," in *Kleists Dramen: Neue Interpretationen,* ed. Walter Hinderer [Stuttgart: Reclam, 1981], 215–16).

10. The translation is left in all its awkward literalness because the theme of writing instruments, here as elsewhere in Kleist, is crucial.

11. Samuel, *Prinz Friedrich von Homburg,* 180.

12. Hackelwitz is, significantly enough, twice the scene of contradiction between serious fall (the threat of death) and the revelation that nothing serious has taken place. Thus the Elector, whom eyewitnesses have seen fall in battle, reappears soon after in Hackelwitz (296E; 2.7.618, 626). Homburg himself had fallen with his horse near Hackelwitz (287E; 2.1.376–78), and although the wound is "Nichts von Bedeutung!" ("Nothing meaningful") (287E; 2.1.379), the Elector later takes it to be a serious injury.

13. And no less by Kleist criticism; see, e.g., Samuel, *Prinz Friedrich von Homburg,* 193, 196. E. M. Oppenheimer ("How Prince Friedrich Learned to Write," *Carleton German Papers* 5 [1977]) sees this as "progress towards the conjunction of composure and composition" (63). In an essay that pays all due attention to the writing scenes in *Prinz Friedrich von Homburg,* the conclusion runs counter to that presented here, for Oppenheimer distinguishes *Schriftskepsis* from *Sprachskepsis* (55) and, moreover, sees the second scene of writing as the place of reason (62) and reconciliation "of the letter with the organic, with life" (60).

14. It is difficult, therefore, to see how Raimund Belgardt could regard this as simply "a new knowledge" and an "action of understanding" (see "Prinz Friedrich von Homburgs neues Wissen," *Neophilologus* 61 [January 1977]: 104).

15. The phrases that appear in these lines (*Fassung, mich fassen, sich fassen*) have to do with writing, *Fassung* as "phrasing," *sich fassen* as the verb "to express oneself" or "to compose." They echo a similar cluster of the same terms in act 3, scene 5, where *Fassung* and *fasse dich* have rather the sense of pulling oneself together. The use of the same terms in the later scene has, then, obvious ironical

reverberations. Thus the somewhat awkward translations that attempt to keep the play of words (see Helmut Arntzen's essay "'Prinz Friedrich von Homburg,'" 230, one of the few in the *Homburg* literature that displays a critical sensitivity to the question of language and contradiction).

16. See Erika Swales, "Configurations of Irony: Kleist's *Prinz Friedrich von Homburg,*" *Deutsche Vierteljahrschrift für Literaturwissenschaft und Geistesgeschichte* 56, no. 3 (1982): 420.

17. Others see this, rather, as the moment when Homburg finds the inner truth of his soul; see, e.g., Hermann Reske, *Traum und Wirklichkeit im Werk Heinrich von Kleists* (Stuttgart: W. Kohlhammer Verlag, 1969), 102.

18. See Ellis, *Kleist's "Prinz Friedrich von Homburg,"* 96.

19. An image noted by several of Kleist's readers; see, e.g., Ilse Graham, *Heinrich von Kleist: Word into Flesh* (Berlin: Walter de Gruyter, 1977), 184–85.

20. Thus the breath of wind that here promises to unveil is not only later (339E; 5.10.1835) but also earlier, and far more explicitly, the force of dispersal (See Arntzen, "'Prinz Friedrich von Homburg,'" 234–35).

THE PRINCE OF HOMBURG
High up, like the spirit of glory,
She lifts the wreath on which the chain swings back and forth,
As though she wished to crown a hero,
I reach, inexpressibly moved,
I reach my hands out to possess the wreath
I wish to sink before her feet,
But just as the fragrance that above the valley floats
Disperses in the cold breath of a wind,
The group evades me. . . .

         (278E)

DER PRINZ VON HOMBURG
Hoch auf, gleich einem Genius des Ruhms,
Hebt sie den Kranz, an dem die Kette schwankte,
Als ob sie einen Helden krönen wollte.
Ich streck, in unaussprechlicher Bewegung,
Die Hände streck ich aus, ihn zu ergreifen:
Zu Füßen will ich vor ihr niedersinken.
Doch, wie der Duft, der über Täler schwebt,
Vor eines Windes frischem Hauch zerstiebt,
Weicht mir die Schar. . . .

         (1.4.172–80)

If Homburg is ready here to sink before the feet of his "spirit of glory," the chain that in the play within the play celebrates Homburg's valor is at the close of act 1 what binds that spirit's blessings away from him, to the Swedish victory chariots. The sphere on which Fortune is said to roll, the "Kugel," later becomes those bullets ("Kugel") obsessively mentioned as the instrument of Homburg's impending execution (see Ellis, *Kleist's "Prinz Friedrich von Homburg,"* 73, 75). Many intelligent close readings have stressed the inexhaustible multiplicity of interpretations that *Prinz Friedrich von Homburg* makes possible (see, e.g.,

Roland Heine, "'Ein Traum, was sonst?'" 286–87), its ambiguity (Valentine Hubbs, "Die Ambiguität in Kleists *Prinz Friedrich von Homburg,*" in *Kleist-Jahrbuch, 1981–82,* ed. Hans Joachim Kreutzer [Berlin: Erich Schmidt Verlag, 1983], 184–94), and its irony (Swales, "Configurations of Irony"). It is not simply a question here, however, of establishing ambiguity or irony in yet other, less noticed moments of the text but rather one of marking what is at stake.

21. It is not without a certain irony, then, that Kleist called *Prinz Friedrich von Homburg,* also a "Schauspiel."

22. In point of fact, not that such facts are necessarily relevant to understanding *Prince Friedrich of Homburg,* although they help to fathom its misunderstanding, Kleist did write his own epitaph in writing this play. Thus his posterity, however sympathetic, engraved his tombstone with the opening line of Homburg's final monologue: "Now, oh immortality, you are fully mine!" ("Nun, o Unsterblichkeit, bist du ganz mein!"). The reasoning, one can only suppose, was that the poet had in his pocket at the time of his death Klopstock's "Then, oh immortality, you belong entirely to us" ("Dann, o Unsterblichkeit, gehörst Du ganz uns") (Samuel, *Prinz Friedrich von Homburg,* 202). Left out of account was the possibility, however unbearable, of Kleist's radical irony—intentional or unintentional—as he wrote *Homburg,* as he took his own life.

23. The joke in *Prinz Friedrich von Homburg* is no static form of contradiction. Excellent commentaries have been written on contradiction in this text, Helmut Arntzen's essay ("'Prinz Friedrich von Homburg'") probably the most thorough among them. But the joke in *Homburg* is a movement, an invasion, a gesture that effects a dislocation, one that cannot be contained in the posing of two fixed opposites.

24. Erika Swales, "Configurations of Irony," offers a good sense of the way in which the multiplicity of readings of this scene are indicative of its tendency to undo any fixed perspective. See also Jochen Schmidt, *Heinrich von Kleist: Studien zu seiner poetischen Verfahrensweise* (Tübingen: Niemeyer, 1974), 94. It is somewhat unfathomable that a vast number of readings see this scene as a positive moment of resolution. Charles E. Passage reads it as "a conclusion in joy and glory" (*The Prince of Homburg* [Indianapolis: Bobbs-Merrill, 1956], xvi); Hans Mayer as a harmony or synthesis between the state of nature, law, and feeling (*Heinrich von Kleist: Der Geschichtliche Augenblick* [Tübingen: Neske, 1962], 70); Walter Müller-Seidel as a *Versöhnung* (*Versehen und Erkennen* [Cologne: Böhlau, 1967], 178, 186). Elmar Hoffmeister reads the Elector's last gesture as a "'poetic' sense of justice" rather than a "whimsical arbitrariness" (*Täuschung und Wirklichkeit bei Heinrich von Kleist* [Bonn: Bouvier, 1968], 50); Ilse Graham as personal grace bestowed by the Elector on "his son" (*Heinrich von Kleist,* 90). Also exceptionally long is the list of those who read the close of the play as a triumph of some particular force, say, the individual or the state, heart or law. Just two examples are: Roger Ayrault, *Heinrich von Kleist* (Paris: Aubier-Montaigne, 1966), 191–92; and Benno von Wiese, *Die deutsche Tragödie von Lessing bis Hebbel* (Hamburg: Hoffmann und Campe, 1967), 92.

25. An "all the same" that is as different as possible from Müller-Seidel's description of resolution: "The ring closes on itself. Dream becomes reality and

reality becomes dream. It is an all-sided reconciliation in the poesy of this summer night" ("Prinz Friedrich von Homburg," in *Das deutsche Drama: vom Barock bis zur Gegenwart,* ed. Benno von Wiese [Düsseldorf: August Bagel, 1958], 409).

Chapter 6. Soothsaying and Rebellion

1. All references to *Michael Kohlhaas* are from Heinrich von Kleist, *Sämtliche Werke und Briefe,* ed. Helmut Sembdner, 3d expanded and revised ed., vol. 2 (Munich: Carl Hanser Verlag, 1964), and, in English, *The Marquise of O—— and Other Stories,* trans. Martin Greenberg (New York: Ungar, 1960). References to the German edition are to page, followed by a *G;* references to the English edition are also to page, followed by an *E.* The translations are often reworkings of the English edition.

2. See the fine text of Helga Gallas, who gives a Lacanian reading of the story in which the horses serve as "phallus metaphors" in Lacan's sense (*Das Textbegehren des "Michael Kohlhaas"* [Hamburg: Rowohlt, 1981], 74, 80, 88).

3. This would seem to be the thrust of many of Kleist's readers (see, e.g., John M. Ellis, *Heinrich von Kleist: Studies in the Character and Meaning of His Writings* [Chapel Hill: University of North Carolina Press, 1979], 85, 88; Harry W. Paulin, "Kohlhaas and Family," *Germanic Review* 52, no. 3 [1977]: 170–82; and Benno von Wiese, "Heinrich von Kleist: *Michael Kohlhaas,*" in *Die deutsche Novelle von Goethe bis Kafka,* vol. 1 [Düsseldorf: August Bagel, 1964], 61). Yet the reversal by means of which Brandenburg suddenly takes up Kohlhaas's cause is not reason for celebrating the well-being of the law. This reversal is muted, if not indeed once again reversed, when the charges against Kohlhaas are shifted to the aegis of the Holy Roman Empire. Saxony, as we shall see, also performs an abrupt about-face, for reasons that become evident, wishing suddenly to save Kohlhaas, almost immediately after charging him for his crimes through the Emperor. The reversal of the positions of the two electors is symptomatic of the rupture that is there at the center of power to begin with. In a sense, this is the subject matter of the rest of the story in the tale within the tale, which concerns the fundamental undoing of the authority of both.

4. Otto F. Best makes the point that in terms of the chronology of the events, the question of the gypsy's fortunetelling has been there from the very beginning ("Schuld und Vergebung: Zur Rolle von Wahrsagerin und 'Amulett' in Kleists 'Michael Kohlhaas,'" *Germanisch-Romanische Monatsheft,* n.s. 20 [1970]: 181). It is this invasion from the very beginning of what the text displaces to the end that undoes such readings as those of Benno von Wiese ("Heinrich von Kleist: *Michael Kohlhaas*") and Charles E. Passage (*"Michael Kohlhaas:* Form Analysis," *Germanic Review* 30, no. 3 [1955]: 181–97), who try to locate a turning point in the course of the action, a sequence of events that represses the question of the soothsayer.

5. This is a favorite point of Kleist criticism, and there is a long list of readers who, well before Greenberg, tried to dismiss this section of the narrative. To name just a few, see Paulin, "Kohlhaas and Family," 180, which also mentions

Heinrich Meyer-Benfey, "Die innere Geschichte des 'Michael Kohlhaas,'" *Euphorion* 15 (1908): 101–3; and Clemens Lugowski, *Wirklichkeit und Dichtung* (Frankfurt: Diesterweg, 1936), 204. See also Gerhard Fricke, "Michael Kohlhaas," in *Studien und Interpretationen: Ausgewählte Schriften zur deutscher Dichtung* (Frankfurt: H. F. Menck, 1956), 214–38; and Friedrich de la Motte-Fouqué, "Zeitung für die elegante Welt," 24 November 1810, in *Heinrich von Kleists Lebensspuren*, ed. Helmut Sembdner (Bremen: C. Schünemann, 1957).

An equally enthusiastic group of readers reviews that literature with a claim to seeing what the passage is all about. Several claim to see the episode as the beneficient assertion of an otherworldly power—e.g., von Wiese, "Heinrich von Kleist: *Michael Kohlhaas*," 62–63; and Walter Silz, *Heinrich von Kleist: Studies in His Character* (Philadelphia: University of Pennsylvania Press, 1961), 185. Elmar Hoffmeister reads the gypsy as the figure who makes justice possible (*Täuschung und Wirklichkeit bei Heinrich von Kleist* [Bonn: Bouvier, 1968], 51), as does Robert E. Helbling (*The Major Works of Heinrich von Kleist* [New York: New Directions, 1975], 208). John M. Ellis's *Heinrich von Kleist* should be consulted for a most thorough review of earlier interpretations. He properly dismisses those readings where the disruption of the unity of the work is criticized (71, 172–73). Ellis goes on to read this episode as the introduction of the "inconsequential and irrational" (81), forcing us to see a "second world [that] for all its surface oddities, is the real world in which we and Kohlhaas live" (82). Clifford A. Bernd, before Ellis, gives an excellent gloss of the critical history of the question and proposes his own interpretation, "that Kleist had intentionally wished to make the element of confusion an integral part of *Michael Kohlhaas*" ("On the Two Divergent Parts of Kleist's *Michael Kohlhaas*," in *New York University Department of German Studies in Germanic Languages and Literature,* ed. Robert Fowkes and Volkmar Sander [Reutlingen: Eugen Hutzler, 1967], 54). Thus Bernd, while intelligently distancing himself from the refusal to read on the part of those before him, offers "confusion" under the aegis of clear, intentional meaning in writing.

6. *Michael Kohlhaas* is riddled through with such lacunae on the part of the narrator-chronicler, moments of the text that gain what significance they may have precisely through their absence. Consider the following, for example: "He [Kohlhaas] had also the satisfaction of seeing the theologian Jakob Freising enter his jail as a messenger of Doctor Luther with a letter in Luther's own hand—without doubt a very remarkable letter which, however, has been lost" ("Er [Kohlhaas] hatte noch die Genugtuung, den Theologen Jakob Freising, als einen Abgesandten Doktor Luthers, mit einem eigenhändigen, ohne Zweifel sehr merkwürdigen Brief, der aber verloren gegangen ist") (179E; 100G).

7. See Gallas, *Das Textbegehren,* 80, 88.

8. See 123E; 43G.

9. The magic circle appears in an earlier passage, but there it is far closer to a conventional double bind that threatens to rupture "the order of the state" (131E; 51G). In the palace of the Elector of Saxony five of his inner circle gather to weigh the matter of Luther's intercession. That Kohlhaas has violated the law no one denies. That the chamberlain Kunz originally misused the sovereign's name

(131E; 51G) and that a long list of other members of the government are also implicated are made equally evident. Thus if the state wishes to "own the authority to crush the horsedealer" (131E; 51G), it must first prosecute its own. This dilemma of the "magic circle," as Count Kallheim puts it, along with "the thread of outrage that threatens to spin out indefinitely" (130E; 50G), might nevertheless find a solution in the forgetting of an amnesty. No such solution offers itself to the magic circle of the Jüterbock marketplace, where the stakes are more than a particular act of authority and its challenge. For the story of the roebuck, the scene of pledges and predictions, is the circle that encloses all the others.

10. From the very first this question of the pledge has been anything but simple. The castellan demands a pledge to ensure that Kohlhaas will resolve the matter of the pass. Kohlhaas answers, strangely enough, by asking what pledge he should leave in place of the blacks. The steward replies that he might as well leave the blacks themselves. It is therefore Kohlhaas himself who places the blacks in the position of the pledge, and the blacks, according to the strange logic of the double displacement in the exchange, end up serving as pledges for themselves (91E; 12G).

11. The historical name was Kohlhase. The historical sources have been reprinted several times; see, e.g., the critical apparatus of Heinrich von Kleist, *Michael Kohlhaas*, ed. John Gearey (New York: Oxford University Press, 1967).

12. Can one simply, then, read the gypsy, as Otto F. Best does ("Schuld und Vergebung," 186), as the "objective correlative" for the relationship of intended revenge between Kohlhaas and Saxony? (Karl Schultze-Jahde also sees the episode as bound to a happy conclusion of revenge ["Kohlhaas und die Zigeunerin," *Jahrbuch der Kleist-Gesellschaft* 17 (1937): 128–31].) The schema of fulfilled revenge with Saxony is as satisfying as that of justice with Brandenburg, but the operation of the capsule and its paper never lets all the loose ends of the story be comfortably digested. All the more impossible to accept is Peter Horwath's reading of the gypsy episode, in which Kohlhaas's refusal to give up the prediction to Saxony is understood as a gesture of love and justice ("The 'Nicht-um-die-Welt' Theme," *Studia Neophilologica* 39 [1967]: 261–69).

Chapter 7. *The Unclosable Wound*

1. John M. Ellis's excellent essay "Der Zweikampf" is a long meditation on the conventional reader's sense of a happy ending to this tale. Ellis stresses the other, ironical reading possible through a patient working out of various moral and aesthetic ambiguities especially in the figures of the main characters (*Heinrich von Kleist: Studies in the Character and Meaning of His Writings* [Chapel Hill: University of North Carolina Press, 1979], 54–66).

2. All references to "The Duel" are from Heinrich von Kleist, *Sämtliche Werke und Briefe,* ed. Helmut Sembdner, 3d expanded and revised ed., vol. 2 (Munich: Carl Hanser Verlag, 1964), and, in English, *The Marquise of O—— and Other Stories,* trans. Martin Greenberg (New York: Ungar, 1960). References to the German edition are to page, followed by a *G;* references to the English edition

224 Notes to Pages 159–65

are also to page, followed by an *E*. The translations are often reworkings of the English edition.

3. See Jochen Schmidt, *Heinrich von Kleist: Studien zu seiner poetischen Verfahrensweise* (Tübingen: Niemeyer, 1974), 251; and Denys G. Dyer, *The Stories of Kleist* (New York: Holmes and Meier, 1977), 172.

4. This point of the potentially infinite deferral of proper interpretation could hardly be missed by Kleist's readers. See, e.g., Ellis, *Heinrich von Kleist*, 65–66; Dyer, *The Stories of Kleist*, 193; Robert E. Helbling, *The Major Works of Heinrich von Kleist* (New York: New Directions, 1975), 154; Donald Crosby, "Heinrich von Kleists *Der Zweikampf*," *Monatshefte* 56 (1964): 199; Denys G. Dyer, "Kleist und das Paradoxe," *Kleist-Jahrbuch, 1981–82*, ed. Hans Joachim Kreutzer (Berlin: Erich Schmidt Verlag, 1983), 218; and Christian Crawe, "Zur Deutung von Kleists Novelle *Der Zweikampf*," *Germanisch-Romanische Monatsschrift* 27 (1939): 425. Peter Horn links the question of the ironical, happy ending to this closing line and gives a fine gloss of earlier, more optimistic readings of this passage: *Heinrich von Kleists Erzählungen* (Königstein: Scriptor, 1978), 203–4. See also Wolfgang Wittkowski, "*Die heilige Cäcilie* und *Der Zweikampf*," *Colloquia Germanica* 1 (1972): 44, which subtly works through the ironization of religious belief in the story.

5. Friedrich Koch quite perceptively locates the problem of trust in "The Duel" as a question of the relationship between the human and heavenly realms. He sees Kleist's figure of God, however, as a "true God who does not disappoint this trust" (*Heinrich von Kleist: Bewußtsein und Wirklichkeit* [Stuttgart: J. B. Metzlersche Verlag, 1958], 133). Just what God's role is has been much disputed by Kleist's readers (see Clemens Lugowski, *Wirklichkeit und Dichtung* [Frankfurt: Diesterweg, 1936], 163; and Gerhard Fricke, *Gefühl und Schicksal bei Heinrich von Kleist* [Berlin: Neue Forschung, 1929], 147). The dispute takes place with good reason, for as Walter Silz points out, nothing takes place in the story that could not have taken place in God's absence (*Heinrich von Kleist: Studies in His Character* [Philadelphia: University of Pennsylvania Press, 1961], 66). It is this absolute unreadability of the presence *or* absence of God in the matter that the closing line of the text insists on. Horst Oppel, on the other hand, sees the text as guaranteeing a "meaningful totality of Being" (*Deutsche Vierteljahrschrift für Literaturwissenschaft und Geistesgeschichte* 22 [1944]: 104), while Hermann Reske sees it as evidence for Kleist's belief in "the human heart as the organ for hearing God" (*Traum und Wirklichkeit im Werk Heinrich von Kleists* [Stuttgart: Kohlhammer, 1969], 121).

6. See Elmar Hoffmeister, *Täuschung und Wirklichkeit bei Heinrich von Kleist* (Bonn: Bouvier, 1968), 30.

7. Even in that specific case not only is von Breysach made legally replaceable by his illegitimate son in the first sentence of the tale and murdered in the second but the entire overture to the duel is a chain of displacements of that authority from the duke to his son; from his son to the duchess (as *Vormünderin*); from the duchess to the Emperor, to whom she defers the authority for the trial; from the Emperor to his court; and from the court to God, who in turn refuses to speak authoritatively.

8. See 303E, 245G; and 316E, 259G.

9. See Geoffrey H. Hartman's knowledgeable and enlightening reading in "The Struggle for the Text," in *Midrash and Literature*, ed. Geoffrey H. Hartman and Sanford Budick (New Haven: Yale University Press, 1986), 6.

10. Gerhard von Rad, *Genesis: A Commentary* (Philadelphia: Westminster, 1961), 314.

11. See *Genesis Rabbah,* vol. 1 of *Midrash Rabbah,* ed. Harry Freeman and Maurice Simon (London: Soncino Press, 1961), 710, cited in Hartman and Budick *Midrash and Literature,* 17.

12. See Gen. 25.26 and 27.36, as well as Hos. 12.4.

13. Von Rad, *Genesis: A Commentary,* 260.

14. "The name Israel . . . is here interpreted very freely and contrary to its original linguistic meaning ('May God rule')" (Ibid., 317).

15. Ibid.

16. Ibid., 318.

Chapter 8. The Style of Kleist

1. *Webster's Seventh New Collegiate Dictionary.*

2. Karl Ludwig Schneider, "Heinrich von Kleist: Über ein Ausdrucksprinzip seines Stils," in *Heinrich von Kleist: Vier Reden zu seinem Gedächtnis,* ed. Walter Müller-Seidel (Berlin: Erich Schmidt Verlag, 1962), 27.

3. The play on *style* is certainly not original with this author: see Jacques Derrida, *Éperons: Les styles de Nietzsche* (Venice: Corbo e Fiore, 1976).

4. Most quotations from Kleist's works are from Heinrich von Kleist, *Sämtliche Werke und Briefe,* ed. Helmut Sembdner, 3d expanded and revised ed. (Munich: Carl Hanser Verlag, 1964), cited as *KL,* followed by the volume and page number. Unless otherwise indicated, the translations are my own.

5. Essentially the interpretation of Jakob Spälti in *Interpretationen zu Heinrich von Kleists Verhältnis zur Sprache* (Bern: Lang, 1975), 62.

6. Katharina Mommsen, *Kleists Kampf mit Goethe* (Heidelberg: Lothar Stiehm, 1974).

7. Johann Wolfgang Goethe, *Goethes Faust* (Hamburg: Christian Wegner, 1963), 145, my translation.

8. Heinrich von Kleist, *The Marquise of O—— and Other Stories* (New York: Ungar, 1960), 243, cited as *TMO,* followed by the page number. The citations are usually slightly modified versions of that translation.

9. From the beginning of the story, the foundling marks the rupture between father and offspring. Thus in response to Klara's earlier announcement Nicolo counters, "The image resembles me, just as you resemble the person who believes himself your father!" ("das Bild gleicht mir, wie du demjenigen, der sich deinen Vater glaubt!") (*KL* 2.208).

10. A translation of the complete text of "Improbable Veracities" appears in the Appendix. For exceptional critical readings of these last pages see Cynthia Chase, "Telling Truths," and Andrzej Warminski, "A Question of an Other

Order: Deflections of the Straight Man," both in *Diacritics,* December 1979, 62–69 and 70–78, respectively.

11. Friedrich von Schiller, *Geschichte des Abfalls der vereinigten Niederlande* (Leipzig: Friedrich Christian Wilhelm Vogel, 1809), 292, cited as *SCH,* followed by the page number. Translations are my own.

12. This paradox is hardly neutral. In the context of Paul de Man's "The Rhetoric of Temporality" (in *Interpretation: Theory and Practice,* ed. Charles S. Singleton [Baltimore: Johns Hopkins Press, 1969], 190–91), it would be the attempt to reduce the allegorical relationship of two texts to a symbolical relationship between story and reality. It would suggest, in other words, an identity between the narrative image and the objective world described, the identity so violently denied in the first two anecdotes.

13. See Helmut Sembdner, *Die Berliner Abendblätter Heinrich von Kleists, ihre Quellen und ihre Redaktion,* vol. 19 of *Schriften der Kleist-Gesellschaft* (1922–39; reprint [19 vols. in 12], Amsterdam: John Benjamin, 1970), 76. Although, like Kleist, I continue to refer to this as Schiller's text, as Sembdner notes, the material that Kleist uses is actually a continuation of Schiller's *History* written by Karl Curths.

14. See also Sembdner, *Die Berliner Abendblätter,* 77.

15. Katharina Mommsen (*Kleists Kampf*) reads the first and last anecdotes of "Improbable Veracities" literally, as stories of miraculous healing and also as texts that directly and unproblematically signify Kleist's personal incapability of being injured.

16. Ernst Cassirer reads *The Critique of Pure Reason* as a guarantor of truth and reason, as a hardly valid source, therefore, for the crisis of 1801 ("Heinrich von Kleist und die Kantische Philosophie," in *Idee und Gestalt* [Berlin: B. Cassirer, 1921]). For a good review of the history of this question see Ludwig Muth, *Kleist und Kant* (Cologne: Kölner Universitäts-Verlag, 1954).

17. It is not a question here, however, of reading Kant in any radical sense but rather of setting him up as a fictional point of stability and limit for the lightning of Kleist's stylus. Kleist's "Hymn to the Sun," Schiller's "Hymn to the Infinite," and Goethe's *Faust* all operated as similar props in our reading of "The Style of God." These illusions of construct are necessary, although they rest, as Nietzsche reminds us, "on movable fundaments, as if on flowing water" ("Of Truth and Lies"). For readings of Kant that put his fundamental constructs into motion see Jacques Derrida, "Le Parergon," *Digraphe* 2 and 3 (1974); idem, "Economimesis," in *Mimesis des articulations* (Paris: Flammarion, 1975); and Jean-Luc Nancy, *Le Discours de la syncope* (Paris: Flammarion, 1976).

18. All English citations from *The Critique of Pure Reason* are from the translation by Norman Kemp Smith (London: Macmillan, 1963), cited as "Smith," followed by the page number. The German citations are from Immanuel Kant, *Kritik der Reinen Vernunft* (Hamburg: Felix Meiner, 1956), cited as *Kritik,* followed by the page number.

19. It was in the years just preceding the writing of the anecdotes that groundbreaking work in the reading of cuneiform took place. In 1788 Carsten Niebuhr published copies of the inscriptions at Persepolis, but it was not until

1802 that Georg Friedrich Grotefend made significant progress in their decipherment. The texts in question, not unlike the anecdotes of "Improbable Veracities," told the same story, but in three different languages. The literature of the time not only speaks of *Keilschrift* but also refers to the writing as "keilförmige Inschriften" (Bruno Meissner, *Die Keilschrift* [Berlin: Walter de Gruyter, 1922], 5–7).

20. For a discussion of the way in which the Jena Romantics took up, preserved, and canceled the Kantian motif of criticism see Philippe Lacoue-Labarthe and Jean-Luc Nancy, *L'Absolu littéraire* (Paris: Seuil, 1978), 376–77; the question of literature as its own criticism is one of the most powerful thrusts of the volume. See also Walter Benjamin, "Der Begriff der Kunstkritik in der deutschen Romantik," *Gesammelte Schriften,* vol. 1 (Frankfurt: Suhrkamp, 1974).

21. Friedrich Schlegel, *Friedrich Schlegel's "Lucinde" and the Fragments* (Minneapolis: University of Minnesota Press, 1971), Athenaeum fragment 238, translation modified; hereafter cited by fragment number. The German citations, taken from Friedrich Schlegel, *Kritische Schriften* (Munich: Carl Hanser Verlag, 1964), are to page number.

22. Lacoue-Labarthe and Nancy (*L'Absolu littéraire*) offer an ambiguous translation of this fragment, rendering "fortlaufender Kommentar zu" as "un commentaire suivi du," as though the commentary of modern poetry were possibly followed by a brief text of philosophy. This leads the authors to conclude, "It seemed indispensable to us to undertake a properly philosophical study of Romanticism" (23). To be sure, the chapter entitled "La Critique" ironizes such a (necessary) stance when it designates anew the relationship between philosophy and criticism (385–86).

23. De Man, "The Rhetoric of Temporality," 202.

24. The relationship of criticism to irony in "The Rhetoric of Temporality" never appears as the explicit subject matter. It must rather be read in the ironical relationship of the critical text to its own form and content. It could be shown that the essay operates by way of endless allegorical and ironical gestures that nullify and consume one another and, thereby, any claims to superior wisdom or enlightenment. To give a brief example, the most obvious instance of this is the way in which the allegory of allegory that constitutes part 1 of the essay is followed by an ironization of that allegory in part 2, 194. (See my essay "Allegories of Reading de Man" in *Reading de Man Reading* [Minneapolis: University of Minnesota Press, 1988].)

25. Benjamin ("Der Begriff"), on the other hand, would seem to read *Kritik* in Schlegel as the path to the "absolute work of art" (84) and irony as an "endless process of fulfillment" (92).

26. The English is from Walter Benjamin, *Illuminations* (New York: Schocken, 1969), 257–58; the German from *Illuminationen* (Frankfurt: Suhrkamp, 1961), 272–73.

Index

Abrams, Meyer, 205nn.6, 8
Absence, 134. *See also* Presence
Absolute, 52; in language, 114; refusal of exterior, 133
Aeneid, 85, 105, 215n.19
Aeschylus, 20
Agamemnon, 85
Allegory of the cave. *See* Plato
Apollo, myth of, 38, 40
Arntzen, Helmut, 215n.26, 218n.9, 219nn.15, 20, 220n.23
Aufhebung, 25
Authority, ix, xi, 115; blind belief in, 140; borders of, 158; crisis of, 23, 165; denial of, 141, 149; desire for immediacy, 143; dislocation of text from, 140; displacement of, 143–44; double bind, 151; of evil, 44; figure of, 138, 164; of God disclaimed, 173; inflexible, 119; and intention, 26; language as, 44; of law, 124; loss by forgetting, 23; of interpreter, x; of Luther, 143; name of, 156; of narrator, x; of origin, 19; of pass, 139, 140; prediction, 150–51; of Prometheus's words, 22; and revolution, 40; structure of laws, 95; and teleology, 20; unknowable source of, 155; unmediated, 152; of voice, x; voice of, 108; will to, 48
Ayrault, Roger, 220n.24

Bacon, Francis, 204n.30
Baker, Carlos, 4, 204n.3, 205nn.7, 8, 207n.23
Baldo, Jonathan, 203n.15
Baudelaire, Charles, 6; "Une Mort héroïque," 202n.10
Beauty: and horror, 12, 15; relation to

agony, 6, 7; Romantic conception of, 5; of work of art, 7
Belgardt, Raimund, 218n.14
Belhalfaoui, Barbara, 216nn.33, 34
Bell, Vereen M., 212n.13
Benjamin, Walter, ix, 227nn.20, 25, 26; angel of history, 194
Bernd, Clifford A., 222n.5
Best, Otto F., 221n.4, 223n.12
Biographical interpretation, 8
Bloom, Harold, 4, 203n.18, 204n.25
Böchenstein, Bernard, 214n.14, 215n.17
Brisman, Susan Hawk, 205nn.8–9, 12–13, 210n.37
Brontë, Emily, ix; *Wuthering Heights,* x, 61–81, 193
Burwick, Frederick, 210n.37
Butter, Peter, 205nn.6–8, 10

Carroll, Lewis: *Alice's Adventures in Wonderland,* 61
Cassirer, Ernst, 226n.16
Causal chain, 62, 63
Causality, rupture in, 186
Chase, Cynthia, 201n.1, 225n.10
Closure, xii, 81, 159; dislocation in, 161; gesture of, 184; opening of, 162; refusal of, 15; and rupture, 53; implied by withdrawal, 48. *See also* Ending, sense of
Contemporary criticism, 8
Crawe, Christian, 224n.4
Critical language, 81
Critical text, 191
Criticism, ix, xi; of adequation, 194, 196; affinity with irony, 193; doubling, 194; as entanglement, 170; as act of Imagination, 18; relation to text, 77
Crosby, Donald, 224n.4

Intentional significance, 176
Interpretation, x; compulsion to, 160; crisis in, xi; diary as, 75; entanglement, 170; impasse of, 73; of interpreter, 80; mediation by, 78
Ione, 36
Irony, 28, 132, 136, 145, 152, 163; and criticism, 193

Jacob: name of, 168–69; struggle of, 167
Jacobs, Carol, 202n.5, 227n.2
Joke, 119, 132, 134, 138, 150–51; intention of, 140; locus of, 123, 124, 127; pledge, 120, 121; presence of, 136
Jupiter, 21; downfall of, 40; and language, 24; rule of, 44
Justice, 38; based on identity, 140; critical point of, 145; giving up, 143; ground of, 173; narration of, 159

Kant, Immanuel, 186–87, 193, 226nn.17, 18
Keats, John, 202n.7
Kermode, Frank, 65–67, 211nn.5, 6
Kleist, Heinrich von, ix; "The Duel," x, 159–70; "The Foundling," 159, 176–79; "Hymn to the Sun," 174–75; "Improbable Veracities," x, 179–90, 195–96, 197–200; *Michael Kohlhaas*, x, 138–58; *Penthesilea*, xi–xiii, 85–114; *Prince Friedrich von Homburg*, x, 115–38, 161, 217n.1; relation to Goethe, 175; "The Style of God," 171–75; suicide of, 159
Koch, Friedrich, 224n.5
Kreutzer, Hans Joachim, 224n.4
Kroese, Irvin, 4

Labhardt, Robert, 216n.33
Lacan, Jacques, 221n.2
Lacoue-Labarthe, Philippe, 201n.1, 227nn.20, 22
Language, 138; as authority, 44; as barrier, 27; binding of, 26; crisis of self-knowledge, 102; critical, 81; double, 21; estrangement, 189; failure of, 9; and intention, 26; and knowledge, 24, 26; in relation to life and self, xiii; literal and figurative, 98, 106, 112; as mirror, 14; as metaphor, 40; of naming, 27, 28; naming itself, 15; necessity, 146; and power, 24, 25; self-reflection of, 81; as sociability, 77; uncontrollable, 188; violence of, 21, 100
Law, x; affirmation of, 158; Amazon, 98; authority of, 124; blacks as signs for, 142, 144; enemy of, 117; immediacy in,

162; inscription, 173; limit of, 116; as literal text, 125; against literature, 127; mediation of, 140; patriarchal, 111; sundering from name, 144; violation of, 146, 158
Linearity, 66, 67, 116, 195
Literary history, 159
Lugowski, Clemens, 222n.5, 224n.5
Luther, Martin, 142, 222n.6

McGann, Jerome, 201n.4, 202n.12
McKibben, Robert, 211n.3
Madden, William A., 211n.4
Mahlendorf, Ursula, 216n.29
Mallarmé, Stephane, 8
Marin, Louis, 202n.5
Mayer, Hans, 220n.24
Meaning: estrangement from sign, 73; indeterminacy, 66; as making present, 27; present as beauty, 16; question of, 146; refusal of, 18
Mediation, 50, 73, 156, 163, 182; of action, 164; crisis of, 165; of God, 170; inefficacious, 141; by interpretation, 78; of law, 140; Martin Luther, 142; mark of, 163
Meissner, Bruno, 227n.19
Memory, 38; *Aufhebung*, 25; gap in, 23; and Hyacinthus's name, 39; and prophetic dream, 39; recall, 24–25; and reflection, 30; against regeneration, 30
Metaphor: captives, 97; of doorway, 61; gesture of, 40; impossibility of, 40; of Kermode's enterprise, 67; language as, 40; for love, 110; of lyre, 17; of man, 16; of other, 38; regulation, 97; sound-object, 109; of surrender, 102; water and fire, 92; of withdrawal, 48
Meyer-Benfey, Heinrich, 222n.5
Miller, J. Hillis, 203n.18, 212n.11
Mimesis, x, 6, 10, 202n.13, 203n.23
Mommsen, Katharina, 175, 225n.6, 226n.15
Motte-Fouqué, Friedrich de la, 222n.5
Müller-Seidel, Walter, 214nn.11, 12, 220n.24
Muth, Ludwig, 226n.16

Name: of authority, 156; for authority of evil, 44; desire to, 43; Hyacinth, 38–39; Jacob, 168–69; mark of, 24; Nicolo, 176, 196; refusal of, 57; sacred, 143
Names: and absence, 68; combinations of, 66, 67; generating differences, 67; and property, 68–69

Uncontainable Romanticism

Designed by Ann Walston

Composed by Village Typographers, Inc.,
in Galliard text and display type

Printed by Edwards Brothers, Inc.,
on 50-lb. Glatfelter Natural text paper
and bound in Joanna Arrestox cloth